MARGARET MITCHELL

Hers is the most phenomenal success story in all of modern American literature. For Margaret Mitchell never set out to carve a niche for herself, either in the public consciousness or in the world of arts and letters. The mantle of bestselling novelist was not one that she sought. Yet it came to her, along with worldwide fame and a considerable fortune.

It took a special kind of woman to make it happen, a woman of extraordinary talent, quiet strength, magnanimity, and brilliance—the dynamic real-life heroine who wrote the epic novel of our time.

MARGARET MITCHELL OF ATLANTA

by FINIS FARR

MARGARET MITCHELL OF ATLANTA

AVON
PUBLISHERS OF BARD, CAMELOT, DISCUS, EQUINOX AND FLARE BOOKS

An abridged version of this book has appeared in *McCall*
Magazine under the title "The Woman Who Wrote 'Gone wit
the Wind.'"
Grateful acknowledgment is made to *The Atlanta Journal an*
Constitution for permission to quote from the *Atlanta Journa*
Magazine; to The Viking Press for permission to quote from
Letters of Alexander Woollcott; to *The New York Times* fo
permission to quote from an article by Lois Cole published i
The New York Times Book Review (© 1961 by The New Yorl
Times Company); to the Atlanta Historical Society for permis
sion to quote from *The Atlanta Historical Bulletin No. 34*
May, 1950; and to The Macmillan Company for permission t
quote from a report by Professor Charles W. Everett on th
manuscript of *Gone with the Wind.*

AVON BOOKS
A division of
The Hearst Corporation
959 Eighth Avenue
New York, New York 10019

Copyright © 1965 by Finis Farr and Stephens Mitchell.
Published by arrangement with the author.
Library of Congress Catalog Card Number: 65-22974.

ISBN: 0-380-00158

First Avon Printing, November, 1974
Third Printing

AVON TRADEMARK REG. U.S. PAT. OFF. AND
FOREIGN COUNTRIES, REGISTERED TRADEMARK—
MARCA REGISTRADA, HECHO EN CHICAGO, U.S.A.

Printed in the U.S.A.

Contents

Author's Note

The foundation of this book is in the papers of the Margaret Michell Marsh Estate and in an unpublished memoir by Stephens Mitchell. I am grateful to Mr. Mitchell for generous permission to use these materials, and am also under a heavy debt to Lois Cole, Margaret E. Baugh, and the many other friends of Margaret Mitchell in Atlanta and New York who graciously helped in writing this biography by sharing with me their memories of its subject.

F. F.

I

Atlanta Carnival

Early in December 1939, the mayor of Atlanta announced
from his office at City Hall that Thursday the fourteenth
would be a municipal half-holiday, and at the nearby State
Capitol the governor declared Friday the fifteenth a holiday throughout all Georgia. Public opinion would have allowed no less, for an event of deep emotional significance
was about to take place. This was the world's first showing
of a moving picture that had been made from a novel
about the Civil War and Reconstruction called *Gone with
the Wind*. And all the world knew the producer had passed
up Los Angeles in favor of Atlanta because that city
was both the scene of the story and the home of the author, Mrs. John R. Marsh, who had written the novel under her maiden name of Margaret Mitchell.

The Macmillan Company had brought out *Gone with
the Wind* on June 30, 1936. It was now history that the
book had enjoyed an instantaneous, explosive success
beyond all previous records in the publishing trade, and
that within a month David O. Selznick had bought the
motion picture rights. Now, at last, after three and a half

years the Technicolor film was ready for release, and in Atlanta a carnival had begun. Official banquets would be given; there would be a costume ball, sponsored by the Junior League; the stars of the picture would parade through town; citizens would hang thousands of Confederate flags on homes and places of business; every shop window was to carry some sort of display related to *Gone with the Wind* or its author; and taxi drivers would ply their trade dressed in sugar scoop coats and planters' hats, while waitresses served their customers in hoopskirts that filled the aisles between the tables.

An influx of notable visitors commenced on Wednesday, December 13, with the arrival of Howard Dietz, who had charge of advertising and publicity for Metro-Goldwyn-Mayer, distributor of the film for Selznick International. He was followed by Vivien Leigh, the hitherto little-known British actress who played Miss Mitchell's heroine, Scarlett O'Hara. With her came the rising London star Laurence Olivier, who had not appeared in the film but was welcomed to the festivities as Miss Leigh's fiancé. In the party was Olivia de Havilland, who had taken the role of Melanie Wilkes, the second heroine. Clark Gable, cast as the hero Rhett Butler by popular demand, was to arrive next day. Of the four star players, only Leslie Howard would be absent: he had gone home to join the British Army. But Miss de Havilland's party was enough for one day, as she brought with her the producer and his wife, a number of the supporting actors, and two dozen assorted celebrities from California and New York. After a welcome by Mayor William Hartsfield at Municipal Airport, the visitors marched to a line of limousines that carried them into town, with motorcycle engines bellowing at the convoy's head. They went to the Georgian Terrace Hotel, a retreat for dowagers at Peachtree Street and Ponce de Leon Avenue, a mile north of the business district. Here they encountered a strong force of reporters that included representatives of every large newspaper in the country, as well as those from the three local papers and the wire services. Graciously answering questions, the celebrities invariably asked a question of their own, which was, "When can we meet Margaret Mitchell?"

That was indeed a question, for Miss Mitchell was doing her best to keep out of sight. She had issued a statement expressing happiness at the many fine things planned for the *Gone with the Wind* festival and the motion picture première. It was wonderful, she said, to see how the whole town had joined to "make the celebration a great success." But Miss Mitchell herself would not be much in evidence; the occasion, she thought, belonged to the moving picture people rather than to the author of the book. She "hoped to attend one or two small affairs," but did not say where these small parties would take place. The showing of the picture was what Miss Mitchell looked forward to. Her statement concluded, "I wrote a book about old Atlanta without ever having seen it except in my mind. Now, I will see the old streets of the little Atlanta I wrote about, and the old houses which have been gone for seventy-five years, and the people. It will be a strange and unbelievable experience."

One of the small affairs Margaret Mitchell felt bound to attend could hardly escape notice, for it brought together three Pulitzer Prize novelists at one table. They were Miss Mitchell herself, and her Southern colleagues Julia Peterkin and Marjorie Kinnan Rawlings. The occasion was the lunch given on Thursday by the book buyer of Rich's department store for the Macmillan people in town for the fiesta. The publishing group included president George P. Brett, Jr. and his sales manager Alec Blanton, with their wives; chief editorial executive Harold Latham; and his associate Lois Cole, a close friend of Margaret Mitchell, with her husband Allan Taylor, who also had been a friend of Margaret's since their days together on the *Atlanta Journal*. This gathering was reported in the papers, but not thrown open to indiscriminate coverage and so the wire services did not carry a story of the accident that marred the party at Rich's store: someone pulled back a chair just as the guest of honor was about to sit in it. Miss Mitchell took a fall that jarred her spine; she made light of it and carried on through the lunch, but was in pain when she got back to her apartment. During these days, Margaret had pain from another source, although only her doctors and her husband knew it, for she was suffering from abdominal adhesions that would require an operation to correct, and had postponed the surgery from month to month as Selznick postponed the release of *Gone with the Wind*. Margaret Mitchell felt she owed it to Atlanta to be there on "the night."

Clark Gable, America's most popular male motion picture star, landed at half past three on Thursday afternoon with only an hour or so of winter sunlight remaining for the grand climax of the opening ceremonies. Gable stepped from the plane with his wife at his side; like Olivier, she was not in the picture, but was nevertheless a sparkling addition to the festivities, for she was Carole Lombard, a beautiful and intelligent woman at the height of her career as a screen comedienne. The Gables were troupers; standing beside the plane they smiled with what appeared to be genuine joy, though almost blown to pieces by a high cold wind, while greeters loaded Carole's arms with flowers. "Atlanta and her people are in the spotlight of the world," said Mayor Hartsfield.

The final automobile parade was to assemble downtown, where the Gables would join the other notables. It would then proceed to the Georgian Terrace, and the governors of five states would confer a welcome from a platform in front of the hotel. The cars would go slowly so that everyone could see the stars, but by the time they reached the hotel, it seemed that most of the 300,000 onlookers had jammed into the intersection of Peachtree Street and Ponce de Leon Avenue. The behavior of the crowd was exemplary, for all present knew the proceedings were being broadcast on a national network. They could see the microphones on the platform built out from the granite loggia of the Georgian Terrace, with announcer Lambdin Kay wearing a jimswinger coat and ten-gallon hat, and behind him seated in a row the governors of Florida, Alabama, Georgia, South Carolina and Tennessee. Darkness was beginning to fall as the automobiles delivered the stars at the side entrance on Ponce de

Leon Avenue, so they could go through the lobby and appear on the platform one at a time; but first came Mayor Hartsfield. A roar of applause testified to his popularity. "Words can't express the pride I feel in Atlanta and her people," said the mayor, and then he brought on the actors, starting with the players of minor parts, such as Laura Hope Crews, the accomplished character woman who had the role of Aunt Pittypat Hamilton. Each ovation was greater than the one before, and by the time Miss Leigh and Miss de Havilland had taken their bows the crowd was giving the rebel yell. The *Journal* had published instructions of the proper utterance of this terrifying ululation, noting that Miss Mitchell had written the yell as "Yee-aay-ee!" but stating that any string of vowels would do, if "emitted high and hard." Whatever method individual onlookers used, their massed voices were overwhelming when Mayor Hartsfield finally said, *"And now—"* and noise blotted out further words as Clark Gable stepped forward. A reporter described the scene: "He came at last through the December dusk, and the thousands who had waited so cheerfully while they stamped their feet in the penetrating cold, broke into a roar of adulation for the powerful, smiling man with the black moustache, who stood in the gleam of headlights. There was communication between this happy, attractive stranger and all the mob he smiled and bowed to . . . No matter what the figure may be on this Gable's contract, it is too small. The man is simply magnificent."

Barely intelligible through the continuous applause and cheering, Gable said he wanted to pay tribute to Margaret Mitchell for writing the book that had brought them all together, adding his hope that while in Atlanta he might have the honor of meeting Miss Mitchell. It was more than a seasoned actor's instinct for saying the right thing; Gable knew how to handle an audience, but he was sincere in this remark. He may have expected to meet the author that night at the Junior League Ball. If so, he was disappointed, for Margaret had declined the League's invitation ten months before, when the ball was still in the planning stage. Certain people who believed they knew the inside story said there was a "feeling"—polite Southern synonym for quarrel—between Miss Mitchell and the members of the League, based on a disagreement now long in the past. At any rate, when Gable got to the ball, what he found was impressive even to a man accustomed to the splendors of Southern California.

As they stepped from their cars, guests saw that the exterior of the Atlanta Municipal Auditorium was covered with Confederate colors and flags, with one huge United States flag draped down the center above the marquee. Beneath this flag was a fifteen-foot representation of the municipal seal with its phoenix and the motto *Atlanta Resurgens,* referring to the city's rising from the ashes of the Civil War.

The floor of the Auditorium's main hall is about the size of a football field, with a roof of Zeppelin-hangar height. At three sides rise banks of seats for musical and sporting events, and the opening for a tremendous stage takes up most of the east wall. For this occasion the ball committee had sensibly abandoned any idea of trying for coziness, and had gone in for grandeur. Smilax and laurel climbed the walls as a ground for swags of red and blue, the colors of the Confederacy. Repeated everywhere was the display of three grouped flags—the familiar battle flag of the South; the Confederate national banner, a formal-looking flag that is seldom seen; and the flag known as the Stars and Bars. Set off against the decorations, perhaps half the five thousand people attending the ball were in Civil War costumes, or approximations of them. There were many, to be sure, wearing family heirlooms, such as that displayed by Colonel Telamon Cuyler, who wore the full-dress uniform of his great-uncle, Colonel Algernon S. Hamilton of the 66th Georgia Volunteers. The gowns of grandmothers and great-aunts were much in evidence, and all the officials and attendants were in costume, the doorkeepers appearing as Confederate generals, and the multitude of Negro footmen and butlers wearing period evening dress. Stephens Mitchell, Margaret's brother, amused his friends by telling them he was dressed as Governor Bullock, who was accused of robbing the people of Georgia during Reconstruction days.

The stage pageant took place before a Corinthian-columned façade which the program identified as that of Scarlett's home, Tara Hall. Nobody minded that it was much more elaborate than the rambling, chance-grown North Georgia manor house that Miss Mitchell had described. Nor was there anything in the novel resembling the waltz and polka performed by fifty debutantes and their escorts, emerging from a screen of magnolia, boxwood, and wisteria to the musical background of the Ebenezer Negro Baptist Choir.

But the primary attractions were the crowd itself, which would soon start general dancing to the music of Kay Kyser's orchestra, and the moving picture people, now to be introduced again as they had been at the Georgian Terrace. The master of ceremonies was Major Clark Howell, editor and publisher of the *Atlanta Constitution*. At the end of the pageant, he called for lowering of lights, and then began presenting celebrities, who stood in their boxes while a spotlight from the ceiling picked them out. As the actresses stood in turn, it was seen that these ladies had wisely decided Atlanta would have enough of their Civil War costumes in the picture. Tonight they wore contemporary gowns. Vivien Leigh, for example, was in black velvet with a diamond and pearl clip at the V neck, and epaulets of ermine tails on the shoulders. Some actresses who had not appeared in the picture were equally decorative; among these was Claudette Colbert, one of the most beautiful women in America, who had come with the Herbert Bayard Swopes of New York simply to see the fun. Miss Colbert wore flame-colored velvet, while in a nearby box Carole Lombard was stunning in black velvet that clung to her superlative figure.

At one point it seemed that something had gone wrong. The time had come to introduce Olivia de Havilland, and she had not yet arrived at the ball. By accident, Miss de Havilland had been overlooked in the assigning of escorts and was still waiting at the Georgian Terrace a mile away. When Miss de Havilland realized what had happened, she told the hotel office she would go to the ball by herself if they would get her a car and driver. Her call was taken by Edmund Miller, the night auditor, a quiet, middle-aged man who lived at the hotel. Middle-aged he might be, but the thought of Miss de Havilland going unescorted to the party was abhorrent to him. Summoning a hotel car and chauffeur, he handed the actress into the tonneau and got in beside her as though he did this sort of thing every night of his life. Policemen helped the car through traffic, and they entered the hall just as Major Howell was about to pass over Miss de Havilland's introduction. Instead of taking time to go around to the box entrances, they hurried directly to the floor, where Mr. Miller delivered Miss de Havilland to Captain Jack Malcolm of the traffic squad, who lifted her up to Laurence Olivier, who in turn lifted her over the railing and into the box with effortless ease. This swift passage from floor to box delighted the crowd.

Clark Gable's appearance ended the presenting of visitors when Major Howell said, "I want to make this introduction in typical Junior League fashion. I present to you—Carole Lombard's husband." Gable rose and bowed smiling amid laughter as butlers swiftly removed the chairs from the main floor for the grand march. On the stage, Kay Kyser brought down his baton; five hundred costumed men and girls stepped off, marched around the hall, and the dance began.

By ten o'clock next morning the visiting reporters were nervously alert. With the Junior League Ball on record, their interest again focused on Margaret Mitchell, who was to appear that afternoon at a party given by her friends and former colleagues of the Atlanta Women's Press Club. This was the other small affair to which she had referred in her statement. Aside from the members of the Press Club, only invited persons would be present, including the Macmillan people, the actors and screen executives, the mayor and governor, and the guest of honor. It was to be a tea party in the lounge of the Piedmont ...ng Club, a fortress of Atlanta social position that ...nveniently across the street from the apartment building in which the Marshes lived. This was a hard gate to crash and a number of visiting reporters and photographers, milling around on the club's driveway, made no attempt to conceal their annoyance at being excluded.

Getting ready for this tea was a greater ordeal for Miss Mitchell than she would have admitted to the friends who had worked so hard to make it "the nicest party of the week." The doctor had strapped her in bandages to support the back she had wrenched in falling the previous day, and she put on a black dress and a small black hat with two pert upstanding bows that John Marsh called rabbit ears. Just before starting across the street to the Driving Club, Margaret Mitchell laid out the dress she had decided to wear at the opening that night. It was pink tulle, with a bouffant skirt topped by a tight-fitting bodice, and rows of narrow pleating to set off its "sweetheart" neckline. She also laid out a white velvet evening coat that was threaded with gold and silver and fastened from neckline to waistline with white velvet buttons; silver slippers; long kid gloves; and a white velvet evening bag. The florist had delivered a small bouquet of camellias, now waiting in the icebox as Miss Mitchell crossed Piedmont Avenue to the club.

An anxious photographer stopped a smart-looking young woman as she walked up the club driveway, and suggested she help him get inside so he could take pictures of Margaret Mitchell. "Why, I'm Margaret Mitchell," said the lady. He refused to believe it, missing his chance for the pictures he was complaining about. A few minutes later, this photographer managed to get past the outer door and made a disturbance in the hall. The people in charge were about to throw him out, when Miss Mitchell heard of it. Not wishing to be reported as an unapproachable female Grand Lama, and because of a sympathy for all working journalists, Margaret went into the hall and posed for a few pictures.

After that, Clark Gable met the author who had furnished him the greatest role of his career. He drew her aside and they talked in an anteroom for ten minutes. As he left the building, reporters asked Gable what he thought of Miss Mitchell, and he replied, "She's the most fascinating woman I've ever met." The news of this brief meeting appeared on the front pages of the late editions under headlines eight columns wide. But such prodigious display did not seem out of proportion at the time either in Atlanta or the rest of the country. There was enchantment in the air—a spell compounded of an entire city's excitement, affection, and pride—city and nation understood that somehow, though no one knew quite how to put it in words, Rhett Butler himself had met the woman who had created him.

Then at last the moment came for the answer to the question of what "Hollywood" had done with the great and famous story of *Gone with the Wind*. The scene was Loew's Grand Theater; on Peachtree Street in the upper segment of the business district, diagonally across from one of Margaret Mitchell's favorite places, the Atlanta public library. All police leaves had been cancelled and hundreds of traffic officers were on duty, as on the previous night around the Auditorium. The Grand would hold only a few more than two thousand people, less than half the attendance at the ball. Nevertheless, the traffic moved more slowly, because, in the tradition of première performances, the arrival of the audience was part of the show. Those who watched numbered about twelve thousand, standing behind barricades in the open space formed by the juncture of Peachtree Street with Forsyth Street, Pryor Street and Carnegie Way. Without this bonus from the rambling plan of downtown Atlanta, many of the onlookers would have been disappointed. As things turned out, they had a good view of the dignitaries and celebrities arriving at the theater, a massive Romanesque structure that had been built forty-six years before. Now it was illuminated by nine 4,000,000-candlepower searchlights that brought into relief the white classical columns, five stories high, that had been added to the theater's front wall, supporting an architrave that carried two three-story-high medallions framing enormous faces of Clark Gable and Vivien Leigh. The reflected glare brought an unearthly shade of green to the lawn of artificial grass that extended across Peachtree Street.

At the edge of the lawn where the ticket holders descended from their cars stood the master of ceremonies Julian Boehm, a genial insurance man with an infallible memory, who called out names over a loudspeaker, and momentarily detained the more prominent for an exchange of pleasantries. These colloquies went out on the radio as well as to the crowd in the street. When Mr. Boehm asked Clark Gable for a few words, he said, "I appreciate the welcome, but I think this night should belong to Margaret Mitchell."

She arrived a few minutes after her leading man, and those who did not know her were struck by the smallness of her stature. Margaret Mitchell Marsh was one inch under five feet tall, and her husband John towered over her at more than six feet while she made a brief, conventional, and cordial reply to the announcer's greetings. "God bless our little Peggy Marsh!" cried Julian Boehm, and turned to her husband, asking, "Aren't you proud of your wife, John?" "I was proud of her even before she wrote a book," John Marsh replied. They walked on into the crush of the lobby. The social columnist who wrote in the *Atlanta Georgian* as Polly Peachtree reported "Ermine to the right of us, to the left, front and rear. Top hats and tails ... Sartorial elegance ... Silver foxes, sables, fabulous jewelry, orchids . . ." Amid this opulence, Margaret walked down the aisle. With a pink ribbon in her hair, she radiated a feeling of youth, vitality, modest happiness, and keen expectancy. Ushers led her to a seat beside John Hay (Jock) Whitney, who rated this place of honor as backer of Selznick International. In the same row, Gable had settled in his chair; he was exhausted, and went quietly to sleep as soon as the lights were dimmed.

Clark Gable must have been the only person in the house who slept through the picture. Everyone else sat in the grip of magic as Miss Mitchell's story unfolded—and thought it no wonder that the film took just ten minutes short of four hours, not counting the intermission, for Selznick and his people had managed to get in every important episode, and nearly every character. The audience saw Scarlett O'Hara struggling to survive the war in Atlanta and at Tara, the home plantation the author had imagined as being near Jonesboro, about twenty miles south of town. They saw the approach of Sherman's armies, the wounded stretched by hundreds at the railroad station, the abandonment and burning of Atlanta, and its occupancy by Federal troops. At this point, the story was only one-third told; faithfully following the novel, the picture went on through the early years of Reconstruction, with the rebuilding of Atlanta influencing Scarlett O'Hara's emotional life, which revolved around her relations with Rhett Butler and the secondary hero Ashley Wilkes. The enchanted audience sometimes gave direct response to images on the screen: Henry MacLemore of the United Press wrote that "When Sherman's legions started their march to sea, Loew's Grand Theater sounded like a pit of angered snakes." He also recorded that he believed applause lifted the roof several inches when Scarlett shot the Yankee straggler who invaded Tara Hall. Before their eyes the novel marched to its end—the enigmatic conclusion which had caused thousands of readers to write to Miss Mitchell, asking, "Is this *really* the end?" The unforgettable scene had Rhett leaving Scarlett, presumably forever, his love extinguished by her callousness and greed. Scarlett cries, "If you go, what shall I do?" and Rhett answers, "My dear, I don't give a damn." But Scarlett has not given up. She will never give up. "I'll think about it all tomorrow, at Tara," she says to herself. "I can stand it then. Tomorrow, I'll think of some way to get him back. After all, tomorrow is another day."

The house lights rose, the audience stood cheering and applauding. David Selznick stumbled into a hallway where his friends found him with tears in his eyes. In front, Mayor Hartsfield was holding his arms high for silence. He called for the stars and the producer, then asked Clark Gable to escort Margaret Mitchell to the stage. "The applause that now went up," a reporter wrote, "was not for Gable or for Leigh, magnificent as they had been, but for her alone."

Margaret Mitchell feared and detested public speaking, but no one would have known it from her appearance, nor would anyone have suspected that bandages supported her back. Her blue eyes seemed to flash into every part of the theater as she began to talk into a microphone, using her everyday low and agreeable tone of voice, in the rhythm of ordinary conversation, but with an indefinable element that gave it charm. She began, "I think everybody who knows me—and I'm sure about three-fourths of the people here do know me—knows that I am not a speaker, and so please excuse me if I stumble through what I am going to say. That is that I want to thank you, for me and my poor Scarlett, for all the grand things that everybody has done—the taxi drivers, the librarians, the bankers, the Junior League, the girls behind the counters, the boys in the filling stations. What could I have done—and my Scarlett—without their kindness and their helpfulness! You know everybody thinks it's just when you are dead broke and you are out of luck that you need friends. But really, when you've had as incredible success as I have had, that's really when you need friends. And, thank Heaven, I've had them. And I've appreciated everything people have done for me, to be kind to me and my Scarlett."

Now Miss Mitchell was done with talking about herself, and turned to the performers. "It's not up to me to speak of the grand things these actors have done," she said, "for they've spoken so much more eloquently than I could ever do. But I just want to speak for one moment about Mr. David Selznick. He's the man that every one of you cracked that joke about, 'Oh well, we'll wait till Shirley Temple grows up and *she'll* play Scarlett.' I want to commend Mr. Selznick's courage and his obstinacy and his determination in just keeping his mouth shut until he got exactly the cast he wanted, in spite of everything everybody said. And I think you're going to agree with me—that he had the absolutely perfect cast."

Miss Mitchell bowed, and waved a white-gloved hand as the applause again crashed over her. She had indeed experienced incredible success since the publication of her magical book, and now stood at the high point of her life.

Had the fame, the adulation, and this evidence of genuine love from a whole city made her a happy woman? Those who knew her best would have been most hesitant in offering a ready answer; for there was much, very much, in Margaret Mitchell and her life that did not meet the eye.

II

Childhood on the Hill

Margaret Munnerlyn Mitchell was born on November 8,
1900, at 296 Cain Street between Jackson Street and
North Boulevard. Some of the houses, like that of her
Grandmother Stephens at the corner of Cain and Jackson
streets, had been there before the Civil War. Nearly all of
wartime Atlanta had been burned, but this block escaped
destruction even though a line of Confederate entrench-
ments ran through its back yards. The Stephens house, in
fact, had been used by both sides as an army hospital.

In 1903, Mr. Mitchell moved his family to 179 Jackson
Street, a spacious Victorian structure with long porches,
flower and kitchen gardens, fruit trees and a stable for a
cow and pony. From the time she could walk, Margaret
had a playmate and adviser in her brother Stephens.
Though five years older, Stephens did not object to his sister accompanying him on expeditions around the interior
of the block, which their grandmother owned. As a little
girl, she followed Stephens when he did his chores, caring
for the pony, milking the cow, tending the tomatoes, let-

tuce, corn and beans in the garden, while Margaret herself gathered fruit and flowers.

Margaret was a shy child, and though Mrs. Mitchell sympathized she refused to allow her daughter to indulge in reticence at the expense of courtesy. That would not do among people who understood and valued good manners as the Mitchells did, and to make certain that Margaret never gave the impression of unresponsiveness, Mrs. Mitchell insisted that she conquer all symptoms of timidity or shyness at an early age. Sometimes, Margaret remembered later, the lessons in behavior were emphasized by a smack with a slipper. Little Margaret might have been shy, but she was interested in people, and at about the age of eight acquired a commanding observatory when she helped Stephens build a tree house in a tall pine. Here they could climb in fair weather, hauling their kittens up after them in a market basket and sitting on a platform to inspect the neighborhood and enjoy the sensation of being above everything they saw.

From early childhood, Margaret could tell a story, and almost as soon as she could talk was able to gather her playmates around her as she told her tales. Grown people observed that the children sat in absolute quiet, absorbed in the stories she invented, which leaned heavily on the supernatural. One boy said he was afraid to walk home alone after an especially terrifying ghost story. It seems likely that these tales came from the stories of Perrault and the Brothers Grimm that Stephens read to her until she knew them by heart.

"Probably the only remarkable thing about Margaret's childhood," her brother was to say later, "was that it was so unremarkable. It was serene and happy in a way that was possible only in a world where one felt absolutely secure. Our experiences were those of most children across the country who were raised in the same general circumstances. We made our own ice cream in summer, and spent our five-cent allowance at the corner store only after anguished thought. We had lemonade parties on the front lawn with the neighboring children and went to school and obeyed our parents.

"Margaret told stories and wrote them, and wrote and produced her own plays with the children around, but so do probably the majority of children. She was a tomboy, but on occasion played happily with dolls. She read a great deal, as will any child properly encouraged. She always liked to ride, first on her Texas plains pony, later on her bicycle or horse."

Margaret loved to go for a drive, but best of all, as her brother observed, she loved horseback riding. Thinking of this years afterward, Margaret said:

"When I was a little girl and went out on my pony every afternoon, my boon companion was a fine old Confederate veteran. He looked exactly like a stage Confederate—white hair and goatee—jimswinger coat—and a habit of gallantly kissing ladies' hands—even my own grubby six-year-old hand. He and a young lady who had reached the beau age were the only two people in my part of town who had time to go riding, and we three went riding together. We never went into the country that we didn't pick up some other old veteran to go with us. Frequently we had several veterans in our cavalcade. Their families and my mother encouraged us to ride together in the belief that we'd keep each other out of mischief. But I regret to say we didn't. There was still plenty of fire and dash left in the old boys. They still had hot tempers and bullheads and they still dearly loved a fight. And the day seldom passed that the young lady who accompanied us didn't turn her horse and race for home. She realized, even if I didn't, that the company of quarrelsome old gentlemen was no place for a lady. But at the age of six I was not concerned about being a lady. Besides, I was too fascinated by the way the veterans shouted at each other. Each one bragged about his own regiment and low-rated all others. I recall one time when we flushed an old gentleman who had been with Wheeler's cavalry. He was a tough, wiry little old fellow. And another veteran who had been in Stuart's cavalry remarked that the boys in Wheeler's cavalry were worse chicken thieves than Sherman's men ever were. Of course, after such an insult, they went at each other at the tops of their voices and with their riding crops. The language they used was highly entertaining and instructive to a small but interested girl. They refought the old campaigns, and argued about the tangled, bewildering muddle of politics in the Reconstruction days. So how could I help knowing about the Civil War and the hard times that came after it? I was raised on it. I thought it all happened just a few years before I was born."

From the time she could remember anything, Margaret and Stephens made frequent visits in the summertime to the farm near Jonesboro, Clayton County, that was the inheritence of their great-aunts, the Misses Mary and Sarah Fitzgerald. These two spinsters, widely known and respected as "Miss Mamie" and Miss Sis," had an important influence on Margaret, both by example and because they had taught Margaret's mother. The great-aunts had gone to Charleston for their educations and returned to bring learning and literature to the back country. Their Catholic religion was an almost exotic thing in that region at that time, and they were devout. Old ladies now as Margaret knew them, the Misses Fitzgerald still held family prayers every night, one saying one decade of the Rosary, and the other the next, with each child and servant called on to recite a decade. In the daytime there was a short catechism lesson to learn and recite, and the Angelus to say, and the grace before meals. It is no wonder that the great-aunts remained in Margaret's memory as persons of unassailable integrity. And in the community, the old ladies stood so high in general estimation that people said, "Having one of the Misses Fitzgerald for a character witness at a trial is the same thing as winning the case." In 1948, long after they had died, Margaret wrote to a friend, commenting on how the Southern women of previous generations had seemed to have "the quality of rising to any situation which the good Lord saw fit to sent their way." In this connection Margaret recalled that "Mother often remarked that my Aunt Mary could sit on her back porch shelling a panful of butterbeans and if the President of the United States or the King of England or the Pope of Rome drove up into the back yard she could rise and

28

greet them and make them feel at home. And I hope you will notice that Mother took it for granted that the King of England, the President and the Pope would be good enough Georgians not to come and ring the front door bell but would drive up into the back yard."

At the Clayton County farm, as well as in Atlanta, Margaret must have felt the nearness of the Civil War. Over the folds and hollows of these foothills blue and gray troops had advanced and retreated, fought and died. It was beautiful country. The forest grew from red earth all around, and a creek wandered by at the bottom of the hill below the farm. She could stand on its banks and looking up at the house make it a place of romance, and feel the love of Georgia land that was always one of her deepest emotions.

And both at the farm and in Atlanta were gatherings of friends and family connections on Sundays. The mid-day dinner would perhaps have a roast, with peas, string beans, sweet potatoes, other vegetables from the garden, fresh and preserved fruits, hot biscuits and plenty of ice cream. Naps were taken afterward, but there would always be a sociable gathering later in the afternoon. In those days people provided their own entertainment by actually talking to each other, and one of the favorite topics was the Civil War. As a grown woman, Margaret recalled these occasions in one of the few formal interviews she ever gave. Reading from a radio script she had prepared for her friend Medora Field Perkerson, she said, "When I was a little child, children were not encouraged to express their personalities by running and screaming on Sunday afternoons. When we went calling, I was usually scooped up onto a lap—told that I didn't look like a soul on either side of the family—and then forgotten for the rest of the afternoon while the gathering spiritedly refought the Civil War. I sat on bony knees—fat, slick taffeta laps—and soft, flowered muslin laps. I did not even dare to wriggle for fear of getting the flat side of a hair brush where it would do the most good. I should add, while I'm talking about laps and knees, that cavalry knees were the worst knees of all. Cavalry knees had the tendency to trot and bounce and jog in the midst of reminiscences and this kept me from going to sleep, fortunately for 'Gone with the Wind.' I heard about the fighting and the wounds and the primitive way they were treated—how ladies nursed in hospitals—the way gangrene smelled—what substitutes were used for food and clothing when the blockade got too tight for these necessities to be brought in from abroad. I heard about the burning and looting of Atlanta and the way the refugees crowded the roads and trains to Macon. I heard about everything in the world except that the Confederates lost the war."

At this point Margaret said she was ten years old before she heard that General Lee surrendered and had refused to believe it—an example of the humorous exaggeration she delighted in. Later on it was a source of annoyance when taken up by newspapers and reprinted as fact. In truth, Margaret as a child knew that the South's cause was the Lost Cause. And from her earliest years her mother taught her that what had counted was how one behaved when facing the fact of defeat.

The other favorite topic for Sunday afternoon discussions was family history, which required a good memory for genealogical detail. In this, Margaret's father was especially gifted. He filled a ledger with family anecdotes and records from which he could quote at any time as accurately as if the pages of his beautiful and regular handwriting lay before him. Margaret was conscious from childhood of her father's store of family information; she recalled his command of it in describing a scene that took place in the Spring of 1940. Writing to Colonel John W. Thomason, the famous Marine Corps artist and author, and biographer of General J. E. B. Stuart, Margaret reported that a number of relatives gathered under a rose arbor to indulge in "the Sunday afternoon diversion of climbing up and down the family tree and venturing out onto limbs and twigs which will hardly bear any weight." Margaret's contribution had been a remark that she thought John Thomason might be distant kin of the Mitchells.

"Yes," said Eugene Mitchell, "Colonel Thomason is

probably distantly related. One of his relatives wrote Cousin Aurelia some years ago for information about our Thomason branch, the Elbert County, Georgia, ones. His branch went to Alabama, I believe. My father, Russell Crawford Mitchell, married Deborah Margaret Sweet. He was the son of I. G. Mitchell, born in Madison County, Georgia. I. G. was the son of William Mitchell, who was born near Lisbon, South Carolina, in 1777. William married Eleanor Thomason of Elbert County, Georgia. Eleanor was the daughter of John Thomason of the same place. This John Thomason was born in the North of Ireland, came first to Pennsylvania and then moved to Guilford Court House, North Carolina. After the Revolution, he moved to Georgia, settling in Elbert County. His wife was Eleanor Nelly Diamond and their daughter was the Eleanor Thomason who married William Mitchell. Some of their children stayed in Georgia, some moved to Alabama." An aunt now spoke up: "Nelly Diamond's mother was a Stuart, one of the Royal Stuarts. The old folks told me that Nelly was an enormously fat woman. They said the family joke ran, 'What was the largest precious stone ever to cross the Atlantic?—Nelly Diamond.' "

Eugene Mitchell was born in the Jackson Hill neighborhood in 1866. He graduated with honors at the University of Georgia in 1885, and took a law degree the following year. By the time Margaret was born, he had become one of the leading lawyers in Atlanta. In partnership with his brother, Gordon Forrest Mitchell, he made a specialty of drawing wills and examining land titles. Perhaps he might have become wealthy with those of his clients who benefited from the rising value of Atlanta real estate. But Eugene Mitchell was no speculator. He told his son the panic of 1893 had come upon him as a young married man, "and taken out of him all daring, and put in its place a desire to have a competence assured to him." But he was courageous when principle was at stake. Stephens Mitchell recorded of his father that he "had daring in his desire to stand for the right. He never hesitated to take unpopular stands on public issues, nor to place himself in danger of violence, at a time when Atlanta had dangerous mobs, and when rioting and lynchings were common."

Eugene Mitchell entered the law at his father's insistence though he had wanted to be a writer, and he did write historical articles that showed with admirable clarity how vast a fund of information he had gathered by reading and in talks with older members of the family and their friends. One of his interests was to study the picturesque names attached to certain Atlanta neighborhoods and suburbs. In and around the city he could explain the naming of Bull Sluice, Tight Squeeze, Rough and Ready, Slabtown, Snake Nation, Lick Skillet and Beaver Slide. Farther afield, he hunted the sources of Ty Ty, Social Circle, and Plum Nelly, a place so called because it was on the border "plumb nearly" in Tennessee. Mr. Mitchell relished the color and blunt humor of such names as proofs of Georgia's pioneer vitality. And he applied the insight and keenness of mind that made him a good historian to his profession; other lawyers said his legal papers were models of clearness and conciseness, and it was impossible to misinterpret a will that Eugene Mitchell had drawn. Discussing this phase of practice, he once said to his son, "In drawing a will, just look after the grammar, and the law will look after itself."

Margaret Mitchell loved and respected her father, though she resembled him too closely for complete understanding. Important factors in Margaret's personality came from Eugene Mitchell: her interest in history and respect for truth, and her feeling that a contract was inviolable. Margaret also inherited her humor from her father, though this might not be readily evident, for Mr. Mitchell's sense of fun did not lie near the surface, and his manner could be frosty.

Stephens Mitchell has recorded his opinion that what was remarkable about Margaret, and gave her character and ability, was the variety of her ancestors. He wrote, "We know a good deal about our forebears, and when I stop and think about them, and think about Margaret, I believe I can see how each of the personalities behind us made its own contribution to her sum-total. Though we

32

owed most, of course, to the characters of our parents, and their influence on us, behind them lay these others who formed us."

To begin with, behind Eugene Mitchell was his father, Russell Crawford Mitchell, who had grown up on the family farm at Flat Shoals, about fifteen miles from present day Atlanta, attending West Georgia College, and started in life teaching school to support his study of the law. On admission to the bar, Russell Mitchell went to Texas, practicing at Alto from 1857 to 1861, when he joined I Company, First Texas Infantry. He became a first sergeant, and saw action at Gaines Mill, Second Manassas, and a number of smaller but equally dangerous engagements. He marched into Maryland in the invasion of September 1862, and was present on the seventeenth, the bloodiest day of the war, on the terrible field of Sharpsburg behind Antietam Creek. Here he was shot in the head; the bullet went through his skull, but did not damage any brain centers. The brigade surgeon, Dr. Roach, came upon Russell as he partially recovered consciousness, wiped the bloody face, and remarked, "This boy is my cousin." They put him on a wagon carrying salvaged muskets and he survived a jolting ride of 150 miles to Staunton, Virginia. He then went to recuperate at the home of his brother Dr. Madison Mitchell, in Thomasville, Georgia. Among the volunteer nurses was a Florida girl named Deborah Margaret Sweet. She fell in love with the sergeant of the famous Texas Brigade, and he with her. The announcement of their engagement coincided with his orders to rejoin the army.

The military authorities now marked Russell Mitchell for light duty, assigning him as wardmaster in the medical corps. When Atlanta lay under siege in the late summer of 1864, he was with the Institute Hospital at Ellis and Courtland streets. He left on the army hospital train, and went through the last campaigns in Tennessee and Alabama. Shortly after the surrender he married Deborah and settled in Florida, hoping to resume the practice of law. Unhappily there was no opening for legal talent, and further annoyance came from a difficulty with a bureaucrat. This person interfered with Russell Mitchell's attempts to start in business, and expressed doubt as to the validity of his word. Russell gave the fellow a beating and threw him into a mud puddle. The Federal occupying authorities put a price on Russell Mitchell's head; he escaped to Atlanta, and lay low until the thing blew over. As soon as it was safe, Deborah Mitchell followed her husband to Georgia. He made no further attempts to practice law, but went into the lumber business and prospered, along with the city, until his death in 1905.

Russell Crawford Mitchell's father was the Reverend Isaac Green Mitchell, a Methodist minister who owned a farm twenty miles from Atlanta. He donated the church building to his congregation, and lived in the parsonage next door, at Forsyth and Garnett streets in the center of the city. His father William Mitchell had been a farmer near where Atlanta is now, who had served in the Eighth Regular Infantry at New Orleans in the War of 1812. This William Mitchell's father, Thomas Mitchell, had been an officer in the Revolution, and is buried near Atlanta in Henry County.

One can see that the Mitchells believed in doing their duty, and that this duty, as they saw it, included attending wars. Margaret once said to a relative who inquired about ancestors, "You can tell your children that they have a fine, plain American background." It is all of that, and in all branches. Margaret's grandmother, Deborah Sweet Mitchell, for example, had Scottish and Huguenot forebears, some of whom were Loyalists in the Revolution, though most of them took the Congressional side. Horry County (pronounced Oh-REE) on the Carolina coast is named for one of Deborah's Huguenot ancestors. Some of the Scottish ancestors came to North America as refugees after Culloden; and one was a respected and prosperous pirate. Grandmother Deborah Mitchell died before Margaret was born; Stephens recorded that "She was a woman of monumental memory, an ability that came to Father and to Margaret, who got her grandmother's family history from her father, and stored it away."

Margaret's mother, Maybelle Stephens, was born in Atlanta on January 13, 1872. After early childhood in the Jackson Hill neighborhood, she went to Bellevue Convent in Quebec, where she learned to speak good French. A devout Catholic, Maybelle Stephens admired the intellectual nuns and enjoyed the ordered life they provided their pupils in Quebec. In Atlanta, she had become conscious of being a Catholic in a largely Protestant community. Maybelle studied this matter with a depth of thought unusual in a girl of her years, and reached a decision: it was all very well for an American Catholic girl of a good family to be educated in Canada, or even in Ireland, or France; but where good schools in America were open to people of her faith, they should seize the opportunity and enter them. Accordingly, in her last year at Quebec she got permission to return home, and finished her education with a year's study at the Atlanta Female Institute.

Though primarily concerned with things of the mind and spirit, Maybelle Stephens liked the outdoors, played a sound game of tennis, and rode well. After her marriage at the age of twenty she devoted most of her time to intellectual pursuits. Her son remembers his mother as one who read widely, with particular emphasis on history. Stephens Mitchell also recorded that "She knew her religion thoroughly and insisted on its being taught and preached correctly. This did not make her too popular with some of the clergy. This never worried Mother at all. She believed that the church was wide enough to use intelligent laymen and women in it, and it turned out that it was. She was one of the founders of the Catholic Laymen's Association at a time when it amounted to something. She believed in the role of the lay apologist, and she, with those like her, made a bright chapter in the history of the church in Georgia."

It is not surprising that Maybelle Stephens Mitchell was among the founders of the movement for women's suffrage in Georgia. She grounded her argument on economic justice: having inherited some property, she objected to paying taxes without the privilege of voting how the money should be spent.

Indeed, one of Margaret's first memories was connected

with the cause of women suffrage as, many years later, she told Mrs. Sidney Howard in a letter about a series of articles in the *Atlantic Monthly* by Mrs. Howard's sister.

"The last one, 'Parents and Parades,' appealed to me especially. My earliest memories are of my mother and the woman's suffrage movement. Mother was small and gentle but redheaded, and nothing infuriated her as much as the complacent attitude of other ladies who felt that they should let the gentlemen do the voting. Our family was fortunate in that the menfolks were heartily in favor of woman's suffrage. The first time I was ever permitted to stay up later than six o'clock was on the tremendous occasion of a suffragette rally which was presided over, I believe, by Carrie Chapman Catt. The cook went home sick, all the relatives had gone to the meeting, and there was no one to look after me. Mother tied a Votes-for-Women banner around my fat stomach, put me under her arm, took me to the meeting, hissing bloodcurdling threats if I did not behave, set me on the platform between the silver pitcher and the water glasses while she made an impassioned speech. I was so enchanted at my eminence that I behaved perfectly, even blowing kisses to gentlemen in the front row. I was kissed by Mrs. Catt, if it was she, and called the youngest suffragette in Georgia and the future of our cause. I was intolerable for days afterwards and, only after being spanked, was permitted to witness a parade of such as your sister described. Please tell her how much I enjoy her articles and how many happy childhood memories they recall."

Maybelle also had a perceptive and deep-rooted social sense. "She could make people feel at home," her son wrote later. "No matter what type of people she was with, she could adapt to them. She had manners in a city that was only beginning to know that there was such a thing. She dressed quietly and was soft-spoken. She knew the world and its perils and was willing to speak of them in a day and time when things were done but not spoken of. She realized the perils of drink and warned against them, but she knew that Prohibition was wrong, and that total abstinence, if universally applied, would make a dull world. We had to learn how to drink and how to be mannerly about it.

"She realized the strength of sex and had only one suggestion for control of it—early marriage. Mother told us she had no remedy for things the world had found none for, and this included gambling and the taking of chances in general. She said that all her family had been gamblers and that none of Father's were, and that she hoped we would be gamblers in life, and lucky ones. She was fond of quoting some lines by James Graham, Marquis of Montrose, that her father had liked:

> He either fears his fate too much
> Or his deserts are small
> Who dares not put it to the touch
> To gain or lose it all.

She insisted that we fight for our rights, even though we were bested. Time and again she said that courage was the only virtue worth worrying about, for it comprehended all the others. Her influence over both of us was very strong."

Margaret took pleasure throughout life in thinking of the Irish ancestry her mother handed on. Maybelle Stephens' father John Stephens had been born in 1833 in Kings (now Offaly) County in central Ireland. He came to North America at the age of seventeen, following other Stephenses who had been sent for by the first member of the family who settled in Louisiana in the 1790s. Soon there were Stephenses from Louisiana to New York, and by 1850, when Margaret's Grandfather Stephens arrived, they were well established and prospering.

Among them was John's uncle Thomas Stephens, a successful New York merchant, who paid for the youth's passage and then sent him on to another uncle who had a store in Augusta, Georgia. John graduated from Hiawassee College in East Tennessee. At the outbreak of war, he enlisted in the Confederate Army, saw combat along the Coast, and later was appointed to the staff of the Commissary General. In 1864, John Stephens was a desk officer in Atlanta at the time the Federal troops began their approach to the city and thousands of people were abandoning their homes in the countryside. Among the refugees coming into the city was Annie Elizabeth Fitzgerald, a guest at the Commissary General's home. Annie and the young staff officer fell in love, and were married as fighting neared the town. When the siege began, Annie went out on the last train to Macon. John left Atlanta with the army and served till the final surrender.

After the war, John Stephens worked hard as an accountant, saved money, and with a partner established the successful wholesale grocery business of Stephens & Flynn. He bought land in the Jackson Hill section, and started a horse car line to provide transportation to this part of town. He then joined a pool of speculators trying to corner the cotton market. They were destroyed in the trading, and Grandfather Stephens survived with only his lands and his horse car line. In the early Nineties electric street railways made horse cars valueless, and so when John Stephens died in 1896 he left a comfortable estate, but no great fortune. His friends remembered him as a slender, erect, blond man with reddish hair and beard, who bore a remarkable resemblance to George Bernard Shaw.

Grandmother Annie Fitzgerald Stephens was to have a great and mostly unhappy influence on Margaret's life. Basically a kind and good woman, as age came on she began turning into an imperious dowager. She regarded the horse car line as private transportation, and would send a servant to hold the Jackson Street car in front of the house until she was ready to get on. After her husband sold the line, Grandmother Stephens continued to expect this service, and the children would often see her on the porch, shouting a command for one of the new electric cars to wait. But the motorman would ring his bell and whirl his crank, and the car would go grinding around the corner without Grandmother Stephens.

This strong-willed and fearless Annie Fitzgerald Stephens had a remarkable father. He was Philip Fitzgerald, who had been born in Lagistown, Ireland, in 1798. His family had joined the rebellion which collapsed in that year with the capture and suicide of its leader, Wolfe

Tone. The English caught Philip Fitzgerald's grandfather, and tortured him to death, but Philip's father got away with his family to France, and then to North America. Philip Fitzgerald made his way as a tutor and schoolteacher, at last settling in Fayetteville, Georgia, one year after Indians left the town. Here he taught school until he saved enough to become a merchant. He prospered, bought farms, and set up as a planter. In some respects his career resembled that of the typical Irish back-country speculator described by W. J. Cash in *The Mind of the South*, a sociological study that Margaret Mitchell admired. Philip Fitzgerald was dour and dry, but he had varied abilities. Although short of stature, he was powerfully built and held his own in the rough community by his skill as a wrestler. When necessary, he could take a knife or pistol from a drunken frontier bully, get him down, and put the boots to him. This formidable aptitude for self-defense was masked by innocent violet-blue eyes, a rice-white complexion, and cornsilk-yellow hair. Margaret inherited the eyes and hair, though after babyhood the yellow hair turned brown with a touch of red.

Though well equipped to survive on the frontier, Philip Fitzgerald differed from Professor Cash's Irish adventurer in two important respects—his cultivated literary taste and his belief that women as well as men should receive good educations. He told his daughters they might attend any school to which they were willing to travel. Two of them went to Charleston, but Annie Fitzgerald preferred the Fayetteville Female Academy in Georgia, as did Scarlett O'Hara. When they came home, the educated daughters found plenty to read, for Philip Fitzgerald had assembled a library that was wide-ranging for the place and time. He also regarded good furniture as essential, and his descendants treasure the pieces that survived the Civil War.

The mother of Philip Fitzgerald's brood of daughters was Eleanor Aveline McGhan, who belonged to one of the Catholic families Lord Baltimore had planted in Maryland. In her maturity, as a West Georgian with a Maryland background, Eleanor McGhan disliked the backwoods atmosphere of Clayton County. In old age she told

Margaret's mother she spent all her young married life at a place not much different from a small African village, over which she found it her duty to exercise unbounded care and attention; and this was to be somewhat the attitude of Scarlett O'Hara's mother in *Gone with the Wind*. The old lady recounted a dream that had come to her repeatedly at the Clayton County plantation. Troops were streaming past the house, in retreat, and over the horizon British troops hurried after them. It was so real that she believed it would happen. And it did happen, exactly as she had dreamed, except that the men coming over the horizon were United States troops—and that was worse. But Philip Fitzgerald lived after the war to build another fortune from the ruin that came from the freeing of his slaves, the burning of his corn and cotton, and the decline in land values. The tradition of his refusal to accept failure was an important part of Margaret Mitchell's heritage.

Common sense, respect for learning, willingness to work in expectation of suitable rewards—these were in Margaret's background as it came to her from both sides of the family. And there was something in it beyone these virtues. This additional quality was integrity, the elemental soundness that brought these people through honorable lives to deaths that they did not fear. And there was more than this: something that escapes definition just as it does analysis, a kind of gallantry or grace. It comes from the Irish blood of the Fitzgeralds, McGhans, O'Reillys, and MacCartans; from the Highland Scottish ancestry, from the sturdy Scotch-Irish, the English, Huguenots, and French—all bequeathing to Margaret Mitchell the quality of romance.

"It has always been a satisfaction to me," Stephens Mitchell wrote, "that ours was one of the families that could refer to parents, grandparents and great-grandparents who had lived in or near the city without embarrassment— in fact, with pride. Ancestors are not much mentioned in Atlanta. There are Southern cities where the opposite is true. But not in Atlanta." Margaret agreed with her brother about the soundness of their forebears in Georgia and other parts of the country, and respected these people, and honored them in memory. Yet even here her humor would break out, so that she once gave a short list of Southern terms and their translations which indicated a certain amount of affectionate irreverence. According to Margaret, in the South the phrase "prominent clergyman" merely meant "minister"; a "distinguished member of the bar" was simply a lawyer; and the phrase "old and prominent" invariably preceded the word "family."

III

Age of Innocence

Atlanta had started when the wilderness was surveyed for a railroad in 1837. Small houses sprang up around the planned railhead, and soon the settlement was informally called Terminus because it was to be the end of the road. By the time the line was finished the village had grown so much that the settlers decided it should have a real name, and in 1842 the place was christened Marthasville for the little daughter of the governor of Georgia, Martha Lumpkin. In 1845 the citizens asked that Marthasville be given a dignified name with a touch of the classic in it. After some thought, the name Atlanta was chosen because the railroad had joined it to the ocean.

The new name was happy and beautiful, but the inhabitants continued bustling at their tasks like true sons of Martha. This was apparent to Dr. John Stainback Wilson, who made perhaps the first sociological study of the city, in 1871, under the title *Atlanta As It Is Today*. Dr. Wilson, who had introduced the Turkish bath to the community, was editor of the medical section in *Godey's Lady's Book*, and so commanded respect when he said: "Our people are emphatically a business people who come here to *work,* and therefore the devil does not find many workshops here in the form of idle brains."

Three decades later that was still the spirit of Atlanta as it entered one of its great periods, and Margaret Mitchell's childhood began. The towers rising across the narrow valley, the bustle of trade, the roar of traffic—all were there to remind the little girl she was a citizen of no mean city. Yet, signs of material prosperity, numerous as they were, did not tell Atlanta's whole story—do not tell it, to this day. In some ways a baffling city, Atlanta has always had an undeniable and perhaps indefinable charm. Visitors and residents alike have succumbed to this spell, which seems to be in the air. At the height of her fame, Margaret said, "Atlanta is difficult to describe. But it is a grand place, and a place one can love."

The year Margaret was born metropolitan Atlanta numbered some 89,000 inhabitants, six times the population of thirty years before. In 1910, Atlanta saw its first season of opera, with Caruso, Farrar, Homer, Scotti, Fremstad, and other stars from New York under Giulio Gatti-Casazza's management. The leaders of Atlanta society gave dinner parties and balls before and after *Tosca, Aïda, Madama Butterfly, I Pagliacci, and Hänsel and Gretel;* the performances took place in the new auditorium, later to house the Gone With the Wind Ball.

Margaret was an observant little girl growing up in an exciting city and enjoying the show her lively fellow citizens put on. It was summed up by Peachtree Street, which had burst into architectural and social glory with the prosperity of the Nineties. Now, in Margaret's childhood, Peachtree unrolled three miles of splendid houses, like the streets of magnates' homes in other flourishing provincial cities, such as Euclid Avenue in Cleveland and Summit Avenue in St. Paul. Peachtree Street stood comparison with the finest, and this was part of the exciting present in Atlanta; the past was also there for Margaret, in hundreds of ways.

Indeed, there was a place in the city where the past

seemed to occur again before one's eyes. This magical place was the Cyclorama, a building that housed a huge historical painting that is still one of the sights of Atlanta. It stands in Grant Park, named for the engineer who planned the city's fortifications in the war. The Cyclorama shows the climax of the battle for Atlanta on September 1, 1864. A team of German artists came to town in 1885 to make preliminary sketches on a platform forty feet high at the intersection of Moreland Avenue and the Georgia Railroad, from which they surveyed the scene of battle. Guided by official reports and military maps, the artists put into their tremendous painting a feeling of absolute reality. Coming up out of the entrance passageway in the center of the circular building, around whose walls the painting spreads as one continuous scene, the visitor has the sensation of standing on a rise of ground in the middle of the battlefield and being able to see for miles in any direction. Off to the northwest, columns of smoke are rising from Atlanta; near at hand a detachment of Federal cavalry gallops down a ridge, with General James B. McPherson in the lead, his pistol drawn. In half an hour, McPherson will be dead. But now the battle pauses and one sees the panorama: flags, guns, horses, twisted railroad tracks, wounded men, dead men. It is easy to understand the effect this combination of theater and history must have had on Margaret as a child: to the diligent and attentive little girl, her hand clutching her brother's, the Cyclorama must have come with the impact of enormous wonder.

Margaret also saw records of the war in brick and mortar. Her mother would take her for a drive into the countryside, and stop on a back road when a ruined chimney could be seen above the scrubby second-growth timber. Pointing to the column of blackened brick, Mrs. Mitchell would say, "That is one of Sherman's sentinels." Then she would give Margaret the familiar speech about the difference between the people who had been, so to speak, defeated by defeat and those who refused to "go down in the world and disappear." One's obligation to life was to turn in a good performance; that was the hard path, and the only path, by which one attained validity and self-respect.

Margaret's memory was that Mrs. Mitchell first began pointing out Sherman's sentinels when her daughter was only six years old. Writing in 1936 to the historian Henry Steele Commager, Margaret recalled one hot September afternoon when she returned from the opening session of first grade to announce that she saw no reason to learn arithmetic. Mrs. Mitchell thereupon took Margaret for a drive on the remote and quiet Jonesboro Road. There had once been people hereabouts, and Margaret's mother "talked about the world those people had lived in, such a secure world, and how it had exploded beneath them. And she told me that my own world was going to explode under me, some day, and God help me if I didn't have some weapon to meet the new world. She was talking about the necessity of having an education, both classical and practical. For she said all that would be left after a world ended would be what you could do with your hands and what you had in your head. 'So, for God's sake go to school and learn something that will stay with you. The strength of women's hands isn't worth anything but what they've got in their heads will carry them as far as they need to go.' Well, I never could learn the multiplication table above the sevens but I was frightened and impressed enough by her words to learn enough rhetoric to land a job on a newspaper some years later."

By the time she was eleven, Margaret had progressed in some ways beyond her age. She had gone through Shakespeare, though perhaps not so much from precocious appreciation as to earn the small sums of money Mrs. Mitchell paid her for the reading of each play. Margaret found Scott and Dickens to her taste, and she read the *New York Sun,* to which Mr. Mitchell subscribed, and the three young people's magazines that came to the house, *The Youth's Companion, Saint Nicholas,* and the British publication, *Chatterbox.* Along with Stephens she read the works of George Alfred Henty, a boys' author who did not patronize his readers. In addition to this Margaret read the adventures of Tom Swift, and many stories about the Rover Boys. Stephens did not share her liking for the Rover Boys books, maintaining the plots were all the same and the style bad. Margaret gave a careful answer: "Well, if it is a good plot, it will stand being read over a good many times, and the style doesn't matter so long as you can understand what the characters are doing."

Verse as well as prose attracted Margaret; in her scrapbook she pasted copies of "About Ben Adhem," "Curfew Shall Not Ring Tonight," "The Night Before Christmas," "A Leap for Life," "Kiss Her and Tell Her So," Byron's "Marco Bozzaris," Bryant's "Song of Marion's Men," "Nebuchadnezzar" by Erwin Russel Jones, "Home" by James Montgomery, "Romance" by Jean Ingelow, "Little Britches" by Ambassador John Hay, and "The Blue and the Gray" by Francis Finch.

Though she read and wrote for hours at a time—indeed, she dictated stories before she could write—Margaret was a tomboy. Until she was eleven or twelve, she frequently wore boy's pants in the wintertime because of her mother's fear that her skirts would catch fire, as they did on one occasion from an open grate in the Jackson Street house. In spite of her preference for tomboy ways, Margaret was sent to dancing school and learned ballroom etiquette at an early age. Because of this good teaching in childhood, and her natural grace, Margaret always danced well; John Marsh said this was the first thing he noticed about her.

Margaret liked to dance, but was even more fond of riding. She did well with the Texas pony, and in 1911 graduated to a larger mount, a strong swift animal who proved to have one fault—lack of a sure foot. This flaw came to light when he fell with Margaret, cracking her leg and grinding her face into the gravel of North Boulevard. The scars wore off, and there seemed to be no serious consequences, but the leg injury was to plague her in later years.

In 1909, Mr. and Mrs. Mitchell decided the Jackson Hill neighborhood had seen its best days, and bought a lot on Peachtree Street, about a mile north of Ponce de Leon Avenue and three miles from the central business district.

Eugene Mitchell held the property vacant for two years, then built a handsome house into which the family moved in 1912. This place was large enough to be called a mansion; architecturally, it was an acceptable example of the Classical Revival style that had appeared in some parts of the South forty years before the Civil War. Eugene Mitchell and his friends knew the style had not been characteristic of their city until they themselves asked their architects to use it. But they *liked* the classical, as a reaction against the architectural pomp and circumstance of Victorian Atlanta. The ground floor of 1149 Peachtree Street stretched for seventy feet, with a sitting room and a music room opening into a spacious central hall. This open plan of the main floor led Margaret to write and produce a series of plays to entertain her friends, using the sitting room as a stage, with the audience in the hall and music room. Among the productions were: *The Cow Puncher;* an echo of Southey called *The Fall of Ralph the Rover; In My Harem;* and *A Darktown Tragedy.* Producer Mitchell cast for Author Mitchell from a stock company of ten or a dozen boys and girls, often reserving a good part for herself, such as that of "Zara, a female crook and one of the gang" in *Phil Kelly, Detective.*

As she wrote more and more, the process of writing fascinated Margaret. She planted a circle of privet around an oak tree behind the house and worked on plays and stories in this magic ring when the weather was good. Indoors, her bedroom served as author's workshop; she would write something every day and filled so many school copybooks with stories and plays—though many were not completed—that her mother began to store the books in tin bread boxes. The number of boxes increased as time went on, and they accumulated in the cellar. Margaret's plays reflected the influence of the crook shows and melodramas she saw when taken on trips to New York or when road companies came to Atlanta. In the stories, Margaret showed she was reading the romantic adventure fiction of George Barr McCutcheon and Richard Harding Davis. An ambitious story dealt with a hero called Silver Spurs, an "outlaw and Rolling Stone" who rode his horse

47

o to thwart a "cold, unscrupulous, revengeful" villamed Con Liddel. Margaret had a feeling for titles, ering "When We Were Shipwrecked" to "When You and I Were Cast Away." She believed in a fast start. "Forest and Foothills," a story written before the move to Peachtree Street, began: "Julia Weston waited where Sam had left her—alone, she thought, in the great woods. She leaned up against a tree, nearby, thinking. Suddenly someone caught her hands, and another hand was placed over her mouth ..." On the first page of this manuscript the ten-year-old author wrote: "To my *dear* friend, Florence Noyes, my first long story is dedicated." The brisk start was evident, too, in "The Little Pioneers," which she wrote, with minor eccentricities of spelling and punctuation, at the age of twelve: " 'Hold on, Margaret, hold on. Can't you wait on a fellow?' The speaker, a red face boy, on a wirey little poney was urging it to its upmost speed, in order to catch up with a girl who was galloping in front of him." In this story, the children take refuge behind the walls of a frontier fort. The Indians attack, and "Every little while one, bolder than the rest, would clamber over the stockage, only to be shot or beaten back by the brave defenders."

Margaret selected the backgrounds for her plays and stories from a list of twenty-nine "Locations" set down in the back of a school notebook. These settings included Africa, Alaska, China, Egypt, Hades, Mexico, Russia, Turkey, South America, and Paris. In addition, she noted the topical key-words Crook, Civil War, Smugglers, Shipwreck, "Society" (her quotation marks) and Sepoy Rebellion. Keeping notebooks and listing ideas and place names is a sign of the bent for professional writing—the instinctive practical approach. Another sign that an author has been born is the ability to bring off a long and consistent piece of writing in childhood, such as Margaret showed in her plays, and in the novel *The Big Four,* which she seems to have finished at sixteen. Extending through fourteen chapters on more than four hundred copybook pages, *The Big Four* was a story of girls in boarding school. Here Margaret turned from Indians, bandits and burglars to things in her own experience. This was good; yet Margaret mistrusted her gift and set down in her clear and honest handwriting at the end of a copybook: "There are authors and authors but a *true* writer is born and not made. Born writers make their characters real, living people, while the 'made' writers have merely stuffed figures who dance when the strings are pulled—That's how I know that I'm a 'made' writer."

Margaret entered Washington Seminary, a leading private school for young ladies, in 1914. Like most Washington Seminary girls, Margaret was a day pupil. Once the mansion of a wealthy citizen, the school stood only a few blocks north of her home on Peachtree Street. Her best subject was English, under an able teacher, Eva Wilson Paisley, who recognized Margaret's talent and encouraged her to write. But Margaret had many interests away from her composition books and classrooms. From a tomboy she was growing into a belle; she had become graceful and pretty, with the enchantingly humorous manner of Shakespeare's more independent heroines. Not only the boys of Margaret's social group, but also her parents began to enjoy her company immensely, and Mr. and Mrs. Mitchell liked to take her with them to New York, on trips to the mountains of North Carolina, and to the seashore.

In the spring of 1917, the dogwood, azalea, and wild iris bloomed, as usual, along the streets of Atlanta. That spring the United States declared war on Germany, and so entered the European conflict that had begun in 1914. People of the Mitchells' sort met the fact of war with uncomplicated patriotism; in most cases, a young man's greatest worry would be that the fighting might be over before he could get there. Laurence Stallings said it in a few words: "It was an innocent man's war, a simple matter to Americans, despite the millions of Europeans who lay dead between the Vilna and the Marne." To Stephens Mitchell in Atlanta, it appeared that "There was a social duty on the young men to go to war and there was a social duty on the young ladies to see that the soldiers had as nice a time as they could. Most of the young officers in the regiments at Fort McPherson, near Atlanta, were young university students or recent graduates. Margaret could entertain these young men. She had a big house, servants, a car that would hold seven people and, if you crowded enough, quite a few more. She was a good dancer and, just as important, a good conversationalist, and she also had the gift of listening to other people. There was no girl in Atlanta more popular with the young officers."

In that spring Atlanta suffered a terrible fire. It started near the Mitchells' old Jackson Street house, spreading across lots by ways of barns and arbors. Then a high continuous dry south wind swept the blaze along the crest of Jackson Hill and the Boulevard for twenty blocks to Ponce de Leon Avenue. The flames moved at the speed of a man walking, from time to time leaping ahead several hundred feet and turning back to the main body of fire. People rushed from their houses carrying children and the ill and old, not knowing which way to turn or whether they dared run back for a few possessions. Firemen began blowing up houses to make a burned-over zone which they hoped would stop the progress of the flames, and the shock of explosions added to the general terror. Margaret and her brother turned out to help, he with soldiers from Fort McPherson, she as a volunteer in the refugee center at the Municipal Auditorium.

The big hall held a scene of massed confusion. Rescuers had picked up furniture, clothing, and other things abandoned in the streets and carried them to the Auditorium, which looked like an enormous rummage sale, with lost children wandering among the piles of tables, chairs, and bedsteads. There were no plans for such a disaster, and the volunteers functioned strictly according to their own intelligence and character. Facing the emergency, Margaret made herself a co-ordinator of rescued furniture and lost children, sitting on a desk and looking like a child herself with her pigtails and schoolgirl's middy blouse. Explosions, fires, soldiers—men, women, and children fleeing from a holocaust—homeless people seeking shelter—every aspect of the disaster found a place in Margaret's mind, and waited there to emerge with remarkable vigor as the refugee passages in *Gone with the Wind*.

Margaret's family lost thirteen houses in the destruction of the Jackson Hill neighborhood. This was a severe financial blow. Nevertheless, Margaret and Stephens continued to give bright and gay parties, first for the officer candidates, and then for the young lieutenants when they had completed their courses. Stephens Mitchell wrote in his personal history that "The sites of most of these parties would be our home or at the Capital City Club roof garden or at the Piedmont Driving Club, which, during that summer were lovely, really lovely. The outdoors, the wind that blows across Atlanta, the starlight nights, orchestras under the stars, great groups of young people, all of them having a good time—that would be a striking scene for anyone. Mother insisted that I spend whatever of my cadet's pay and officer's pay I had on having a good time, and she wanted Margaret to have a good time, because she said, 'You are seeing the end of an era and are able to see it under very attractive circumstances. Don't let the chance of seeing this go by you. Don't try to save a dime and lay the dime aside. For all we know, after this is over, the dime or the dollar or the million dollars will be worth nothing. Things have a habit of disappearing during wars, but what you have seen and what you have done are something that will always be with you, and that you can remember, and its remembrance will have a much greater value than denying yourself the sight of it.' That season we danced to 'Poor Butterfly,' 'The Girl on the Magazine Cover,' 'Long, Long Trail,' 'Where Do We Go from Here' and 'Over There.' The city was never the same after that year. The war changed everything."

When she returned to Washington Seminary in the fall of 1917 for her senior year, Margaret was much concerned about the war and the men with whom she had danced who were preparing to go overseas or who had already arrived in France. She knew that like Stephen Crane's hero, these young amateur soldiers were going to touch the great death—and some would do more than touch it. An untitled story in one of her copybooks had this passage: "God, it couldn't be true! Yet there the crumpled telegram lay on the floor under the poor bed with its too thin coverings. The shabby room was bitter cold—the carpetless floor was cold as she knelt down to retrieve the telegram and smooth it out in the dull hope that she had misread. But the words were unchanging— 'The War Department regrets to report the death in action of Private William Southern.'"

Margaret did not finish that story; but by the time she became a senior, she had acquired a literary reputation at Washington Seminary for a story called "Little Sister" which was published the previous June in the school annual, *Facts and Fancies*. Here Margaret drew once more on her childhood imaginings of banditry; but she treated this material with a realism that made the piece a shocker for a school publication. As usual, Margaret seized the reader's attention with the opening paragraph: "Peggy lay in the sand behind some mesquite bushes, hugging her father's big rifle to her breast and watching Alvarado's men move about in the house. Since the later hours of the night before she had lain there and though now the early Mexican sun was burning her blue eyes and blistering the little arms that so tightly held the big gun, no thought of changing her position had entered her mind." The reader next learns that Alvarado and his gang have massacred Peggy's parents; the little girl has escaped unnoticed, with the rifle, and has lain in hiding all night. She has heard the carousing of the bandits, and the raping of her older sister: "Long she watched the lights in the cottage, shivered and hid her head at Big Sister's screams." Knowing it will mean her death, the child plans to kill the bandit chief, and at dawn, "a hard-faced Peggy with dry eyes" is waiting. Then the story ends: "Within the house there was a general stir. Someone had heard the whisper of the wind, and as if by magic, a Mexican appeared, ran across the porch and bent his head to the ground intently a moment, then called excitedly inside. Out in the early morning sunlight hurried the bandit leader, tossing away a cigarette as he came and hastily buckling on his gun belt. At the words of the scout he raised his head, listening anxiously. Crowd-

52

ing behind him came the rest of his unkempt band, stopping short at his upraised hand for silence.

"With infinite care Peggy slid the gun up to the level of her eyes and found the man across the sights. Coldly, dispassionately she viewed him, the chill steel of the gun giving her confidence. She must not miss now—she would not miss—and she did not."

Besides being a remarkably workmanlike story for a young girl to write, "Little Sister" revealed that Margaret's relations with her fellow students were not uniformly good. She had submitted "Little Sister" in the *Facts and Fancies* short story contest, and the editor had rejected it. Nevertheless, the story was published, presumably because Mrs. Paisley used her authority to get it into the annual. On the whole, it seemed to Stephens Mitchell that "Margaret did not like Washington Seminary." In his record of this period, Stephens wrote: "She did not get an invitation to join any of the school sororities, but she had begun to meet people outside school circles and she never lacked for men friends. At the end of her school days, we find a girl who had not made a social success at her school, though she came of an old family who had sufficient means to provide her with the proper things for a young girl entering on her social life in the city. But at school she had made enemies as well as friends. The judgment of adolescents was wrong, but it led to much bitterness. There are people in Atlanta who have always disliked Margaret Mitchell and will always dislike her. Margaret never forgot who were her enemies."

Margaret passed the entrance examinations for Smith College and graduated from Washington Seminary in June 1918. That summer in Atlanta, Margaret fell in love. The young man was Lieutenant Clifford Henry, who had left Harvard in his senior year. His parents were Mr. and Mrs. Ira W. Henry, of New York City and Sound Beach, Connecticut. Mr. and Mrs. Mitchell approved of Clifford Henry, though they suffered private anxiety when Clifford and Margaret told friends they were engaged and he gave her a family ring. Stephens Mitchell, being a young man himself, and preparing to set out for France, could understand how Clifford Henry felt: "He liked the soft Southern nights of Atlanta, the drives, the dances, our house with its wide terraces, the moonlight with the strolling Negro guitar players under the deep shadow of the oaks." It was a marvelous time to be alive.

Both her fiancé and her brother had gone to France by early in September, when Margaret set out with her mother for Smith. They left Atlanta two weeks before Margaret was due at college in Northampton, Massachusetts, in order to shop in New York and visit an aunt in Connecticut. Though she had brought grace and gaiety to many parties, Margaret was starting her higher education in a serious frame of mind. She intended to take all the available science courses, enter a medical college after Smith, and become a doctor. But there was nothing about these plans in Margaret's first letter to her father and grandmother. Writing on September 8 from the house of her Aunt Edyth (Mrs. Edward Ney Morris) on the Shore Road, Greenwich, Margaret told of "a riotous time tramping up and down Broadway and 5th Ave., peeping into every window and 'shopping.' Then we went to the Museum of Natural History where we renewed our old friendship with the brontesaurus and stuffed Hypies . . . When we took the Greenwich train, we sat opposite a man who looked vaguely familiar and I noticed that he was looking at us. Our Southern accent marks us anyway. But when I pulled off my glove and changed the heavy ring from one hand to the other, I caught his brown eyes and grinned for I knew who he was. He arose and came over to us—

" 'You are Miss Mitchell, aren't you?' he questioned, smiling.

" 'You are Clifford's father.' And it was!

" 'I recognized the ring,' he laughed. 'Cliff was so fond of it.'

"And then we all began to chatter. I liked him immensely and I believe Mother does too. He is a pleasant man, with a quiet sense of humor and he is more forceful than Clifford. He's no plain New Yorker, but very cosmopolitan and well educated. He is intensely proud of his son, though he tries not to show it and he handed me some letters from him that he had in his pocket. Well, he invited us to meet Mrs. Henry (who was then out of town) at luncheon at the Waldorf Wednesday. After that we are going to the theatre. Well, I hope I like the Madame as well as I do the father for I certainly like him. Funny meeting, wasn't it? Of course he had seen some awful snapshots of me. He's so much like Clifford in looks. If you get any letters from Cliff to me, *please* hustle them up here.

"Perhaps I'll like the North—I'm going to try to like the place I must live in for nine months, but it will be rather difficult. Perhaps Northampton is different from Greenwich. I hope so anyway for I want to get to a place where the individual and not the millions count."

Two days later, Mrs. Mitchell wrote to her husband: "Margaret's letter will tell you how we met Mr. Henry and will take luncheon with him and his wife tomorrow. Dear, you must have had no youth or forgotten it if you attach so much importance to the affections of seventeen years. The Henrys so far as I have seen are good people, well travelled, educated, how much or how little money I do not know, but respectable. The boy is over in Europe perchance for life. Why worry over what can't happen for four or five years and 99 to 100 will not happen at all. Can you remember how many girls Stephens has been in love with since he was seventeen? Youth has ways of its own for its own education. I will tell the Henrys when I see them that they must not say anything of Margaret to any one, so as to leave both their son and Margaret freedom to change their minds if they so desire. Margaret herself is not ignorant of the natural manner of seventeen to change its mind. So put *your* mind at rest about this affair, as there can come no harm of it."

The following week, Mrs. Mitchell took Margaret to Northampton and saw her installed as a freshman at Mrs. Pearson's house, 10 Henshaw Street. Then as now Smith College had a justly earned reputation of being a place that challenged the brightest minds among America's young women. Margaret had met a sophomore at Greenwich who told her Smith wasn't as difficult as some people thought; still, it must have looked large, and impersonal, and—*Northern* to Margaret as she said good-by to her wise and kind mother at the Northampton railway station. That was the last time she would ever see her mother alive.

IV

Mr. Eugene Mitchell Requests

Settling down at college—everyone who has done it can imagine how Margaret felt as she dug in at 10 Henshaw Street, and learned to refer to it as "Ten Hen." Installed on the second floor, she acquired several roommates, including Dorothy Brooks from Syracuse, New York, and Madeleine ("Red") Baxter from Woonsocket, Rhode Island. Ten Hen was the same sort of refuge as the houses at the great British public schools, the basic, cellular establishment of student life. Outside was College, big and exciting, but not especially friendly until one got accustomed to it. Chartered in 1871, and opened four years later through the bequest of Sophia Smith, the college had high intellectual standards together with a reputation, in Eastern undergraduate circles at least, for elegance, dash and style. A provincial young lady might be proud to enter such an institution, while feeling some anxiety as to her ability to make a dent in the place. Margaret felt this anxiety, but concealed it; her mother's training saw to that.

In late September and October, a mysterious danger

overran most of the world, including Northampton. This was the epidemic of Spanish influenza, a disease that attacked the throat and lungs. There had been a premonitory outbreak in May and June; now, as Margaret settled to the college routine, the invisible wave of Spanish influenza came again. The outbreaks were attributed by France to Spain, by Spain to France, and by America to eastern Europe, but everywhere the symptoms were the same: aches throughout the body, pains in the head, fever, nausea, and paroxysms of coughing. The onset was sudden; then in a short time the patient either got well or died. Throughout the United States, authorities forbade crowds to gather, and closed the schools, so that many a boy and girl enjoyed a serene and unexpected holiday bicycling through quiet streets in mellow October weather.

The health officers put Smith College into quarantine, then suspended classes. On October 5, Margaret wrote: "Now we can't leave Hamp, even visit other houses, or go to Allen Field for sports. We *can* hike and we do. I'm realizing Stephens was right about his little fellow out-hiking the big ones. I believe I'll be a good walker soon for I'm developing a strong second wind. These Yanks are strong on cross country 'Tramps' and as the fields and woods are beautiful now and in the open it's far safer, I intend to stay out a good deal." Margaret returned to this letter before sealing it and added: "Late in night. Your money order and telegram came a while ago. Thanks muchly for the money order. I hope I can get the cash. You see, I was down to my last cent and just about desperate because everybody had treated me so nicely (fed me, I mean) and I had not repaid them. Then there was the wash and worst of all, all the societies are howling for coin. In fact the wolf was at the door but I didn't need this much."

Walking on the hills around Northampton, Margaret felt the hush that had descended on the country; it would have seemed like a stillness that covered the world, except for news from places like Saint Mihiel. As part of a great offensive, the American 102nd Infantry attacked machine-gun nests at a point on the way to that Meuse River town. Enemy fire disabled the 102nd's captain, and Lieutenant Clifford Henry took over, leading troops with much gallantry in hand-to-hand fighting. Command passed to a sergeant when fragments of a bomb from a German airplane tore Clifford's legs and stomach. They took him to a hospital; a French general came and made a speech about la France and la Gloire and gave him the Croix de Guerre. A Harvard classmate in the next bed later reported that Clifford Henry told him he thought what he had been put on earth to do had been accomplished. On October 16, he died. The telegram Margaret had imagined in her story was a reality now: it came to the Henrys in Greenwich, and Mr. Henry sent word of its contents to Northampton. The parents got letters of condolence from President Wilson and President Lowell of Harvard, former President Roosevelt, and many cabinet and government officials. The blow almost broke Ira Henry; he wrote to Eugene Mitchell that his only ambition now was soon to join his boy. Margaret wrote to her father, "It does my heart good to think that we weren't mistaken in Clifford, that he was even better stuff than we thought. It makes me feel very proud that such a man cared for me . . . I feel so dreadfully sorry for the Henrys." Every year for the rest of Mrs. Henry's life, Margaret sent flowers on the anniversary of Clifford's death.

Margaret's brother was luckier than Clifford Henry, and came home to Atlanta the following January. He found that the wave of influenza, subsiding in the first weeks of 1919, had touched his father. However, Mr. Mitchell was beginning to recover when his son got back to the big house on Peachtree Street, which was fortunate as there were no nurses procurable, and no hospital beds. Shortly after Stephens returned, the disease struck Mrs. Mitchell. Worn and weak from nursing others, she was seriously ill by January 23. On that day, she dictated a letter to her daughter. Stephens took down the words at his mother's bedside:

"*Dear Margaret,*

I have been thinking of you all day long. Yesterday you received a letter saying I am sick. I expect your father drew the situation with a strong hand and dark colors and

I hope I am not as sick as he thought. I have pneumonia in one lung and were it not for flu complications, would have more than a fair chance of recovery. But Mrs. Riley had pneumonia in both lungs and is now well and strong. We shall hope for the best but remember, dear, that if I go now it is the best time for me to go.

"I should have liked a few more years of life, but if I had had those it may have been that I should have lived too long. Waste no sympathy on me. However little it seems to you I got out of life, I have held in my hands all that the world can give. I have had a happy childhood and married the man I wanted. I had children who loved me, and, as I loved them, I have been able to give them what will put them on the high road to mental, moral, and perhaps financial success, were I to give them nothing else.

"I expect to see you again, but if I do not I must warn you of one mistake that a woman of your temperament might fall into. Give of yourself with both hands and overflowing heart, but give only the excess after you have lived your own life. This is badly put. What I mean is that your life and energies belong first to yourself, your husband and your children. Anything left over after you have served these, give and give generously, but be sure there is no stinting of love and attention at home. Your father loves you dearly, but do not let the thought of being with him keep you from marrying if you wish to do so. He has lived his life; live yours as best you can. Both of my children have loved me so much that there is no need to dwell on it. You have done all you can for me and have given me the greatest love that children can give to parents. Care for your father when he is old, as I cared for my mother. But never let his or anyone else's life interfere with your real life. Goodbye, darling, and if you see me no more it may be best that you remember me as I was in New York."

Mrs. Mitchell then directed Stephens to sign the letter "Your loving Mother."

A telegram called Margaret home, but Mrs. Mitchell had died before her daughter got off the train in the Atlanta station on January 25. As Margaret descended the

Pullman steps, she saw Stephens walking toward her. She looked in his face and said, "I know it. I knew it while I was on the train. Let's go on out and take charge of things now." At 1149 Peachtree Street, Eugene Mitchell was a problem to himself and others. Still weak from illness, he went into shock when his wife died, and made a slow recovery. "Father seemed in complete despair," Stephens noted. "It took weeks for him to recover from his first grief, although he would get up and stagger around and even go downtown." Just so was the death of a beloved and necessary woman to affect Gerald O'Hara in *Gone with the Wind*.

As for Margaret, the sorrow of her mother's death never left her. But she tried to comfort her father by remaining outwardly cheerful in a manner which owed something, of course, to the resilience of youth. A few days after the funeral, Stephens and Margaret went to their father's bedroom to hear his plans for the future. Mr. Mitchell made his decisions known without first asking his children what they might wish to do, and the young people listened without comment as their father turned on his pillow and said to Margaret, "Go back to Smith. I want your brother, now that he is out of the Army, to stay with me. I think I will want you to come back, but do not miss the year you have begun."

Accordingly, Margaret returned to Northampton. She still talked of medical studies; but what impressed her classmates were the collected photographs of young men in uniform on her bureau. During fall term, Margaret had met a number of Amherst students and other Eastern college men, and her friends could testify that the Mitchell charm worked in New England just as it did in Georgia. Margaret understood the importance of young men to young women; but in the first weeks back at Smith after her mother's death, she concentrated on studies and midyear examinations. "You should see the despair of the girls when they return from Exams," Margaret wrote to her father. "Most of them are weeping or swearing. Mrs. P. always gives us a big bowl of soup after exams, so we cluster around the table and swap miseries."

Smith looked after physical fitness, and Margaret reported she had been rejected for "strong gym" and put in a less difficult division; this suited her, as she felt she was "not quite husky enough" for advanced gymnastics. Much of her correspondence with her father through this period would seem familiar to anyone who has been at either end of transactions involving term bills, medical and dental expenses, allowances, and telegraphic money orders. But in these early weeks, physical training was staple news; shortly after being rejected for strong gym Margaret was writing, "Well, now I am in 'Foot' gym. My ankles are rather weak and I couldn't perform for an hour in flat slippers—so into foot gym I went. It's screamingly funny to see twenty huskies in stocking feet, wriggling their toes with apparent aimlessness or walking on heels or toes, or trying to follow exactly a line in the floor. But what I am most expert in is picking things up with my toes. You needn't laugh for it's no easy job—just you try to pick up a pencil or marble in your stocking feet. The gym teacher says I'm as good as a monkey—a dubious compliment! Anyway, it's helping my feet so I should worry about how funny I look in action!"

Here Margaret showed a lifelong characteristic—a willingness to make herself the butt of a story to cheer a friend. In this case the friend was her father, for Margaret was growing up, and learning how grief can lie in wait and leap out; it happened to her on February 17 when thoughts of her mother suddenly occupied her mind. In her sorrow she remembered Eugene Mitchell and wrote, "Dearest Dad—It hurts so much when I think how Hellish things must be for you now. For I'm beginning to miss Mother so much now. I only had her for eighteeen years but you loved her for twenty-six years and I know how lonely you must be now. I wish I could make up just a little for her in the place in your heart. But try not to brood too much, Dad—it only makes things harder. And write to me often, too, please for you don't know how much I want to hear from you." Margaret then turned to practical things, knowing this would appeal to Mr. Mitchell's fondness for considering concrete matters, great

62

or small. "I am enclosing my receipt for the grub and board—So far, I haven't received any flunk notices but I haven't taken French yet. Three girls here flunked out and two of them are going home today. I'm boning hard for French for I have just gotten my glasses. They are good ones and I certainly need them."

Margaret conquered the mid-year examinations with something to spare, but it was a harsh winter at Northampton. On March 17 she wrote to her brother, "Steve, sometimes I get so discouraged I feel that there is no use keeping on here. It isn't in studies, for I'm about a 'C' student—but I haven't done a thing up here. I haven't shone in any line—academic, athletic, literary, musical or anything. Of course, I suppose my year has been rather broken up with the Flu and Clifford's and Mother's death but in a college of 2500 there are so many cleverer and more talented girls than I. If I can't be first, I'd rather be nothing. At any rate, I've learned a lot and I suppose that's what I came here for. It does seem that I could have done better tho. Better luck next time." On March 18 she wrote to her father, "I now see why Steve had objections to my coming north to college. Of course, as I haven't laid eyes on a man since I arrived, this doesn't apply to me. But it does seem strange that the college required (up to last week) chaperones to go with girls to the movies at night but lets them leave town and go to New York unchaperoned. I fear that I am becoming rabid on the subject of propriety. Another peculiar thing is that unless you and your date are content to sit in a stiff New England parlor with perhaps two or three other couples the only thing left for you to do is walk. To be sure, there are 'approved' eating places but you can't eat for three blessed hours! The prevalent idea in New England seems to be that of Sparta—that so long as nobody finds out, you're all right. Well, anyway, I love Smith, even tho it is barbarous and I wouldn't take anything for my year here. It has showed me how much nicer home is—and that there are nice places besides home."

As the second term of Freshman year crawled through February and March, Margaret's letters continued to express anxieties, hopes, and occasional joys in phrases that were sometimes girlish, sometimes pointed and mature. At last spring came back to New England and Margaret's spirits lifted. With Red Baxter and other cronies she went for picnics, cooking frankfurters by the Connecticut River; the girls also relieved the monotony of college fare with fudge cake at the Fruit Farm, or tea with poached eggs at the Copper Kettle. Margaret had not been serious in writing that she had not laid eyes on a man since entering college. She had by now a considerable acquaintance among the youth of Harvard, Dartmouth, and Amherst who were beginning to descend on Northampton in visitations connected with spring glee and mandolin club concerts and dramatic society plays. Margaret liked these visitors as dancing partners and escorts, and evidently they liked her, for Red Baxter stated that whenever an expected "date" was prevented from getting to Northampton, Margaret could always produce a nice Amherst man to fill in.

Margaret made a private estimate of each young man she met—a measurement against specifications of an acceptable husband. For instance, she wrote home of meeting the son of a Midwestern soap manufacturer at a party in Greenwich, and dismissing him, from the height of her nineteen years, because he was only seventeen. Not long afterward another Midwesterner came to call on Margaret at Northampton. She had met him when he passed through Atlanta in an officer training class, and he had now reached the suitable age of twenty-three. He said he was starting on a job in Hartford, and he showed an interest in Margaret as serious as it was sudden. Margaret wrote to her family of this young man, "He really means business. Is there any way of looking him up? He told me to. His father is a big corporation lawyer and president of the Chamber of Commerce. He hasn't a cent and I'm not in love with him. 'The beauty of the whole thing,' he remarked, 'is that both of us have plenty of time to think about it.' Please look him up, if you can. He swears his folks are all right but then he may be a rough neck. It felt awfully nice and natural to be proposed to. But don't worry. I shan't elope with him."

Margaret's next piece of news about male visitors had to do with a group from Dartmouth who had come to Northampton for a dramatic show. One of Margaret's friends at Ten Hen was determined to stay out after hours with some of the Dartmouth boys, and enlisted two housemates to go along. In her letter of May 29, Margaret described what happened. "Men were gotten and after the play the three left in high excitement to meet them. We promised to cross their names off the theater list and leave a French window open down stairs. We did as we promised, climbed up the stairs and every one went to bed—except me. Some how, I couldn't help feeling that they would have trouble getting in, and visions of them sitting on the Chapel steps all night stirred my heart. So I sat up for them. The house was dark and still and the campus was quiet. Still they didn't come. At 2 o'clock I heard them try the door and then a frightened giggle or two and profanity from the boys who had visions of taking the girls to a hotel.

"My hunch had been right—something was wrong. I leaned out and whispered that I'd come down and let them in some way. A chorus of relieved whispers floated up. I crept down the stairs and oh! how those three flights creaked. And every time they creaked, I wished to Heaven I had paid more attention to the Law so I would know exactly how culpable the accessory to the act was. Imagine my horror when I found the French window that we so carefully opened was locked. That meant that Mrs. Pearson had gotten suspicious. Not opening it, I carefully raised a window and on sticking my head into the night, I butted into a face—

" 'Oh! my Lord!' I gasped.

" 'It's one of the gentlemen of the party!' reassured a deep voice.

" 'Aren't you all gentlemen?' I giggled—Whereupon he wanted to brain me for unseemly levity—at 2 o'clock and Mrs. P. close by. I told them I'd open the front door and finally I got it open. It was so dark I could not see and as I was quite sure I wasn't going thru life not knowing what those boys looked like, I stepped on the porch. Then—

horrible to relate, the door slammed to, locking automatically. Maybe I wasn't petrified! Standing out there bare footed and some what negligee—locked out! But one of the girls climbed in the window I had opened and unlocked the front door again and I scooted upstairs thanking my stars. Then they came up and talked till 4 and kissed me effusively for being a guardian angel. But you don't catch me being accessory again! It's too hard on the nerves!"

In the midst of final examinations a week later, Margaret's Hartford suitor came up for a Saturday evening call. She wrote that it was "a very solemn occasion—as it was the last time I will see him before going South. The romantic scene was there all right but I never felt so many mosquitoes in all my life. He seems perfectly sure that a few years from now I'll be his'n. It makes no difference to him that I haven't the slightest inclination that way—he merely grins and says he hopes I'm not expensive!

"On Wednesday, I have no exam, so I think I'll go horseback riding for relaxation and to get away from this house. Every body's nerves are pretty bad by now and there is no conversation except 'crams' and 'flunks.' I must run study like a good little Freshman and a dutiful daughter."

With the posting of final grades, Margaret saw that she had passed into the Sophomore class by a safe margin. There followed the buying of yard-long railroad tickets, the packing of trunks, and the hiring of expressmen to load them in wagons and check them to home towns; in those days nobody traveled light. There were farewells—those college partings that leave a faint and sad emotion to the end of life. Margaret had not found it easy at Smith. Yet, at the end of this college year in which she met with shock and loss, she must have felt additional sadness from knowing that she would never come back to Northampton as a student. Years later she would sit on a platform at a Smith commencement in a group of distinguished men and women, and receive an honorary degree. But her formal education ended with the close of Freshman year.

In Atlanta, Eugene Mitchell welcomed his daughter and told her to consider herself hostess and housekeeper of 1149 Peachtree Street. If Mr. Mitchell had an idea of marrying again, no one heard of it, and the thought never entered his children's minds, for they saw him as married to their mother till the end of time. So Margaret became mistress of the mansion at the age of nineteen. In addition, she agreed to her father's plan for her to make a formal entrance into Atlanta society, and accepted membership in the Debutante Club for the winter season of 1920–1921. A roster of girls whose social standing was unassailable, the Club was also something in the nature of a waiting list for the Atlanta Junior League. In Margaret's case, membership in either organization would seem a matter of course.

But as always in society, there was the question of money; and financially Eugene Mitchell stood some distance below the top. Stephens Mitchell told his sister she had grown up in a town where "First you assume that all rich people are good people, and then, with that as an axiom, all the means by which they became rich are blessed and sanctified." He said the white people in the metropolitan area had serial numbers running from 1 to 200,000 and that each person knew his exact rank on the scale, because his number depended only on the amount of money he had. Margaret saw good sense in her brother's observation. She had given up her dream of becoming a doctor, so that becoming a young society matron was second choice. Nevertheless, Margaret liked parties, and in the main liked people, though she was later to say, "Not meeting somebody is one of my favorite things." But having accepted the role of debutante, she played it straight as a girl whose object was a suitable marriage. Among her preparations for making an impact on the world of society was a careful study of fashionable dress, which she began in the summer of 1919, more than a year before her debut. "When a girl is making a social career," she said, "clothes are a uniform, to be worn like a soldier's—always well done—never sloppy."

Margaret's approach to life in starting out as a young

adult did seem to have a sort of military stoicism. Sometimes after returning from a party she would kick off her slippers, lean back in one of the big armchairs in the drawing room, and say to her brother, "Did you ever see so many horse-faced people in your life, and so many dumb-bells? You may be right about those serial numbers. Still, that might not be such a bad thing. This is a democratic society and the people on top are just the same as the people on the bottom. The only difference between them is that one has money and is afraid he'll lose it and the other hasn't any money and hopes desperately to make it. So at least they have that bond in common."

And yet the city was a delightful place as the summer of 1919 passed by. Young Atlanta danced; as elsewhere in America, the end of the war had given young people a feeling that pent-up forces were about to be released, together with a hunger for richness of experience that caused a change in standards of behavior. A good party must have plenty of boys who came without girls, "stags" who ranged the edge of the floor or herded in the middle of it, and cut in on the girls as they danced by. At the height of the party, a popular girl might go only a few steps with each cutter-in, and if she went all the way around with one partner, she might doubt her popularity. Every stag got a welcome whether he was a schoolboy or an elderly debutantes' delight of thirty or thirty-five, and to extend that welcome, girls used a flow of collegiate slang and society chatter known as a "line." A girl had to dispense her line continuously, and it must have become hard labor by four or five in the morning, even for a young woman with the energy and determination of Margaret Mitchell. She was in demand; her qualities of wit, charm, and sympathy were already evident—the qualities that were to mark her personality throughout life. But Margaret's popularity with men did not lead to equal favor with less attractive young ladies, or with their mothers.

In this summer, with Margaret not altogether happy and yet not altogether unhappy, the household on Peachtree Street received an addition that was to bring on trouble as surely as acid turns litmus paper red. Eugene Mitchell's mother-in-law, Grandmother Stephens, arrived for an indefinite stay. Mrs. Stephens, in her seventies, was not prepared to recognize Margaret as an adult, even though the girl was mistress of the house and prop and comfort of its owner. The friction began when Mrs. Stephens criticized Margaret's friends. Instead of silently accepting the implied condemnation of her taste, or getting rid of the people under criticism, Margaret stood her ground and argued for right of selection in a tone that the old lady thought disrespectful and improper.

It was not a continuous quarrel, but Mrs. Stephens and the aunt who accompanied her sat like masked batteries at the dinner table, ready to fire a barrage of disapproval at any time. Although it was inevitable, Margaret did not detonate the final explosion until the two older women had lived in the house for almost a year. In the meantime, she found that Grandmother Stephens' conversation had its own interest when immediate personalities were not involved, for old Mrs. Stephens had a stock of what Margaret later called "eye-witness information" about the Civil War and Reconstruction in Atlanta. One story that made an impression concerned a fugitive from federal justice, Doughboy Taylor. He had married Cousin Lizzie Stephens, and Doughboy was his real, baptized name. He served with Kirby Smith's forces, and when General Smith surrendered, "Dobe" refused to lay down his arms, but kept on ambushing and killing Federals. Union Army agents pursued him from Texas to Georgia, where he reached Atlanta and knocked at Grandfather Stephens' door in the night. Mr. Stephens hid him in an attic. Margaret's grandmother described the way she would carry Taylor's food up a ladder and find him crouching with a pistol in his hand. After a few days Mr. Stephens got a horse and buggy, put the fugitive under a rug and smuggled him to Apalachicola. From there Dobe Taylor made his way to Brazil. There was talk in Atlanta, and the occupying authorities charged Grandfather Stephens with complicity in the escape. They locked him up for several months in McPherson Barracks, but got nothing out of him, and lacking evidence to hang him finally let him go.

The year 1920 came in with rumors of hard times. Eugene Mitchell feared a depression but continued his plans for Margaret's social career. He had one reason for optimism in the acquisition of his son as an associate when Stephens completed the legal studies he had begun at Harvard before the war. Nevertheless, Margaret entered the year of her debut with a feeling that funds must be spent with care. In addition to this uneasy feeling, there came two misfortunes that brought lasting trouble and sorrow. One was an accident: for the second time Margaret had a bad fall while riding. She said, "The horse sat on my stomach." The fall injured the same leg and ankle that had been hurt in 1911, and she never fully recovered from the combined effects of these accidents.

The other misfortune was one that Margaret might have avoided had she been a saint instead of a girl with her own way of looking at things and an independence of spirit that could become implacable on occasion. When it finally came, the crisis in her relationship to Grandmother Stephens began with the usual criticism of friends, introducing a long argument that sharpened into a quarrel. Although it was by then half-past eleven at night, Grandmother Stephens and the aunt went upstairs, packed some bags, called a taxicab, and moved to the Georgian Terrace Hotel. Thus began one of the most painful and harmful of all estrangements, an unhealed breach between close members of a family. The disagreement branched out to include contention over property that Margaret's mother had held as trustee. Margaret and her brother waived their claims in this matter, but still bad feeling increased, until some of the Stephenses asked Margaret "not to claim relationship with our side of the family." There were disagreements about the use of burial sites and, on occasion, actual wrangling at the graveside. Yet even here Margaret's humor came into play; and she was able to tell J. P. Marquand, as she looked back on the worst of the family fights, that she could understand the cranky New

Englanders he satirized in *The Late George Apley*. They were exactly like certain Georgians.

Mr. Mitchell and his son gave parties for Margaret at the Peachtree Street house and at the Capital City Club and the Piedmont Driving Club. In those days debutantes were objects of great interest and there was newspaper publicity—in defiance of the old rule that a gentlewoman's name appeared only at the times of her birth, marriage and death. The *Journal*, for example, printed a page of photographs in the Sunday rotogravure section under the heading "Following the Fads of Atlanta Debs." A picture showed Margaret perching on the cowcatcher of a locomotive, waving a trainman's hat, with the caption: "Miss Margaret Mitchell believes that driving a locomotive would be next to skimming the clouds in an aeroplane."

Further attention came to Margaret on March 13, 1921, with a photograph and description of "The Apache dance by Miss Margaret Mitchell, one of the prettiest of the debutantes, and A. S. Weil, a student at Georgia Tech." The *Journal* society reporter said this performance was the most striking feature of the Micarême Ball given by the Debutante Club for the benefit of the Home for Incurables. Supposedly the rough dance of Paris hoodlums and their girls, an Apache number was considered daring, and this notion colored the report in the *Constitution:* "One other debutante offering herself and all she was on the altar of charity was constantly *hors de combat* because of the strenuosity of the Apache dance—Margaret Mitchell, you know."

A number of older ladies, including Margaret's grandmother, objected to the dance and clucked, "What can Eugene Mitchell be thinking of to allow it?" The fact was that Margaret knew she was putting herself in a vulnerable position by doing this dance, and volunteered to learn the number with Mr. Weil because she was a good dancer, and her code would not allow her to step aside from anything that was going to be hard work, and possibly an irritant to the elderly. But so far as some of the older women were concerned, Margaret had done something even more reprehensible: she had joined with two or three other girls in objecting to the use of hitherto unquestioned authority by senior committeewomen in deciding which charities should get the proceeds of the ball. Margaret's argument was that the girls did the work, and so should have the privilege of allocating the funds. Without question, at this time Margaret fell from favor with many of the city's ruling dowagers.

Margaret found out how she stood a few months after the ball, when the Junior League announced its new probationary members and her name was not on the list. In Atlanta at least, acceptance to membership in the League was a sign of high social standing. It followed that rejection after having been a certified debutante must be an intentional omission, and in Margaret's case especially pointed because some of her relatives were members. The withholding of Margaret's membership was not a mere teapot tempest. No matter how clearly Margaret could see through the social pretensions of the League, the fact remained that recognized authority had closed a conventional door in her face. As victim of this snubbing, which she did not forget, Margaret showed no waning of confidence in herself, and continued to be one of the most popular girls in town so far as men were concerned. During these months Margaret had two serious suitors, one from outside the state, whose parents she visited. But although Margaret talked in a practical vein about the matrimonial purpose of coming out and making a show in society, she was romantic at heart and would not marry a man she did not believe herself in love with. It also seems reasonable to suppose that Margaret enjoyed flaunting her popularity with men before the girls and women who disapproved of her. This does not mean, however, that she had no women friends. At a later time she wrote: "Every day I thank the Lord that I really like women and enjoy them. A woman who doesn't like women can't have much fun."

Stephens Mitchell worried about his sister, occasionally showing it to such an extent that she reproved him for being over-protective. Stephens feared that life had beleaguered his sister with problems she was too young to solve. He saw her as a girl who needed a mother to launch a counter-attack on the older women who had snubbed her, and he felt that Margaret was under intolerable strain trying to run a large house without enough money.

The shortage of money had come gradually, a creeping anemia that attacked Mr. Mitchell's bank account as North Georgia settled along with the rest of the South into the poor times of the 1920s. Around Atlanta the economic villain was the boll weevil. According to a folk song this creature was just a-looking for a home, which it found in North Georgia cotton, puncturing the young plants to hatch a wormlike embryo that ate the interior of the pod or boll, thus earning a name while destroying a crop. The resulting hard times closed hundreds of financial institutions, which became known as boll weevil banks. Mr. Mitchell's office did not turn into a boll weevil law firm, but there was little work, for a time, in his specialty of real estate contracts, and Margaret felt the trouble in her father's worried manner as well as in reductions of household funds.

One evening Stephens Mitchell was reading in the downstairs living room when the doorbell rang. Stephens himself went to the front door and admitted the visitor, a tall, thin, pleasant-looking young man with a good smile and an easy, deliberate manner. The caller introduced himself as John Marsh, and said he had come to see Margaret. Stephens had not criticized any of his sister's friends, but some had impressed him more favorably than others. He liked this young man, however, almost on sight. And as they waited for Margaret to appear, Stephen learned that John Marsh had come to Atlanta from his home town of Maysville, Kentucky, after serving overseas in the Medical Corps, and that he was a graduate of the University of Kentucky and a former teacher of English, now working as a copy editor on Hearst's *Atlanta Georgian*. This young man soon became a constant visitor at the Peachtree Street house.

Shortly after John Marsh's first call, Margaret went to a commencement dance at the University of Georgia, where she met a handsome fraternity man named Berrien Kinnard Upshaw. Little Margaret Mitchell fascinated big and broad-shouldered Upshaw, and he began paying court to her. As the son of a well-to-do North Carolina insurance executive, he was socially acceptable; what Margaret, Stephens and their father did not know was that he was a dangerously unstable man. But Upshaw was in one of his good periods while courting Margaret and the uncontrollable factors in his personality remained out of sight. He met John Marsh, and got along well with that easy-mannered gentleman; Upshaw told others he considered Marsh his best friend in Atlanta. As for Margaret, she was in a mood to take Berrien Upshaw as seriously as a woman can take a man; and in August, an Atlanta society editor burbled, "Peggy Mitchell is writing another drama, 'They Lived Happily Ever After.' Playing opposite her, Berrien K. Upshaw."

When Margaret told her father she was planning to marry Upshaw, he objected in emphatic terms. He had made no objection to Upshaw's having a place in his daughter's train of admirers, but it was quite another thing to consider him as her husband. There was nothing to put a finger on, but Mr. Mitchell's instinct told him there was something wrong about Upshaw. Stephens agreed, but decided the one way to make certain that Margaret married the young man would be to object to him. Stephens knew his sister. He said nothing and hoped for the best, and did not discuss the marriage with other people, then or later. But he never forgot a comment from a girl with whom he was dancing one night on the roof of the Capital City Club, who said to him, "I saw the announcement of Margaret's engagement. It's a great mistake. She's in love with John Marsh and doesn't know it."

On September 1, 1922, Grandmother Stephens suspended hostilities to the extent of attending a trousseau tea. That was on Friday. On Saturday, at half past eight in the evening, Margaret walked beside her father down the stairway of 1149 Peachtree Street to marry Berrien Kinnard Upshaw at an altar constructed of palms, ferns, Easter lilies, and other white flowers. Smilax entwined the balustrades and draped the doorways; baskets of pink roses and gladioli stood about. Attended by bridesmaids and two little flower girls, Margaret wore white satin with long pearl ornaments arranged at either side. Neck line and sleeves carried pearl trim and orange blossoms set off the white satin court train, while a Russian pearl coronet supported her veil; the bridal bouquet was an arrangement of Richmond roses and lilies of the valley. They knelt before an Episcopal clergyman; thus Margaret gave evidence that she had left the Roman Church. The best man was John R. Marsh.

After a wedding trip by automobile to the Grove Park Inn at Asheville, North Carolina, and a visit to the Upshaws at Raleigh, the newly married couple came back to Atlanta—to quarters that had been prepared for them at 1149 Peachtree Street.

This attempt to settle at the bride's former home showed the doom the marriage carried in it. The inadvisable situation bred a strained atmosphere so distressing to Eugene Mitchell that he took to his bed. Stephens was courteous, privately unhappy, and embarrassed. Berrien Upshaw's performance as a breadwinner was sketchy, his temper grew uncertain, and within a few months he left the Peachtree Street house and Atlanta. He never came back. And Margaret never uttered any reproaches or explanations about him; but she kept a loaded pistol near her bed every night of her life after Upshaw's departure until news came, years later, that he had been found dead on the ground below a hotel window in the Middle West.

In December 1922, however, Margaret's determination to present a cheerful countenance during the Christmas holidays to her father and brother kept her outwardly serene. But the situation was bleak. Behind her lay a college career abandoned, a social failure, and a marriage to be regretted. Now, if ever, was the time to recall the words of her mother under the ruined chimneys on the Jonesboro Road. Life itself was the enemy. You fought it, or you might as well be dead.

V

Newspaper Days

One morning in December 1922 the editor of the *Atlanta Journal Sunday Magazine* found himself looking across his desk at a young person whom he at first took to be the editor of a school paper come to ask for a trip through the plant. His caller was Margaret Mitchell, who had lost flesh under the stresses of recent months and weighed only a little over ninety pounds. She was wearing a dark tailored suit which made her look even smaller than she was, and her reddish brown hair was long and done high on the back of her head. But Angus Perkerson noticed that her bright blue eyes were determined. And she soon made the object of this determination plain: she proposed to become a feature writer for the *Sunday Magazine*.

That Margaret was the daughter of Eugene Mitchell spoke well for her; as to experience, she had recently visited a friend in Birmingham, Alabama, who worked for one of the papers there, and she had helped this friend for a week or so. Perkerson did not need to say this was hardly adequate; he was one of the best editors in the country, and set a high standard on the *Journal* magazine.

However, it happened that he needed an extra hand; and so he said, "It would be a question of whether you could get the basic idea of how we work here. We handle a great deal of copy and I don't go in for extensive alterations—haven't time to. What we are looking for is straightforward writing without self-conscious tricks, and it's surprising how few people can do it. You either can or you can't. I'll try you out, and we'll see if you're one of the people who can."

Perkerson thereupon made Margaret a provisional member of his staff, her salary to be $25 a week if she qualified. After Margaret left the office with instructions to return for work next day, he discussed the matter with his wife Medora Field Perkerson, skilled newspaperwoman and mainstay of the *Sunday Magazine*. Skeptical about the practicality of hiring a society girl, Mrs. Perkerson said, "Debutantes sleep late, Angus, and don't go in for jobs." She did not believe Margaret would be on time the following morning, and would not be surprised if the girl did not come back at all. "That may be," said Perkerson. "We'll see."

Margaret arrived promptly at eight o'clock in the morning, and Perkerson soon called her to his desk for her first assignment. This story, so tremendously important for Margaret, proved to be a fashion feature having to do with the length of skirts, a topic of interest then as it is today. World War I had brought short skirts, but by 1923 they had lengthened considerably, and Mr. Perkerson wished to tell his readers what the prospects were that skirts would again begin to shorten, and when this would take place. He therefore told Margaret to go and see Mary Hines Gunsaulas, a well-to-do Atlanta woman who was back from a three-month stay in Europe with several trunks of Paris clothes. Question: would skirts be shorter again any time soon? Armed with notebook and pencil, and accompanied by a photographer, Margaret set out to get the answer.

Mrs. Gunsaulas welcomed Margaret, posed for pictures in her Paris frocks, and incidentally mentioned that she had been in Rome the day the Black Shirts marched in and Mussolini took over the government. Many times in the years after she had given up newspaper work would Margaret laugh over the way she received this piece of news.

"Mussolini was not even a name to me then." Margaret would say, "but it sounded interesting and I listened and asked questions while Mrs. Gunsaulas told more. I came back and wrote my story about skirts and tacked all this other incident onto the end. Mr. Perkerson—I did not call him Angus then—turned the story hind-side before, and started it off with the eye-witness account of Mussolini taking over the Italian government."

If Margaret had failed on this first assignment, Angus Perkerson would have given her further opportunities to qualify for the staff before turning her off. But Margaret had brought back an exact answer to his question: Paris skirts were now twelve inches above the floor, and rising. Moreover, she had written the information about fashions, and the report on Mussolini, in the straightforward style Perkerson said so few people knew how to achieve. After reading her copy, Perkerson walked over to the typewriter table he had given to Margaret as a desk and explained why he was turning the article around. Then he said, "I think this table is too high for you." Margaret answered, "So is the chair." The editor then called the *Journal* carpenter, who sawed bits from the legs of the chair and table until they were comfortable for Margaret to use. Both pieces are on exhibition today in the *Journal's* new offices as a memorial to the most famous of the talented people who wrote for the paper at one time or another. As an Atlanta exhibit the table ranks with the cavernous rolltop desk, at which Joel Chandler Harris created Uncle Remus, which once stood in the *Constitution* office and is now at the Harris home and museum. But at the time the carpenter was working, all Margaret could think of was that she had landed a job: they wouldn't saw up good furniture for someone who wasn't going to stay. Margaret's by-line in the paper was Peggy Upshaw; shortly she changed this to Peggy Mitchell, and under that line her articles became known during the next four years to all readers of the *Journal*.

Those were the years in which Margaret Mitchell grew up. And no better place than a newspaper office could be found to make the maturing process complete and final. Perkerson sent Margaret on every kind of assignment he could think of, for her vivid personality came through equally well in interviews, local-color features, and the stunt stories that were as popular in big-city journalism then as they are today. One of Margaret's first stunt assignments took her to the top of an office building to swing from the cornice in a sort of bosun's chair sixteen floors above the street. This hazardous exploit had the excuse that the sculptor Gutzon Borglum planned to use a similar rig when carving the Confederate Memorial on the high and steep face of Stone Mountain a few miles outside Atlanta. Margaret led off her account of what happened with a parody on the patter of two popular vaudevillians:

Oh, Mr. Gallagher!
Oh, Mr. Gallagher!
Did you see the human fly a-climbing high?
Oh! he took an awful chance
When he hung there by his pants.
Feats of daring, Mr. Gallagher?
Plain d—— foolishness, Mr. Shean!

In the story Margaret explained that the proposal was to "shove her out of a window on the top floor of a very high building that had been selected as an imitation Stone Mountain." Before seating herself in the chair, Margaret put on "an enormous pair of Size 40 overalls." Then they pulled in the swinging chair attached to a hoist on the roof. Margaret seated herself, the inventor of the device strapped her in, and the men on the hoist swung the rig back out the window and down. "A dizzy whirl—buildings, windows, a glimpse of the sky, anxious faces at the windows, all jumbled up for an instant of eternity, a feeling of nausea, and then BUMP! completed the first swing as I came up against the side of the building with an awful wallop. The wall felt good. It was rough and it had hit me a jolt, but it was solid and secure. Before I could catch hold of it, however, Newton's third law of motion asserted itself—for every action there is an equal and opposite reaction—and pendulum-like we started to swing out over the great wide world again.

" 'Hey!' shouted a distant voice. 'Look down this way and smile!'

"Smile! Ha! Smile! Imagine that at a time like this! Except that both hands were so busy holding on to the leather straps I would have laughed in my sleeve at him. I glanced down to give him the most cutting, scornful look in my repertoire, and—What a sensation! The realization of how high above the world I was hit me with a jolt. There was a sickening sensation in the pit of my stomach. I jumped. The seat of the swing slipped from under me, and for a terrible instant I hung there, spinning, with only the strap under my arms between me and the hard, hard street 200 feet below.

"Fortunately Mr. Thomas [the inventor] had fastened me in so tight I could hardly breathe and the strap held. They lowered me down the side of the building and swung me around some more, and after a while they decided that the cause of journalism had been sufficiently served and they consented to pull me back up to the window, and the thing was over. Trembling, I'll admit, but the feel of a solid floor beneath my feet brought back the jolly old bluff and I managed to pull a weak sort of smile and announce: 'Oh, it wasn't so bad!' "

Newspaper photographers traditionally refuse to be impressed by writing colleagues, but Margaret won over the most hardened camera men by the nerve she showed in these stunt assignments. "That was the period when I had no better sense than to risk my neck to keep people from thinking I was scared," she would say in recalling her newspaper days. "The photographers who went along on these assignments were always hoping I would scream or faint or back down and I was just as determined not to. Some of these stunts I thought up myself, but one that I remember in particular was a photographer's brainstorm.

We had gone behind the scenes at the circus to get an animal story. At that time I had never been nearer an elephant than to feed him peanuts, carefully extended at arm's length. I saw the photographer mutter behind his hand to the mahout, who barked something in Hindustani to the biggest elephant I had ever seen. The next thing I knew that elephant had picked me up and, carrying me through the air, had deposited me on his head. I found myself frantically holding onto his ears with both hands—just in case he decided to drop me as suddenly."

Margaret did not spend all her time on the *Journal* acting as a photographer's model. She was a writer; and her second story for the *Sunday Magazine*, which was about a botanical experimenter, achieved print, like her first, almost exactly as she wrote it. This piece ran in the *Magazine* for January 7, 1923, and showed the ability to seize the reader's attention she had first exhibited in her tales of pirates and outlaws. It began: "There's a man on Peachtree Road who can give a strawberry a 'shot in the arm' and make it feel so good it doesn't care a whoop for freezing weather. He has a bunch of these immoderately bold plants with big, red, juicy berries on them growing out in the open air right now—not in a hothouse or under glass but in the chill of this January weather. He is a small man with a kindly face, a white moustache and a shock of Paderewski-like hair on which a battered derby is tilted. A shirt open at the neck, a sailor's pea-jacket and a pair of muddy, kneeless trousers complete his costume." A following interview with Hudson Maxim, the perfecter of explosives and smokeless powder, started off: "Mrs. Maxim, tiny and sweetfaced, was holding Hudson Maxim's bare feet on her lap, drawing on his socks, when the interviewer entered, somewhat abashed.

" 'Oh, don't mind this,' roared the inventor affably, waving one bare foot cordially toward a chair. Hudson Maxim tugged at his white beard and smiled—a sturdy old man with a magnificent leonine head topped with a mass of unruly white curls—a personality as well as a celebrity." In the interview, Margaret reported that the most important thing Maxim told her was that there would inevitably be another world war.

Such figures as derbied botanists and barefoot inventors fascinated Margaret and she had the gift—a rare one, as Perkerson said—of communicating her interest to readers in a simple, modest, and effective style. She wrote about everything—Georgia camp meetings, Confederate generals, bobbed-haired bandits, bootleggers, convicts, politicians, and movie stars. In that category, one of her most perceptive pieces dealt with Rudolph Valentino, the Italian who found that he had become a symbol of romance after his virile performance as a desert chieftain in *The Sheik*. Margaret saw Valentino as a life-worn man of tired but genuine courtesy, to whom money and worldwide fame seemed to have brought but little satisfaction. She said of him, "He was a plain, nice spoken, very weary sort of person. I don't think he quite understood why ladies acted the way they did." Margaret found a happier personality in another popular film actor, Ben Lyon. To her he was "a nice boy" with "a youthful eager face, a ready smile and the sleek, parted-in-the-middle look peculiar to Georgia Tech boys on Sunday afternoons."

Looking over the files with Medora Perkerson on a day in 1945, Margaret laughed at material she and her editor had considered daring and sensational in the 1920s. As she turned the pages, Margaret said, "This type of story always led off with a question: Could a girl be virtuous and bob her hair? Could she have a home and a husband and children and a job, too? Should she roll her stockings, park her corsets, be allowed a latch key? These questions were hot stuff then. Between the younger and older generations swords were drawn. Practically anybody could get publicity by criticizing younger people. There was a passionate interest on the part of both old and young as to what prominent people had to say on those topics. They aren't issues any longer and they are dead because they are victories won by the younger generation of the 1920s."

As a newspaperwoman of the 1920s, Margaret considered herself a member of the younger generation who not only had something to say, but also a place to say it. Mar-

82

garet's working home, and forum of her opinions and impressions, was a locally owned independent evening and Sunday paper. Its competition came from the *Constitution,* a morning paper with a long tradition, and from William Randolph Hearst's lively *Georgian.* In those days, newspaper owners thought any sort of amenity for editorial employees sheer folly and waste. The Atlanta writer William S. Howland has recalled that the *Journal* was "written, edited and published in the old five-story, smoke-stained, rat-infested, roach-ridden, red brick building which rose in grimy ruggedness above the railroad tracks on Forsyth Street. It was just north of the tracks and on the east side of the street, directly opposite the shining clean and highly polished building that houses the *Journal* of today. There were no Diesel switch engines or locomotives in the 1920s. There were only smoke-belching, soft-coal burning steam locomotives. The southern side of the *Journal* building was shrouded constantly with nauseous clouds of black smoke from the puffing engines. In winter, with the windows closed, it was hard enough to breathe without strangling. In summer, when it was a question of open the windows or suffocate, it was next to impossible. It was no uncommon occurrence for a red hot cinder to fall on one's desk. And it required iron concentration to take news over the phone or write news, with locomotive whistles bellowing, engine bells clanging, just outside the window.

"It was, indeed, a rugged physical environment into which Peggy moved to take her first professional writing job. Perhaps most rugged of all was the third floor back office in which the *Sunday Magazine* was quartered. Dark, gloomy, with its soot-begrimed windows looking out on an alley, the *Sunday Magazine*'s single room was later described by Peggy as 'The Black Hole of Calcutta.' "

And so the girl who had been too frail for strong gym at Smith took up the six-day, sixty-hour week that newspaper people worked in the 1920s. Getting up before the cook arrived, Margaret left the house without eating, caught a trolley car and arrived at the *Journal* about seven-thirty each morning to breakfast in the ground-floor lunchroom that she christened "The Roachery." Then, as

Mr. Perkerson put it, "She sort of opened up the office," and was always waiting there when he and his wife appeared. Margaret soon became so deft and quick at the office chores of the newspaper trade that she acquired extra duties in the proofreading and caption writing departments. Among other tasks, she had to paste up and check the proof of the serial story that was a staple *Sunday Magazine* feature, and once when a chapter was lost, wrote a new one to fill in. Margaret also helped out on the *Magazine*'s column of personal advice, which was headed, "Courtship, Marriage and Manners." Mr. Perkerson found that Margaret's engaging personality was sometimes as useful as her journalistic skills. It was welcome, for example, in dealing with the Methodist Bishop Warren A. Candler, a churchman of enormous importance and influence who contributed a weekly department to the *Magazine*. The bishop was a small man, but from his chest there issued a voice of such depth and sonority that when he spoke the office windows rattled. Perkerson appointed Margaret special editor in charge of Candler; the bishop became her devoted slave and made no trouble. Margaret tamed another ogre in the person of an elderly composing room foreman who had grown so cranky that editors hesitated to enter his domain. As Perkerson's ambassador, Margaret became a friend to the touchy old man, and he would behave in a patient and reasonable way if it was she who asked him to hold the forms open for late copy. Perkerson and the men on the desk marveled that "Peggy had him eating out of her hand." Under their own pressures, they had not seen what Margaret felt intuitively: the foreman was old and tired, and hungry for courtesy, appreciation, and the gaiety of spirit that Margaret brought into his gloomy workroom, noisy with the clanking of linotypes, filled with hurrying men, and smelling of hot lead. She was on the paper when the foreman died, and with Medora Perkerson drove thirty miles to the funeral at a country church.

A young woman who could accomplish so much by tact and charm in the office sometimes drew an assignment to act as guide around Atlanta for visiting notables. This was the case one afternoon when Margaret appeared for the hourly lecture at the Cyclorama with an impressively dressed stranger in tow. He was a middle-aged person with a fleshy-looking head and petulant mouth; and he began to display signs of nervousness before the silver-haired Confederate veteran who acted as docent had gone halfway through his talk. At last, the speaker paused, the visitor called out: "What you just said is wrong. You don't know your subject."

"I certainly don't know who *you* are," the veteran replied.

Immediately a furious argument broke out, with raising of voices, flourishing of canes, and indignant looks from the bystanders. Poised and self-possessed, Margaret took the visitor's arm and led him away. Outside they got into a chauffeur-driven Rolls-Royce limousine and continued their tour of the city. Passing through the wholesale warehouse district and into uptown Atlanta, they glided past the Georgian Terrace, where Margaret's grandmother sat among the dowagers on the loggia. Although chauffeurs and limousines were common sights in Atlanta, a Rolls-Royce was unusual, and the ladies asked Mrs. Stephens, "Who is that distinguished-looking gentleman driving along with Margaret?" Mrs. Stephens did not know, and that evening telephoned the Mitchell house to find out. Margaret's answer was a shock: "That was Harry K. Thaw, who shot Stanford White."

It is a comment on journalism—and the same thing could happen today—that Harry Thaw should receive the treatment of a celebrity and command the time of a good reporter as escort while visiting an American city. The son of a Pittsburgh millionaire, Thaw had shot the gifted architect Stanford White in 1904, at Madison Square Garden, out of resentment over imagined injuries to his (Thaw's) wife. He was the first widely publicized murderer to avoid the electric chair on a plea of temporary insanity at a trial filled with psychiatric jargon. Some years later he managed to obtain legal authorization for his escape from an asylum, and remained at large, an object of notoriety and curiosity, until his death in 1931. To Margaret he was merely one more oddity that her profession had thrown in her way. She did get considerable amusement from his challenge to the Cyclorama lecturer, boorish though it was. Thaw had told her that during his confinement he had read deeply in the history of the Civil War, and considered himself an authority.

Those who could appreciate Margaret's telling the tale of her trip around town in Thaw's limousine included the daily staff of the *Journal* as well as her colleagues on the *Sunday Magazine,* after City Editor Harlee Branch began drafting her for straight news reporting. Margaret took this as an honor, and a triumph, too, for Branch himself, not so long before, had told her he could not use women reporters. But she feared there might be a humiliating failure with her first story for the daily, and hung around in anxiety until Branch gave her the traditional "Good night" that meant her piece was satisfactory and she was free to go. After that, Branch asked for Margaret on at least forty assignments; and it was not just for woman's-angle writing, but for her assiduity in digging facts and staying with a story until she had it all. Margaret was modest about her performance in "city-side" reporting, and was surprised when she overheard Branch telling his men they might learn something from a story she had written. But it was true that although Branch praised Margaret's factgathering ability, he also believed she was good at pressing the Vox Humana stop when the material was there. He prized her story on a woman who shot a man, which began with the quotation: "I killed him because I loved him." And Erskine Caldwell, on the *Journal* during part of the time Margaret was there, wrote in a memoir that one afternoon, when he was struggling to get on paper the dreariness of a suicide in a third-rate hotel, the editor told him, "Just give the facts, Erskine. If I want a sob story, I'll call Peggy Mitchell."

Caldwell was one among a remarkable array of writers who passed through the *Journal* offices, mostly in Margaret's time, though perhaps the finest of them, Don Marquis, preceded her. She always thought that Marquis first observed his character Archy the Cockroach in the lunchroom downstairs, and this does seem likely. Among other *Journal* men of note were Laurence Stallings, Ward Morehouse, Ward Greene, Grantland Rice, Morris Markey, Roark Bradford, and W. B. Seabrook. O. B. Keeler, the *Journal*'s famous golf writer and biographer of Bobby Jones, was a warm friend and admirer of Margaret's. Medora Field Perkerson also belongs among the *Journal* people who made a separate mark. Within a few years of the time she worked with Margaret, Mrs. Perkerson was to produce a number of successful mystery novels, two of which were made into films. Another woman who contributed to the *Journal* and later achieved national recognition was Frances Newman, who became famous for her novels *The Hard-Boiled Virgin* and *Dead Lovers Are Faithful Lovers*. But whatever their degree of talent and subsequent renown, Margaret Mitchell's colleagues were one in affection for the girl reporter whom they recognized, in William Howland's words, "as a capable fellow craftsman in the office, and as a gay and buoyant spirit outside the office, quick to share the joys, equally quick to share the burden of misfortune, trivial or tragic."

To Margaret the newspaper trade gave one invaluable privilege in furnishing her the outlet that a writer must have—the license to put down, on her bouncing and jumpy old Underwood typewriter, the satisfying words that said what she wanted to say. But even more precious to Margaret was the connection between her newspaper and her city. The American who has not at some time loved a provincial American city has missed the only emotional experience that never leaves regrets; and Margaret loved Atlanta. Being a reporter she looked from a tower, so to speak, over the gray and green city of trees and stone that was Atlanta in the 1920s, and saw it on its hills and valleys as an enchanted place. She also saw the ugly part, and never forgot it. Once, at the end of an afternoon of reading old files, she closed the big volume, and said to Medora Perkerson:

"Working on the paper was a liberal education. If more women, when they were girls, were in a position to see—as a newspaper girl is—the inside of jails, the horrible things Travelers' Aid discovers, the emergency rooms of Grady Hospital and those sad, desolate sections which used to be fine homes but now are rookeries and rabbit warrens—if more people knew the sad things and the horrible things that go on in the world, there would be a darned sight less complacency and probably not so many of those sad sights and horrible things. Nowadays girls do get out more, people do know more, but even so, one good whiff of the police station on a hot July day would do a lot for a lot of people."

Newspaper work had done more for Margaret than waken her consciousness of human misery. She had a purpose now, and something many people are never so fortunate as to find: the work she was born to do, and plenty of it. With her working life satisfactory, her social life became normal: once again guests laughed and chatted in the house on Peachtree Street. They were mostly her new friends, the newspaper and literary crowd, though Augusta Dearborn, a friend of longer standing, was often there with her future husband, the businessman and artist Lee Edwards. There were the O. B. Keelers, and a *Journal* reporter and friend of John Marsh named Allan Taylor, who came from Tennessee. From Richmond, Roy Flannagan had come to work on the Atlanta papers, and he often visited the Mitchells with his wife, whose departure from the *Sunday Magazine* had given Margaret her chance. These and others made up a group that called itself the Peachtree Yacht Club. This was before the building of dams that made lakes around Atlanta, and there were no yachts in the city. When critics mentioned this, Stephens Mitchell had the answer. "There are no athletes in the Athletic Club," he would say, "and no one drives at the Driving Club. Why should there be yachts at the Yacht Club?"

With such gaiety among easy-going friends, Margaret's first year as a newspaperwoman passed by. All the friends helped, just as she helped them, but those who were close to her knew she had a special admirer among the men who came to 1401 Peachtree Street, which was the Mitchells' renumbered address. This sympathetic and attentive friend was John Marsh, and by 1924 a courtship was in progress. John had given up newspaper work in the spring of 1924, and now had a job in the advertising and publicity department of the Georgia Power Company. And the Mitchells instructed a lawyer to start proceedings for Margaret to divorce Berrien Upshaw. The uncontested divorce was granted on the grounds of cruel treatment.

It was a quiet courtship; though it was obvious that Margaret and John liked each other, they gave no occasion for gossip. Indeed, one aspect of John's wooing escaped notice altogether: an expert copy editor, he would read Margaret's articles and take them to her with suggestions for improvement in usage and style pencilled in the margins. And he was always right—he invariably spotted the loose sentence or redundant word that would occasionally creep into Margaret's copy and escape Perkerson's eye under the pressure of deadlines. He also pointed out inconsistencies, such as "going," "gwine," and "goin'" in the same person's mouth in a single paragraph. John offered praise as well as correction; for example, he wrote "Good!" in the margin of a paragraph about One-Eyed Connelly, the man who made a career of getting into public events without a ticket: "Connelly is a thickset, short man, with a bullet head set on a short, thick neck. His eagle nose is crisscrossed with scars, his face full and placid, and his one green eye shines with the quiet confidence acquired only by one who is convinced in his own soul of the laudability of his life work."

When 1925 came in, Margaret and John considered themselves engaged. It is possible they had come to this understanding some time before, but they felt a public announcement was not called for, and preserved a certain reticence even with close friends. Happy and serene, Margaret was planning to set the wedding date, when trouble came. John had not been in first-class health since an illness diagnosed as ptomaine poisoning had sent him to an Army hospital in France during the war. In recent months he had spent considerable time in the offices of expensive doctors who could not say for sure what ailed him. Now he developed a nervous reaction akin to hiccups that would plague him for a month at a time. Unable to eat, he grew weak and thin. The doctors put him in a hospital, and after many costly tests decided the trouble centered in his gall bladder, which they removed. This major surgery was successful, but John Marsh came out shaky on his feet and debilitated in his bank account. However, things of this sort do not discourage the young, and when John began to move from convalescence into a state of improved health during the months of May and June, Margaret chose the Fourth of July as the day for their wedding.

Without mentioning her first marriage, the society pages gave as much space to Margaret on her second wedding as they had when she married Berrien Upshaw. Not only her home paper, but the *Georgian* and the *Constitution* went into detail about the afternoon ceremony at the Unitarian-Universalist Church on West Peachtree Street. Returning a week or so later from the mountains of North Georgia, Margaret and John started housekeeping in an apartment at 17 Crescent Avenue (now 979 Crescent Avenue, N.E.) in the neighborhood that had delighted Eugene Mitchell with the name of Tight Squeeze.

Perhaps the word for the Marsh apartment was "tiny," for it had only two rooms plus a kitchen and bath. It was on the ground floor of a three-story brick building topped by a steep romantic roof—a building still to be seen on Crescent Avenue, and still populated largely by young people. Around the corner is the intersection of Tenth and Peachtree streets, the heart of Northside Atlanta's shopping district. At the time the Marshes moved in, the neighborhood was already taking on a commerical character, but there were big houses and apartment buildings all around it, as there still are, though the fine old houses now often prove on inspection to be the offices of doctors, architects, and advertising agencies. A few blocks to the southwest was the magnificent new Atlanta Biltmore Hotel, build by one of the Coca-Cola Candlers. This fortress-like structure stood on West Peachtree Street, which runs *parallel* to Peachtree Street, a fact that does not seem odd to Atlantans. In fact, the directory shows fifteen varieties of Peachtree, with an Avenue, a Road, a Drive, a Circle, a Place, and so on, all carrying the name of the great artery that runs up the middle of town. Margaret always referred to her apartment as "The Dump." The Marshes felt compelled to live in modest style because they were in debt, having borrowed to meet John's medical expenses, and to people of the Marshes' sort, in 1925, debt was a horror. Margaret said, "John and I are going to live poor as hell and get out of this jam." It was true that the power company paid John more than the newspaper scale, and the Marshes had a part-time cook-housekeeper. They could afford Lula Tolbert because Margaret was now earning $30 a week, the *Journal* having rewarded her with two raises of $2.50 each. Running on a tight budget and alert for extra income, they had to face a curious decision when John went to the Veterans' Hospital for a general examination and came back with an odd look on his face.

"Peggy," John said, "they've told me I'm eligible for Government compensation—provided I don't object to having my papers made out for what they call psychosomatic illness." This demanded thought, and a consultation with Stephens Mitchell. His advice was, "Some day you two will be on top of the world. I think all of us will be. I don't know why, but I believe it. So, do not take anything now based on a premise that might be misunderstood, and embarrass you, when you are on top." Margaret said, "Steve, that's just what we want to hear." So, with combined salaries, Margaret and John continued to work at the money problem. They also indulged in a mild affection that caused eyebrow-raising in the town when they tacked two calling cards on the apartment door, one reading "Mr. John R. Marsh" and the other "Miss Margaret Munnerlyn Mitchell."

It was a hospitable door. The group that had formed at Eugene Mitchell's house when Margaret became a reporter now made headquarters at The Dump, and its membership grew. At the core of Margaret's crowd were the newspaper people of Atlanta; then there were those from other occupations who liked the high spirits and good talk at the Marshes' place. Stephens Mitchell said he seldom saw any of Margaret's old "social" friends on Crescent

Avenue; nevertheless, many persons of conventional social standing—including Stephens himself and his fiancée, Carrie Lou Reynolds of Augusta—were happy to go there. And then there were always the friends and relations from other parts of the South. Margaret said, "No matter where your relatives or friends are going, Atlanta is on the way." She did not realize at the time what this undoubted truth would eventually mean to her, but somehow wedged all comers into The Dump, either for unscheduled visits or at the big parties—"brawls," as she called them—that she and John liked to give throughout the year, and always at Christmas, when they might entertain as many as a hundred callers.

Hospitable as Margaret was, she preferred small groups of close friends, and thought the ideal social arrangement a dinner party of six. "I am a glutton for the talk of people I like," she said, "and I can't get enough to satisfy me in a crowd." At the smaller gatherings, there was amusement not only in conversation, but in charades and plays with Margaret often in a leading part. The group admired Donald Ogden Stewart's *Parody Outline of History*, and liked to act out such scenes as "How Love Came to General Grant." In this Margaret played the streetwalker who is rescued from her bad life by thinking of the greatness and benevolence of General Grant. The general was usually played by Stephens. They also liked to portray Stewart's version of the Whiskey Rebellion; and one of the properties in this dramatization would be real whiskey. Like most progressive young people of the time, Margaret and her friends believed that the National Prohibition Act was a mistake, and they made a point of not observing it. Margaret had grown up to moderate social drinking, in which she saw no harm. During her newspaper days she learned to swallow a shot of corn liquor with admirable skill and control. However, she found it impossible to forgive anyone who spoiled a party by getting drunk. She was no prude. She liked to see people happy and comfortable, and did not object to a ribald story if it had genuine wit. All she asked in light conversation was civilized taste; and when the talk turned to serious matters, she respected accurate knowledge while gently deprecating contention merely for contention's sake.

At the office, Margaret was working now with the rhythm of a seasoned professional. Late in 1925, Angus Perkerson handed her another assignment based on the Stone Mountain Memorial, but considerably more dignified than swinging in a bosun's chair. This time Perkerson wanted a series of short biographies of the Georgia generals who were to be among the Southern heroes in the sculptured allegory planned for the granite cliff. The scheme has not yet reached completion, but Margaret's essays on the five soldiers are her most substantial writing in the *Journal Sunday Magazine*. In these pieces she demonstrated two things: her care in research, and her perceptive feeling for the period. A significant passage occurs in her account of General Henry Lewis Benning, for whom Fort Benning is named. The words foreshadowed a major factor in *Gone with the Wind*, and had to do with the general's wife, a "frail and slight" woman who was left in charge of a plantation when her husband and the other men-folk went to fight. The mother of ten children, Mrs. Benning was "as brave a soldier at home as ever her husband was on the Virginia battlefields. She saw to it that the crops were gathered, the children fed and clothed, and the negroes cared for. To her fell the work of superintending the weaving of enough cloth, not only to clothe her own children and servants, but also Confederate soldiers. While her husband was away she buried her aged father, whose end was hastened by the war, comforted her sorrowing mother, cared for her bereaved sister-in-law, the widow of her brother, and her brother's children, and nursed sick and wounded Confederate soldiers. And, hardest of all things in those trying days, she went three times to Virginia to bring home her own wounded."

Margaret received congratulations on these essays throughout the holiday festivities of 1925. But when the new year came in, she began to think about leaving the *Journal*. The way had begun to open before John Marsh at the Georgia Power Company, and the need for two salaries lessened as the load of debt melted under the

Marshes' regular payments. Margaret said early in her marriage, and repeated throughout her life, "A married woman must be first of all a wife. I am Mrs. John Marsh." Of course Margaret had loved her job; it had put a foundation under her life, and there was nothing for her quite like the feeling of competence and confidence when she sat down to write a newspaper piece. But she hoped and believed that John would become an important man, and held that one career in a family was enough. Accordingly, she talked matters over with the Perkersons, telling them she wanted her release as soon as Angus could get a replacement. He found a prospect in a talented Atlanta girl named Elinor Hillyer, and on May 3, 1926, Margaret drew her last check as a regular employee of the *Journal*. She agreed to continue for a while as an outside contributor to the *Sunday Magazine,* taking over from Frances Newman a column called "Elizabeth Bennet's Gossip." As Margaret wrote it, the column contained no gossip, but a series of ancedotes about Atlanta, presented in a light conversational tone that was quite worthy of Jane Austen's charming heroine after whom the feature was named. Reading this column was like sitting next to a nice and bright woman at a dinner party, and under Margaret's authorship, as during Miss Newman's, it was one of the most popular features Perkerson offered his readers.

Margaret's years on the *Atlanta Journal* gave her an abiding interest in the problems of newspaper reporters and editors, especially those besetting the people who wrote and edited Georgia papers. For the rest of her life, she never missed the annual convention of Georgia journalists, where she would meet old friends, and listen with close attention to discussions of the craft. This unflagging interest was reflected in the letter Margaret wrote early in 1949 to Dr. John Donald Wade of the University of Georgia Press:

"I think the *Georgia Review* becomes more interesting with each issue and I want to tell you how much I enjoy it ... At a recent luncheon which gathered a number of female authors and newspaper women I was reminded of one of the most amusing and instructive Round Tables ever held at the Press Institute. I wondered if any of the lady society editors who took part in the discussion could write an article for you. The matter they were discussing was what constitutes social news on a country newspaper. One of the greatest problems confronting the country editress seemed to be this: if Mrs. Jones had three friends in for an afternoon to play bridge and the editress put it in the paper, Mrs. Jones was furious because it made it appear that she had had a party and had not invited a number of her friends. On the other hand, if Mrs. Smith had three friends in to play bridge and the editress did not put it in the social column, Mrs. Smith was indignant that the little party she had given was ignored. How to drive the frail barque of the social column between Scylla and Charybdis brought out the most interesting newspaper discussion I have ever heard. It was followed by an almost equally instructive discussion on how one gathers social news in a small town—one editress saying frankly that she walked the back alleys of her town on wash day, and when she saw strange underwear hanging on the line she knocked at the back door and asked the cook who was visiting within. It appeared that one of the most dangerous things to mention was the unexpected arrival of a newly married daughter to her mother's house. On one hand it might be a pregnancy, which would, of course, be public property in no time and no one would be annoyed by this except the prospective mother. On the other hand, the bride might have had a quarrel with her husband and left him. She would doubtless be sent back by her mama with an earful of advice and the whole family would be mortified if the visit was mentioned in the public prints. The lady editress discussed this with stark realism. There were a great many other facets of this problem which I have forgotten now, but all of them showed what social life in the smaller Georgia towns was like at that time (probably 1938 or 1939). Some of these editors will be in Athens this week and I could put you in touch with them."

Though she no longer wrote for the *Journal*, there still remained the question of Margaret's private writing. Margaret had said, "Writing is my trade." She was a professional, and so considered herself. Yet, in later life, she was to hear that her production of a book whose worldwide acceptance went beyond anything ever heard of, was some sort of freak, a sport of nature akin to the performance by the talking horses of Elberfeld. Much of this refusal to believe in Margaret's professionalism as a novelist came from her reticence—the same distaste for revealing private matters that had kept John's courtship from becoming a subject of ordinary talk. As Margaret saw it, writing fiction was a private matter, too. She also had the born novelist's instinct not to talk a story away; she knew the approval of friends can satisfy an author's hunger for applause and thus make him lose the concentrated drive necessary to get his story on paper. So, in the years at the *Journal*, she had not talked about writing fiction. But she was writing it, all the same.

One serious effort that Margaret began in her own time, while on the *Journal*, was a novel of youth in the 1920s. She abandoned the story after thirty pages, but her secretary Margaret Baugh noted the main features of this fragment before destroying it, at Stephens Mitchell's direction, some years later. In Miss Baugh's summary, the heroine is Pansy Hamilton, daughter of Judge Hamilton of an old Georgia family. Pansy's mother is an unsympathetic Northern woman. The other characters are Pansy's young friends in Atlanta, and the opening scene gets them into trouble when Pansy and several boys go for an automobile ride. One of the boys is drunk, there is an accident, and he is hurt. They go to a drugstore for help, and find it closed at the late hour. Pansy climbs the side of the building and gets through a small window. There is a description of the store's interior, dark and full of mysterious smells. Pansy finds bandages and antiseptics, manages to get out the window with them, and the young people are talking about how to get the injured boy home without waking his mother, when the author abandons the story.

Margaret knew she was wise to drop this project. She could have completed it with fast action and convincing dialogue, but would have produced only an imitation of a popular contemporary novel called *Flaming Youth*, as the reviewers would have pointed out. She could do better than that, and so she proved in the completed manuscript of the novella *'Ropa Carmagin*. Years later, in 1937, Margaret asked Miss Baugh to read this manuscript and store it with other papers. Miss Baugh found the novella of somewhere between twelve and fifteen thousand words a fascinating story. The heroine was Europa Carmagin, a girl whose once good family had come down in the world. Margaret depicted the grim and haunted atmosphere in which the Carmagins lived, the old house, the weed-choked garden, the rotting fences around the worked-out fields. The heroine had character that might have sur-mounted all this, but her story could not have a happy end: she was in love with a handsome mulatto. Europa Carmagin was to remain a shadowy figure. As the years went by, magazine editors heard of her and begged for permission to publish her story, sight unseen. But no one ever again read *'Ropa Carmagin*, and the manuscript was destroyed, either by Margaret herself or John at Margaret's instruction, some time after Miss Baugh filed it away.

Like Rudyard Kipling, Margaret had learned her trade in a newspaper shop, and like him she had learned the art of significant detail and the importance of accurate background in realistic fiction. It was the tradition founded by another journalist, Daniel Defoe. This respect for truth as the foundation of convincing stories was what motivated Margaret when she wrote at home during the period immediately before her departure from the regular *Journal* staff. Margaret wished John's career to be the only public achievement in the Marsh family; she was reading for background and inventing stories because she could not help it, but she did not believe she would gain such notice from her writings as to overshadow her husband. But she was writing, and planning to write more. She had been doing this, after all, since she could hold a pencil.

So Margaret continued through the summer of 1926, reading and writing, and visiting the Atlanta public library for certain researches that led her to the oldest newspaper files. As one of the most assiduous patrons of the library, she would leave each evening carrying an armload of books stacked so high that she had to lift her chin in order to see and greet friends at the trolley stop in front of Loew's Grand Theater. And some of the friends would say that any time you saw a stack of books walking up Carnegie Way in front of the library you could say, "Hello, Peggy," and be sure you were addressing Margaret Mitchell. Then came early autumn, and another of the accidents that so often interfered with her private schedule. Margaret sprained her ankle; it was the one that had suffered in the riding accidents of 1911 and 1920, and it did not heal as it should. The doctors spoke of arthritis, then of rheumatism, then of possible pathology in the bone. Unable to walk, Margaret had the ankle in a cast for a time, then spent several weeks in bed with traction on the injured leg. This caused subsequent rumors that she wrote her long novel while flat on her back and encased in plaster. Margaret could not even have written a letter in bed, for at this time in her life, she wrote everything on the typewriter. She had to give up the Elizabeth Bennet column, and never resumed it.

Although confined to the small apartment, first as a bed-ridden patient, then on crutches, Margaret found compensation in reading. She had the writer's insatiable appetite for print, and while she was disabled, John brought home the piles of library books. Most obliging of men and devoted of husbands, he did not mind this chore. But at last it appeared that Margaret had read every book in the Atlanta library. One evening late in 1926 John said, "It looks to me, Peggy, as though you'll have to write a book yourself if you're to have anything to read."

Margaret's reply must have been on the order of "That's just what I'm planning to do." Forces under long development were about to emerge: family tradition, love of locality, a point of view that came from tested personal code, and above all, the need to write—to write in the seemingly effortless style of the born storyteller, the style that put no barrier between the reader and people of the tale—all these elements came together to form a narrative in her mind. And at last with a unified inspiration complete from start to finish, Margaret sat down to write.

VI

Birth of a Novel

She sat at a spindly sewing table in an alcove of the front
room under two small high windows. On the table was her
Remington portable typewriter. At its left, a pile of yellow
paper; at its right, a growing pile of typed sheets. Some
days Margaret typed from early morning until John came
home, and again after dinner until eleven or twelve. On
other days, Margaret did no writing at all. Sometimes the
non-writing days would lengthen to weeks, and a month
would go by with nothing added to the typewritten pile.
Margaret had no deadline. What she had was a story so
nearly complete in her mind that she could write in any
chapter at any time. She would write now toward the beginning, now in the middle, now at the end. In fact, the
first chapter Margaret wrote was the last chapter of the
book. This method of starting resulted from a habit she
had formed on the *Sunday Magazine*. Margaret liked to
end a piece well, and sometimes decided on the close, and
typed it out, before composing the opening passage of an
article. She said this gave her something to push toward; it
was one of those working habits, with a hint of supersti-

tious ritual in it, such as writers often employ to gain momentum. But in the case of Margaret's novel, it turned out that the last chapter came some five hundred thousand words after the first. This was indeed something to push toward. When questioned, Margaret would admit only that she was engaged on "a piece of writing"; it might have been a cook book or a guide to Atlanta, for all the particulars she gave. A few close friends found out she was writing a work of fiction, but not what the story was about.

A new and important friend appeared in Margaret's life about the time she started her book, laid aside her crutches, and began to go out again. This was a young woman named Lois Dwight Cole, who graduated from Smith after Margaret's time and came to Atlanta to run the office end of The Macmillan Company's trade department. She was an addition to the bright people in the town and received invitations to various parties, including a luncheon bridge given by Medora Perkerson. When the guests came to the card tables, Miss Cole found she had drawn as partner a Mrs. John R. Marsh, who was a "small, rather plump person with reddish brown hair, very blue eyes, and a few freckles across a slightly uptilted nose." Picking up her cards, Lois Cole asked, "Do you follow any particular conventions, partner?" Margaret said, "Conventions? I don't know any. I just lead from fright. What do you lead from?" "Necessity," said Lois Cole, at which Margaret gave a sudden grin.

The two girls found they had mutual interests—of which bridge was the smallest—and Miss Cole soon began to drop in at The Dump for tea after work once or twice a week. Here she saw the sewing table, the portable typewriter, and the stacks of paper. She would sometimes find Margaret working in shorts and blouse, sometimes in slacks or a house dress, but always with an eyeshade completing her costume. And always if Margaret was writing when visitors entered, she would rise from the table and cover the typewriter and manuscript with a bath towel, on which she would then toss the eyeshade. Lois Cole was among those to whom Margaret went so far as to admit she was attempting a work of fiction, and one day Miss Cole asked, "How's the great American novel going?" "It stinks," Margaret said. "I don't know why I bother with it, but I've got nothing to do with my time." Lois Cole said, "Macmillan would love to see it. When's it going to be done?" "At this rate it won't ever get done," Margaret said. "And no one's going to want to see it."

Time went on, and a few friends learned one more fact about the work on Margaret's sewing table: it had something to do with the Civil War. This became known when Margaret was again able to visit the basement of the Atlanta public library, where the bound volumes of old newspapers lay on dusty tables pushed against the walls. Margaret complained that these volumes were too heavy for her to hold or handle; the only way she could read them was to lie flat on the floor and prop them on her stomach. "And I'm wearing out my stomach," Margaret said, "just to read the newspapers they printed in this town in the 1850s and 1860s."

As a result of her hours at the library, the typewritten pages began to make a noticeable pile in the living room. She was writing her story by chapters, working first on one and then on another, without regard to sequence in the novel. When Margaret completed a chapter, she stowed it in a large manila envelope, which she stacked on the floor in a gradually heightening mound beside the sewing table. At times she would scribble notes of revision on the envelopes, or write new paragraphs on slips of paper and stuff them in with the original pages. As 1927 passed, and the early months of 1928 arrived, the pile of envelopes grew nearly to the table's height, and Margaret pushed it against the wall and started another. By the end of 1928, one stack of envelopes was solid enough to sit on—and some callers did. The older envelopes by now had accumulated dust and dirt. Yet Margaret knew exactly where each page and paragraph could be found; and when she felt like working on any particular passage, simply lifted it from its place as though she had located it by reference to a cross-filed card index in her head. For a while she used two or three envelopes as a prop under the leg of an ailing sofa. On others she jotted notes that had nothing to do with the work in progress, using the manuscript-fat envelopes as memorandum pads for telephone numbers, recipes, grocery lists and dinner invitations.

Most of Margaret's friends began to accept the business at the sewing table as possibly no more than a mild eccentricity. But some few, aware of Margaret's strength of mind and vividness of fancy, felt that so remarkable a person might well be turning out, in one way or another, a remarkable performance. One of the most perceptive observers near Margaret at this time was Lois Cole. Miss Cole came from the New Haven Dwight family that had scholars and divines among its members; her brother was to be president of Amherst College and ambassador to Chile. Lois Cole, therefore, had an eye for personal excellence and, as an outsider, would not give Margaret Marsh the uncritical admiration and applause that sometimes turns the heads of home-town Southern "characters." Within a few weeks of meeting Margaret, Lois Cole had known that "Peggy" was someone very special indeed. The two liked, respected, and enjoyed each other thoroughly, and a lifetime of amused and affectionate understanding was to result from their shared convictions about the important things in life. Each agreed the other was "a good ear." They also had one of the greatest causes of firm friendship in nearly perfect agreement as to what was and was not funny. In 1961, Lois Cole brought Margaret to mind as she wrote for the *New York Times Book Review:* "It is difficult to put Peggy on paper, to convey her gaiety, her interest in and profound knowledge of people, her range of interests and reading, her devotion to her friends, and the verve and enchantment of her talk. Many Southerners are born storytellers, but Peggy told her tales with such fun and skill that a whole roomful would stay quiet all evening to listen to her."

"If you want your dinner party to be a success, invite Peggy Marsh," said Augusta Edwards. Early in her adult life, Margaret had shown that in addition to sparkle in her conversation, there was warmth in her heart, and the gift of listening. People unburdened themselves to Margaret; you started talking with her and before you were done she knew your innermost problems. A friend said, "One thing about Peggy was that when you were with her, either just talking to her or at a party, you always felt more intelligent and more gay and more sparkling and more interesting than at any other time. Somehow, just being with her, raised us above our ordinary level. And we always felt we were more interesting as people just because we were friends of Peggy Mitchell."

Time went on agreeably enough, and by 1927 John had begun to rise at the Georgia Power Company. That year the Public Utilities Advertising Association established an award for copy in its field—and an advertisement written by John Marsh won the first of the annual prizes. And Margaret kept on filling manila envelopes. She continued to say nothing to friends of what she was doing; her audience was John Marsh. In the evenings, when there had been a day's output, he would read it. Since Margaret's writing for that day might be at any point in the story, John must have taken it in as an usher at a moving picture theater sees the feature attraction, any way but chronologically. But he knew the theme, which Margaret was later to define as "survival." John knew, too, that Margaret's heroine—a girl who echoed Pansy Hamilton with the name of Pansy O'Hara—was to survive the war, and prosper, just as the city of Atlanta survived and prospered.

One night John read a page that would finally appear about halfway through the book, after the burning and temporary abandonment of the town, when a back-country character says to the heroine: "You know Atlanta folks as well as I do. They are plumb set on that town, most as bad as Charlestonians are about Charleston, and it'll take more than Yankees and a burning to keep them away. Atlanta folks are as stubborn as mules about Atlanta. I don't know why, for I always thought that town a mighty pushy, impudent sort of place . . ." And Margaret's heroine mentally agrees: "it was a pushy, impudent sort of place and that was why she liked it."

Such was the simple underlying theme of a woman and a city on which Margaret was constructing her long novel. But this heroine had human needs and passions, and Margaret was writing a love story as well as a fictionalized account of history. She was to bring off the romantic side of the story—if that term can be used for Margaret's blunt and frank presentation of her self-centered heroine's sex relationships—with striking success. As she had shown in the letters she wrote as a freshman at Smith, Margaret knew there was a practical side to love and marriage. Clicking away at the Remington portable, she used this knowledge to keep the love interest in her story on a plane that such material had not up to this time occupied in a novel of the Civil War, except in one book by James Boyd. This was the plane of realistically depicted jealousies and passions. As psychological insight, this aspect of her story was to strike so hard with those who were prepared to see it that one might say a relationship of man to woman was the novel's theme. Stephens Mitchell thought so; after the publication of the book, he said, "The theme is, many a woman has a good man, but she doesn't know it until it is too late."

Stephens observed his sister's reading, and noticed that she had devoured a many-volumed medical report on the Civil War. He himself had begun to cultivate an historical specialty in studying the economic aspect of the war; he turned up little known material, tracing what became of the Confederacy's store of bullion, and into what Northern and foreign bank accounts the profits of blockade-running disappeared. He wrote an essay on confederate manufactures during the Civil War for the *Bulletin* of the Atlanta Historical Society after its founding in 1927. Margaret read Stephens' manuscript with care, for she had not found in the orthodox histories all she wanted to know about the enrichment of profiteers in North and South. She was working a vein of economic motivation into her story; as her mother had told her, where Sherman's sentinels stood along the road, some folks had come through and lived to raise their heads again, while others went down and down and finally turned to trash. It was a question of character, to be sure, but it was also a question of money: where did it come from, who had it, and where did it go?

Stephens knew, then, that his sister's writing would contain something about medical history and something about economics, two topics that the sword-waving type of Civil War novel had so far failed to exploit. He also thought that this long work, whether it turned out well or badly as fiction, would have in it something that he called his sister's philosophy, for Margaret had her own way of seeing things and people. Being close to her, sometimes in almost telepathic sympathy, Stephens understood how Margaret arranged material in her mind, and he recorded: "Her philosophy was made up by the case system. That is a system of studying law where you get no rules and no text, but you study cases which have been tried and decided, and you find out how they turn out, and finally, after reading many cases and discussing them with your fellow students, you make up the rules yourself. Margaret's philosophy was a 'case' philosophy. She did not try to make people fit a rule. She studied the people, and out of that came a rule. She had wished to be a physician and a psychiatrist. She said that she practiced psychiatry on her friends and acquaintances. When she drew characters, it was from her observation of how people behave—it was not from any preconceived notion of how they *ought* to behave. She put them down as they were."

In addition to what she observed of people, and the facts she read in historical books and essays, Margaret of course had purely literary influences working on her. At the time she was writing on Crescent Avenue, she took especial interest in the stories of Joseph Hergesheimer, F. Scott Fitzgerald, and Booth Tarkington. Of these only Hergesheimer was writing historical fiction, as it had been many years since the appearance of Tarkington's costume pieces *Cameo Kirby* and *Monsieur Beaucaire*. Hergesheimer achieved brilliant but essentially literary effects in such novels as *Balisand*, *The Three Black Pennys*, and *The Limestone Tree*, a story of the Civil War. Margaret responded to Hergesheimer's charm, but was in no danger of infection by his decorated style. She knew, however, that an author may offer a colleague a greater danger than that of causing unconscious imitation: he may publish something so good that it takes the heart out of a writer struggling along the same line. The contemporary author Margaret admired more than any other was Stephen Vincent Benét. In 1928, a young friend of Margaret's came hurrying to the Crescent Avenue apartment with a copy of Benét's long poem *John Brown's Body* fresh off the press. It was a writing day for Margaret and the young man found her at the worktable, staring at a sheet of paper in her motionless machine.

"Listen to this!" cried the young man. "Just listen to it!" Margaret put the bath towel over her work and dropped her eyeshade. The young man sat down, leafed through the book, and started reading the passage which begins:

> This was his Georgia, this his share
> Of pine and river and sleepy air
> Of summer thunder and winter rain ...

As he continued, Margaret jumped to her feet and said, "Don't read my any more of that." The visitor looked up in surprise, then down at the book again, and Margaret put her hand on the page. "Please, I mean it," said Margaret. "I can't listen to that." Nine years later she was to describe and explain this episode in a letter to Mr. Benét: "The reason was that you had caught so clearly, so vividly and so simply everything in the world that I was sweating to catch, and had done it in a way I could never hope to do and with a heartbreaking beauty. And, just listening to it made me realize my own inadequacies so much that I knew if I heard any more I wouldn't be able to write ..."

When the depression of 1929 struck Atlanta, many saw no change, for a return of the boll weevil had already impoverished North Georgia. While the disastrous months went by, Margaret was writing about poverty and starvation, as the world learned later. Stephens Mitchell watched his sister observing the hard times that had come to her native town. He noted: "The poor people with no jobs, the heartrending things that went on—educations abandoned, standards lowered, physiques ruined through bad food, nervous exhaustion and worry—all these things impressed Margaret. She could write of the poverty of 1864–1870 with a first hand knowledge of what it was."

It was true that John's job was secure; but raises were to be unknown for several years and the Marshes continued to live modestly. By the end of 1929, Margaret reached completion of the work she was typing at the spindly table below the two high windows. This statement, like many about Margaret's writing, needs immediate qualification: she herself said, "The book was *substantially* finished." It still lacked an opening chapter; others were in unsatisfactory shape; in some cases, she had not made final selection between two or more versions of events. Margaret knew what was necessary to prepare copy for printers, so she knew her thousands of pages were not ready for submission at any publishing house. Perhaps she had abandoned her vast project. Yet she kept the story on her mind, and she kept her unsatisfactory pages in the manila envelopes, as though she had some idea that the day might come when she would wish to see how her ideas had taken shape.

"I hit the book a few more licks in 1930 and 1931," she said later. By 1932, the stacks of envelopes had moved from the front room into closets where they crowded themselves on shelves or hid away behind Margaret's coats and John's evening clothes. In this same year, Margaret and John said good-by to The Dump and moved to a larger apartment at 4 East 17th Street. This was a more impressive building than that on Crescent Avenue, and closer to Eugene Mitchell's house. Stephens had married Carrie Lou Reynolds in 1927, and the new Mrs. Stephens Mitchell was hostess of 1401 Peachtree Street. By the time the Marshes moved to 17th Street, Margaret and her father had achieved a reasonably smooth relationship; before this they had been edgy with each other. Like many a father, Mr. Mitchell did not know how to approach his daughter when he had criticism or instruction in mind, and any suggestion of a peremptory tone would make Mar-

garet's sense of independence flair. But now she was secure in herself as a young woman who had succeeded on a
newspaper, married a good husband, and achieved her
own place in the life of Atlanta. Thus, no longer on the
defensive when dealing with her father, she avoided conflict. Eugene Mitchell had withheld praise from Margaret
when she was a schoolgirl; it gratified her that he now
found ways to let her know his pride in her. Warmth grew
between them, and an affectionate regard.

The year 1932 saw Lois Cole leave Atlanta. Married to
Allan Taylor, she went back to New York to become associate editor in The Macmillan Company's home office.
Margaret regretted that there would be no more evenings
when their husbands worked late and the two wives sat
with their mending baskets. They both loathed sewing, and
sewed with only passable results, but it was easier to turn
the collars on shirts when discussing books, poetry, history,
and people past and present. In December 1933, Margaret
was surprised to receive a formal letter on office station-
ery from her friend, stating that Macmillan would like
very much to see her novel, either when it was finished or
in its present condition, whatever that might be. "It's kind
of her, but Lois doesn't need to do this," Margaret said to
John. She then answered the letter in equally formal
terms, saying she had not finished the book, and doubted
that she ever would, or that it would be worth seeing—
but, if she did complete the story, Macmillan should have
first look. Aside from that, the correspondence between
the two friends was personal.

The envelopes had begun to disappear into closets in
1930. The move of 1932, then, would have been the natural time to throw them out like the rubbish they appeared
to be, but Margaret found storage space at her new home
for the manuscript that "would probably never be worth
seeing." One could theorize at length on her reasons for
preserving the script, while not submitting it to editors.
We know that she could not make up her mind as to
whether or not the book had merit; but it is understand-
able that she dreaded having editors tell her—the bad news
would have to come first from her old friend—that her

years of work had no value. And yet, Margaret must have thought she could be wrong, and that it was barely possible a first-rate publisher might accept the book and, somehow, as in a daydream turned to reality, it might become a success and its author a celebrity. What then? In her newspaper days Margaret had interviewed famous people, and this experience had convinced her that notability was something to be shunned. Morever, if she became the author of a successful novel, she would advance beyond her husband in the world's estimation. And this was not Margaret's idea of a suitable turn of events.

The day to day existence of Mrs. John R. Marsh was a pleasant one. Obvious things account for Margaret's happiness at this period: to begin with, she was living where she wanted to live. It was the city rather than the countryside that gave her the greatest sense of being, as she put it, "Where I belong." Of course Margaret loved the country, too, and liked to drive the back roads and visit small places, such as Jonesboro, and Fayetteville, at whose Female Academy her novel's heroine had received her education. But Atlanta itself was where Margaret most liked to be. Counting suburbs, the city now had a population of more than three hundred thousand. "We're a little town, even if we're a big town, and we love to talk things over," Margaret said, as she settled the new apartment. The principal items of furniture were family pieces; some had survived destruction, and dated from before the war; others were pieces from the Seventies and Eighties in the modified Empire style that now bears the generalized label of Victorian. Like many Southerners, Margaret and Stephens had been enjoying the solidity and elegance of the better "Victorian" furniture long before Northern decorators rediscovered the style. Later there was to be a nationwide revival of interest in the sort of furniture she had at 4 East 17th Street—a result of the moving picture that would be made from the story that lay in the wrinkled and scribbled envelopes on her closet shelves.

John had now been two years in office as head of his department at the power company. Confirmed in executive rank, he knew that his depression-proof job with a public utility would be worth money when good times came back. But there were troubles of various kinds. Grandmother Stephens died on February 17, in 1934. Margaret's sorrow was partly for the quarrel on Peachtree Street; if only she had been older then, she said later, she would have known how to avoid the whole scarifying business. Unhappily the "feeling" that distressed Margaret and others in the family connection did not go also to the grave.

Misfortune struck again in 1934 when an automobile accident occurred. Margaret drove the family Chevrolet with adequate skill and commendable caution, preferring to yield the road when approached from the rear. About a month after Mrs. Stephens's funeral, Margaret pulled over in her usual manner to let another car pass, but its driver plowed into the Chevrolet so violently that Margaret's head snapped back and she sustained a spinal injury. For months she wore a brace. Some years later, she was to enter the Johns Hopkins Hospital for a corrective operation that failed to give hoped-for relief; both before and after the surgery she suffered frequent periods of pain and weakness about which few people ever knew. Close friends eventually found out about the pain and the accompanying physical difficulties, though none ever heard her complain. But she did express her opinion of "the fool who ran into me" with vigorous words.

Christmas of 1934 was one of the best Margaret ever had. It was, indeed, the last holiday season she would pass with nothing to do but select and wrap gifts, hang up decorations—she liked the traditional glittery sort with red and green in the backgrounds—and go to congenial parties. So the Marshes saw the old year out, not knowing that 1935 was to mark the beginning of a fundamental alteration in their lives. In New York, a man who was to be among those who caused this change was returning to his desk at a publishing house on Fifth Avenue.

Harold Strong Latham was a New Englander who moved in youth to Brooklyn, where he attended the crack Erasmus Hall High School. He graduated from Columbia in 1909, and on the following Monday went to work for

The Macmillan Company. This employer divided his time between the advertising and accounting departments, and Harold Latham found it interesting to write circulars and jacket copy, but was not so happy in accounting, where he learned the mysteries of assessing charges against the various titles on the Macmillian list. Though he recognized its importance, he called this aspect of the trade "depressing." The fact was that he longed to be an editor, and the measures he took to achieve his goal were extraordinary. At the time of his retirement from active daily duty at Macmillan in 1952, he revealed the story to a trade journal. "Young Mr. Latham," the article reported, "set out to publish privately a literary magazine. The recollection of this project so appalls Mr. Latham today that he can be persuaded to mention it only because it did result in his becoming an honest-to-goodness editor. 'A prospectus of the magazine happened to fall into the hands of Edward C. Marsh, Macmillan's editor at that time,' Mr. Latham says. 'He called me in and said, "Well, if you want to be an editor *as badly as that*, you'd better come into my department."' So, early in 1910, Mr. Latham did join the editorial staff as an assistant. Ten years later he was editor in chief of the trade department* and a director of the firm." He became a vice-president in 1931.

Up to the 1920s, editors in American publishing houses let writers with manuscripts come to them; but, after World War I, public demand for reading matter caused a sharp increase in the number of books printed. There followed a proportionate increase in competition among publishers for authors to write the books, and editors began to go on scouting expeditions. At the start, Harold Latham scouted only in England, going there first in 1929, with such good results that he returned annually except during World War II. Thus he rounded up a number of writers, including Charles Morgan, G. B. Stern, Phyllis Bentley,

---

* In the language of publishing, the trade department is that which concerns itself with books intended for general sale—fiction, biography, travel, and so on, as opposed to textbooks, scientific works, and titles for special groups and interests.

and Richard Llewellyn, whose novel *How Green Was My Valley* recorded one of the great successes in Macmillan history with a sale of 250,000 copies.

In the first week of 1935, the Macmillan directors considered prospects for the next two years; the depression had receded, and much of the country was enjoying moderate prosperity. From this, the publishers concluded that in 1936, when the books they accepted in the next few months would reach the stores, fair to excellent sales should reward any works that could catch public interest. Therein lay the gamble of the book business, and its fascination: one was never sure what a book would do until people reached into their pockets. At any rate, Harold Latham decided this year of 1935 might be a good time for the first literary scouting trip through the United States by a Macmillan official. The suggestion drew approval from his colleagues and from the chairman of the firm George P. Brett, Sr. Mr. Latham then pointed out that a Southern women, Caroline Miller, had won the Pulitzer Prize for 1934 with a novel called *Lamb in His Bosom;* it might be well to start in the South and see if there were any more Caroline Millers down there; he would then go to the Pacific Coast. With a three-month itinerary drawn up, Mr. Latham started out in April. First stop, Atlanta.

Lois Cole, as associate editor, spoke to Harold Latham about Margaret's manuscript. "No one has read it except her husband, but if she can write the way she talks, it should be a honey of a book." Lois also wrote to Margaret and to Medora Perkerson, asking them to devote what time they could to making her chief's stay in their city pleasant and profitable. Accordingly, when Mr. Latham reached Atlanta, he found that one of his first engagements was to meet some people for lunch at the Atlanta Athletic Club.

Not long after he entered this handsome brick clubhouse, two blocks down the hill from the Atlanta library, he met a small, pretty and agreeable lady whose name was Margaret Mitchell Marsh. Recalling what Lois Cole had told him—a recommendation borne out by Medora Perkerson, who was giving the lunch—Mr. Latham asked Margaret if she had a manuscript he might see. Harold Latham was the first New York editor Margaret had ever met; she had some notion that such a dignitary might be hard to talk with, especially about literary matters. In fact, editors are a kindly and approachable sort of people, marked by eternal optimism and willing to read almost anything. Mr. Latham was an especially good example of the editor with a soothing, reassuring manner as benign as that of a popular professor or minister. (Indeed, he later became a high official of the Universalist Church.) At the table in Atlanta, in a tone of unmistakably sincere interest, he was giving Margaret an opportunity that most unpublished writers would have jumped at. Margaret replied that she had nothing to show. Harold Latham later recorded: "I did not get far at that luncheon."

The next day, he attended a lunch for Georgia writers and reviewers at one of the Atlanta department stores. Here again he saw Margaret, and heard several people say, "Peggy's written something, and she's so clever it ought to be good. Why don't you ask her to let you see it?" Latham cornered Margaret and said, "Look here, you say you have no manuscript and yet all your friends are rooting for you." Margaret's reply was an invitation to ride out and see Stone Mountain, the stupendous outcropping of solid granite, sixteen miles east of Atlanta, which is one of the most remarkable sights in the country.

Seated beside Margaret in the Chevrolet, Mr. Latham again asked to be allowed to read the manuscript, but she would not discuss the matter. Harold Latham then asked Margaret to agree that if she ever *did* have something to show, he should have first look at it. Margaret told him she had already promised this to Macmillan through Lois Cole, and she repeated this promise, though Mr. Latham noted that "her tone implied it was the most remote possibility in the world."

The day after the visit to Stone Mountain, Margaret shepherded a number of writers to tea at which she introduced them to Harold Latham. Again, the editor heard many recommendations that he find out what "Peggy" had to offer. He was too courteous a man to shrug his shoulders, but he had given up hope; perhaps he would find his Caroline Miller somewhere else. Had Mr. Latham settled down in Atlanta, he would have discovered that the members of Margaret's set were not unanimous in thinking she had produced something good, or, in fact, that she had written anything at all. Among these acquaintances were malicious gossips of both sexes. For example, one friend, if we may use the term, had passed word around Atlanta that Margaret had never written a line. Others said that Margaret had pretended to be writing a long book to avoid boring parties. Not everyone respected Margaret, or liked her. This was partly because she herself knew how to hold a grudge, and in part due to the wear and strain of existence that seems to secrete a certain unhappy amount of criticism and hostility into the air we breathe.

The point—a remarkable working of unsolicited luck— is that a member of the anti-Peggy Marsh faction was the final cause of her novel getting into print. For this irony, we have Margaret's evidence as she wrote it to Lois Cole.

"I've gone through deaths and handled funerals, and the very people who call on me for these things are the ones who say, 'Isn't it a shame that somebody with a mind like Peggy's hasn't any ambition?' It never made me especially mad—till the last straw came. After all, when you give your friends something, be it money, love, time, encouragement, work, you either give it as a free gift, with no after remarks, or you don't give it at all. And, having given, I have no further regrets. But this very same situation was what really made me turn over the manuscript to Mr. Latham. He'd asked for it, and I'd felt very flattered that he even considered me. And I'd refused, knowing in what poor shape the thing was. And for that tea, I'd called up various and sundry hopeful young authors and jackassed them (that is a friend's phrase) about in the car and gotten them to the tea where they could actually meet a live publisher in the flesh.

"One of them was a child who had nearly driven me crazy about her book. I'd no more than get settled at my own work than there she was, bellowing that she had gone stale or that she couldn't write love scenes and couldn't I write them for her? Or she was on the phone picking my brains for historical facts that had taken me weeks to run down. As twilight eve was drawing on and I was riding her and some of her adoring girl friends home from the tea, somebody asked me when I expected to get my book finished and why hadn't I given it to Mr. Latham.

"Then this child cried, 'Why, are you writing a book, Peggy? How strange that you never said anything about it. Why didn't you give it to Mr. Latham?' I said I hadn't because it was so lousy I was ashamed of it. To which she replied—and did not mean it cattily—'Well, I daresay. Really, I wouldn't take you for the type who would write a successful book. You know you don't take life seriously enough to be a novelist. And you've never even had it refused by a publisher? How strange! *I've* been refused by the very best publishers. But my book is grand. Everybody says it'll win the Pulitzer Prize. But, Peggy, I guess you are wasting your time trying. You really aren't the type.'

"Well, suddenly, I got so mad I began to laugh, and I had to stop the car because I laughed so hard. And that confirmed their opinion of my lack of seriousness. And when I got home I was so mad still that I grabbed up what manuscript I could lay hands on, forgetting entirely that I hadn't included the envelopes that were under the bed or the ones in the pot-and-pan closet, and I posted down to the hotel and caught Mr. Latham as he was about to leave to catch his train. My idea was that at least I could brag that I had been refused by the best publisher. And no sooner had I done this and Mr. L. was out of town than I was appalled both by my temper and my acting on impulse and by my giving him the stuff when it was in such sloppy shape and minus so many chapters."

At the hotel, Margaret telephoned from the lobby: "Mr. Latham, this is Peggy Marsh downstairs. Could I see you for a moment?" She certainly could, and a minute or or two later the editor stepped from the elevator, looked around, and saw Margaret perched on a large divan. Beside her in its many envelopes was the biggest manuscript he had ever encountered. The pile of envelopes reached to

Margaret's shoulders; and as she saw him approaching, she rose and said, "Here, take the thing before I change my mind."

Latham was delighted to have possession of this mass of paper; but there was no room for it in his bags. He hurried to a luggage shop for an extra suitcase, into which he put the manuscript, unedited, not typed for professional submission, untitled, and lacking a first chapter. Then he went to the railroad station.

On the overnight train to New Orleans, Harold Latham began reading about Mrs. Marsh's heroine Pansy O'Hara and her friends and enemies. To say he found the story interesting would be understatement, for it was elation the editor felt as he read the typed and scrawled pages and added them to a pile on the green Pullman carpet of his stateroom. The train rolled on, Mr. Latham read; he later recorded that he soon knew Mrs. Marsh's novel was "something of tremendous importance." He added, "Any publisher would have recognized that fact. I was fortunate to have come along at the right moment."

Next day in New Orleans, a telegram from Margaret was waiting at Harold Latham's hotel: "PLEASE SEND MANUSCRIPT BACK I'VE CHANGED MY MIND." Latham diagnosed this message as a symptom of author's jitters, and wired Margaret he had started reading her story and was sure she would not wish him to return it without knowing how it came out. He then completed his business in New Orleans, and set out for Austin, Texas. While on the train he typed a letter to Margaret dated April 18. He thanked her for permission to take or send the novel to New York for consideration by his colleagues and one of Macmillan's outside advisers. Margaret had worried about the chewed-up condition of the manuscript, and Mr. Latham assured her he would see that "our readers thoroughly understand its present state." He continued, "I am greatly impressed by it. I see in it the making of a really important and significant book. I have read only a small portion of it, to be sure, but what I have read is very reassuring. So then, I shall take it or send it along and deal with it, when I get back, with the care which it deserves. I have the feeling that we are going to keep at this project until a novel is issued that is going to be regarded as a very significant publication."

Before leaving New Orleans for California, Harold Latham shipped the manuscript to Lois Cole in New York. Miss Cole has recorded that "It was, physically, one of the worst manuscripts I have ever seen." Its yellow paper had faded and was approaching disintegration. Margaret had written over the typescript in pencil, on some pages altering nearly every line. There were versions of the same chapter at variance with each other, and some chapters missing because they were not yet written, or still lying among the pots and pans on East 17th Street, and, as Margaret had explained to Mr. Latham, there was no opening chapter at all. Nevertheless, Lois Cole realized she was reading one of the most fascinating novels of all time. And having read it, she sent the manuscript on to a Macmillan adviser on fiction, and what his report boiled down to was: "Publish as quickly as you can." Early in June, Harold Latham got back to the office and finished his own reading of Margaret's novel, with unwavering enthusiasm. Then came the meeting of the Macmillan Editorial Council. Backed by Lois Cole, Latham assured Mr. Brett and other executives that he had brought in a good book, a possibly great book, and without doubt, a salable book. He recommended they offer Mrs. Marsh a contract and it was so ordered.

On July 17 a telegram went from Harold Latham to Margaret Mitchell Marsh, saying that her novel had inspired unanimous enthusiasm at The Macmillan Company, and urging her to accept and sign the contract that would reach her in a short time. The author's royalty was to be 10 per cent on the retail price of the first 10,000 copies sold and 15 per cent thereafter; and Mrs. Marsh was to receive an advance against royalties of $500—half on signing the contract, the balance on delivery of a finished manuscript. The advance of $500 in the currency of 1935 equals $2000 in the inflated money of the 1960s, about what the average first novel commands today. But Margaret was not thinking of money when Latham's message arrived, along with a jubilant wire from Lois Cole. She had just returned from visiting Bessie Berry,* her cook, Lula Tolbert's successor, who was sick in Grady Hospital, and there had been trouble with an officious, bureaucratic young intern. Emotionally exhausted by this unpleasantness, she read the New York messages and telephoned John at his office. Margaret told John she still could not believe a publisher would actually bring out her story, adding, "I don't see how they can make heads or tails of it." John answered, "You'd better sit down quietly so you'll have less distance to fall when the realization comes over you that someone besides me likes the damned thing." Margaret said, "But I still don't see how they expect to sell any copies." John said, "Don't worry about that. You and I have so many cousins, we'll sell at least five thousand copies in Georgia alone."

* Later Bessie Jordan.

VII

Tide Rising

Both sales and editorial officials at Macmillan considered
Margaret's novel as certain of success as it is possible to
predict in the publishing trade. Soon they were to appropriate $5000 for advance advertising, the equivalent of
$20,000 in the money of the 1960s. And now when we
stand poised with them all, editors, promoters, Margaret
herself, like passengers on a rocket with a fuse sputtering
down to the fuel supply, is a good time to ask ourselves
what, in point of fact, had Macmillan bought?*

For those who do not remember or know the book or
picture, the best answer to that question is in the report
from Macmillan's adviser, Professor Charles W. Everett of
the English Department at Columbia University. His report telling the entire story in a few pages was a model of

---

* Publishers do not buy manuscripts; what the author sells
is a license to print and sell copies of his work. The work
remains his property, and for this reason payments based on
the number of copies sold are called royalties, a compensation
paid the owner for use of a patent or copyright.

perception and conciseness. Professor Everett started by saying, "There really are surprisingly few loose ends, and the number of times one's emotions are stirred one way or another is surprising. I am sure that it is not only a good book, but a best seller. It's much better than Stark Young.** And the literary device of using an unsympathetic character to arouse sympathetic emotions seems to me admirable.

"This is the story of the formation of a woman's character. In the peace and quiet of plantation life before the war, in the crisis of the Civil War, and in the privation of the reconstruction period. Pansy O'Hara inherits an aristocratic tradition and charm from her mother, Eleanor D'Antignac of Charleston. From her father, Gerald O'Hara, who has left Ireland as the result of a shooting, she inherits most of her qualities—aggressiveness, courage, unscrupulousness, obstinacy, and charm. By the time she is born, O'Hara has won a stake in the new world of Georgia and is accepted by his neighbors for his courage and generosity. Pansy has lived her seventeen years in luxury without even knowing that it was luxury. Her greatest problems have been those having to do with clothes and flirtation.

"Then the war comes, to her annoyance, for she is both self-centered and realistic, and it seems like the sort of foolish thing men are always doing. Piqued by the marriage of Ashley Wilkes, the charming and cultivated son of a neighboring planter, Pansy marries Charles Hamilton, one of her beaux and brother of Ashley's bride, Melanie. Charles goes off to war after a week and in five weeks is dead of pneumonia, leaving her with a child coming. She is furious at her predicament and at the way a bereaved widow is supposed to act. After the birth of little Wade Hamilton she goes to Atlanta on a visit, and causes talk by her appearance in public, even though she is helping the Cause. Atlanta is humming with activity as the Confederates try to establish their own foundries and facto-

** A reference to Stark Young's recently published Civil War novel, *So Red the Rose*.

ries. She meets again Rhett Butler, black sheep of a good family, now a blockade runner, and his attentions cause more talk. Rhett has always flouted public opinion, and he alienates Atlanta by insisting, when the ladies treat him as a hero, that all he is interested in is the money he makes, and by saying that the Yankees are bound to win by sheer weight. In spite of her interest in gay parties Pansy is still in love with Ashley, off in Virginia with the army, and she hates his wife, Melanie. The sweet and gentle Melanie defends Pansy from criticism, however. After Gettysburg, Ashley is captured and no news arrives from him for the rest of the war.

"The Confederates under Johnston fall back before Sherman's army, much to the disgust of the residents of Atlanta. Johnston is replaced by Hood, but the Yankees continue to advance. Pansy helps in the hospitals and cares for Melanie, who is about to have a baby, but she hates the smells and the suffering in the hospitals and is upset by the shortage of food and clothes. Rhett brings her presents and teases her by saying all sorts of improper things to her. He knows her feeling about Ashley and is half in love with her himself. He understands her, sees through her, and still likes her.

"After a forty day siege Atlanta falls. On the last day of the siege Melanie has her baby, assisted only by Pansy and a little Negro girl. That night Pansy escapes to Tara, the O'Hara estate, in a decrepit rig secured by Rhett. He leaves her at the edge of town, and joins the retreating Confederate army, making fun of himself for his absurdity in joining a lost cause.

"The twenty miles to Tara take a night and a day to cover, for Pansy goes by back roads to avoid army stragglers. In the jolting wagon she carries Melanie and her day old baby, four year old Wade, and Prissy, the little Negro girl. Almost every place they pass is a heap of smoking ruins, and they have nothing to eat but some early apples they find. Pansy is in terror of what she will find at home. She knows her mother has been ill, but nothing more. At last they reach Tara and find the house still standing. But Ellen is dead of typhoid, Gerald broken in mind and body, and Pansy's two sisters ill with typhoid, Mammy, the old negro nurse, is still there, as are Gerald's valet, Pork, and his wife Dilcey. The author sums up the situation as one in which Pansy finds 'Her father old and stunned, her sisters ill, the children helpless, and the negroes looking up at her with childlike faith, clinging to her skirts, knowing that Ellen's daughter would be the refuge Ellen had always been.' There is nothing to do but take up the load, and Pansy takes it up. She shoots and buries a marauding Yankee straggler and keeps his horse. She finds a few vegetables and yams in the deserted negro truck patches, at the Wilkes place. Prostrated by heat and lack of food in a negro cabin, she vows 'As God is my witness, when this is over, I'll never be hungry again.' Sherman's army comes through again, and she saves the house from fire and hides her money in the baby's diaper. Against incredible odds, she keeps the nine of them alive in spite of the Yankees and the Confederate commissariat. She finds a few neighbors, all in worse plight than she is, bullies the house negroes and her sisters into doing field work and survives.

"After Appomattox, things are a little better. The returning Confederate soldiers are nearly starved, and she begrudges them every hard-won bite they eat. One of them, Will Benteen, a cracker, stays on and helps her run the place. Then comes reconstruction. Tara is assessed for $300 in taxes. A carpetbagging former overseer hopes to buy it in at a sheriff's sale. Pansy knows Rhett has money, and with a new dress made from velvet portieres, she goes to Atlanta to see him. He is in jail, and makes her offer to become his mistress before telling her his money is in England. She meets elderly Frank Kennedy, engaged to her sister Suellen, and learns that he had begun to make money running a store. Using a full battery of lies and wiles, she marries him in two weeks and pays the taxes with his savings.

"Then comes the turning point in her life. She *likes* making money and running people. She takes Frank's business out of his hands, and makes it pay. No credit to old friends who think they have to have things they will never be able to pay for. She borrows money from Rhett to buy a sawmill, and as Atlanta rebuilds, she makes money. She gives Ashley a job, and is still hopelessly in love with him. To her annoyance she finds she is going to have another baby. The Ku Klux arises and strikes back at negro rule. Kennedy dies (one version) or is killed in a Klan raid (alternative).

"After the birth of Ella, Pansy marries Rhett, who really is mad about her, but knows better than to let her get the upper hand by knowing it. With Rhett's money, a quarter of a million, Pansy builds a new mansion, atrocious but fashionable. Her unwomanly behavior calls down on her the contempt of all her old friends until Melanie, who has never forgotten what Pansy did for her, puts up a fight for her.

"She has a third child, Bonnie, by Rhett, and then refuses to have further relations with him. Separate rooms. She forces from Ashley an admission that he loves her, and the scene is overheard by hostile ears. This last scandal would have been too much, but Rhett forces her to receive at a reception with Ashley and Melanie, and thanks to Melanie, whose standing is unassailable, the town is forced to continue paying Pansy outward respect. Rhett has done this for the sake of the beloved Bonnie, who is now killed in an accident, and he slumps into hard drinking and low life. Melanie dies, and Pansy has a last scene with Ashley, who says Melanie was the only dream he ever had that lived. Pansy sees him as a middle-aged tired man with no particular glamor. At last she realizes that she loves Rhett and goes back to tell him the glad news. But he is tired. He won't put himself in jeopardy a third time, after losing to Ashley for years (spiritually) and then losing Bonnie. No one can wait for ever. He doesn't care what she does, and he really means it.

"She decides to go back to Tara. Tomorrow she can think what to do, how to win Rhett back. Tomorrow will be another day."

Having boiled down half a million words to a few hundred, Professor Everett went on, "This book is really magnificent. Its human qualities would make it good against any background, and when they are shown on the stage of the Civil War and reconstruction the effect is breath-taking. Furthermore, it has a high degree of literary finish. Take for instance, in the evacuation of Atlanta, the ridiculous appearance made by the aristocratic Mrs. Elsing in the morning as she drives furiously out of town with her carriage bulging with flour and beans and bacon. Then see Pansy leaving that night—with a worn-out horse and broken down wagon, and those literally beyond price so that only a strong man like Rhett could have secured them. And at Tara Pansy faces starvation. Yet there is no reference made by the author to the previous scene; it simply marks an increase in the tempo. It is perhaps in this control of tempo that the book is most impressive. When the writer wants things to seem slow, timeless, eternal, that is the way they move. But her prestissimo is prestissimo and her fortissimo if FFF. For like King Lear, Pansy learns 'There is no worst, as long as we can say "This is the worst." '

"By all means take the book. It can't possibly turn out badly. With a clean copy made of what we have, a dozen lines could bridge the existing gaps . . . The end is slightly disappointing, as there may be a bit too much finality about Rhett's refusing to go on . . . Incidentally, how about *Another Day* for a title?" Everett concluded: "Take the book at once. Tell the author not to do anything to it but bridge the few obvious gaps and strengthen the last page."

Professor Everett seems to have erred only in recommending alterations for the closing page. Leaving the conclusion open had been a fine stroke of story-telling: the question of whether the two leading characters ever saw each other again was to agitate the country with a consuming interest such as had not flared up since the national excitement in the 1880s over the equivocal ending of Frank R. Stockton's short story, "The Lady or the Tiger." Everett had thought there was too much finality in Rhett's departure; but what Margaret had accomplished was the releasing of her two characters into the realm where fictional creations live outside the stories that gave them birth. Indeed, the urge to furnish Rhett and his infuriating wife with a further written history was to set scores of amateur writers at work on sequels to Margaret's story, which were a source of annoyance for years. When Lois Cole forwarded a copy of Everett's report, Margaret found it hard to believe she was an expert in the control of literary pace.

Upon the arrival of the Macmillan contract, Margaret remarked that the Mitchells were "legal people," and took the two-thousand-word document to her father and brother for professional analysis. But before allowing them to see it she insisted that they agree to accept ten per cent of her future net earnings for acting as her lawyers. "I don't want free advice," said Margaret. After making some minor alterations, Eugene Mitchell told his daughter the contract was in shape for signing.

Stephens recorded later on, "Had we known of all the complications which could have arisen, we would have written in a great deal more than we did." No one could have known, of course, that they were establishing a business that would still be flourishing long after Margaret and John were dead. On the day she signed the contract, which was August 6, Margaret said she hoped the book, despite its being a first novel, would earn $5,000.

She must have had the feeling that at least five thousand dollars' worth of work would go into editing the manuscript. Making her copy readable for typists was only a small part of the tremendous task. Margaret determined to have her story consistent from start to finish in usage, spelling, dialect, places, times, and dates. She wanted her readers to accept scores of characters and hundreds of scenes without once experiencing the halt in reception of narrative that comes when an incident seems to occur out of logical sequence, or when a minor figure in the plot talks out of character. Margaret had tried to give each person in the story an individual voice; and she felt that in printed fiction this was a matter of appearance on the page as well as how the writing sounded to the reader's inward ear. Her editing and rewriting, therefore, must take account of both sight and sound. This determination to deliver a flawless technical performance was one of Margaret's most admirable qualities. She said that putting a first draft on paper was harder than digging ditches; but coming back to it cold—some of it work she had last looked at nearly ten years before—required sheer power of the will.

Harold Latham returned the rough typescript a few days after the exchange of signed contracts between Atlanta and New York. So far in her career, Margaret had written two novels: one was the long work she now proposed to edit and rewrite; the other was the story of Europa Carmagin and her tragic love affair. Latham had received the short novel along with the big one, and thought it publishable as it stood. Unfortunately The Macmillan Company could not use a piece of fiction in that length. Latham added. "The excellence of the novella shows that you can handle more than one type of material and character." Lois Cole, who also read the short novel, said it sent an authentic chill up the spine. But the author put 'Ropa Carmagin away and apparently never again gave it serious consideration.

The big thing now was to get the big book ready. Correspondence grew thick on such topics as the style of art for the jacket, the type face, the end papers—"whatever they are," as Margaret remarked. (They are the linings of the front and back covers together with the first and last pages.) All agreed that Tomorrow Is Another Day would be a good title; but, on checking, it was discovered that there were thirteen books in print with "tomorrow" somewhere in their titles, which threw a favorable light on Professor Everett's suggestion of Another Day. Margaret liked the sound of it, but wrote that she would like to send a few more suggestions for the publishers to think about.

Before settling to her task of editing and publishing, Margaret wanted opinions from her brother and father. Stephens read the manuscript first, from the point of view of his specialized knowledge of Southern economic history. He found she was historically accurate in her treatment of trade and finance, and added, "It is a very competent piece of writing. I am proud of it." From a Mitchell to a Mitchell, this was all that needed to be said. Their father was more emphatic: he said the novel was a work of genius. His only worry was that the descendants of families who got rich in Reconstruction days would take offense. He groaned when he read the characteristics Margaret had given one of the families in her story, and said there was a certain Atlanta tribe whose members would publicly resent this treatment. But Margaret and Stephens thought nothing of the sort would happen, and it turned out they were right. As to history in general, Mr. Mitchell told Margaret she had been thoroughly accurate.

But this did not satisfy the author; she dreaded being caught in an historical error more than she feared criticism of plot and style. So there was nothing for it but to go back to the Atlanta library and check the novel's innumerable statements as to times and places that were matters of historical record. Margaret always maintained that after the checking at the library she was able to cite at least four authorities for each nonfictional statement in her book. This seems excessive; she needed no over-statement in describing her painstaking work, for example, on the military background. Before she was done, Margaret had constructed an hour-by-hour schedule of every recorded happening in Atlanta and the surrounding country for the last twenty-four hours of Sherman's campaign. Indeed, she had put together at least the skeleton of a book that might have been called *The Day Atlanta Fell;* but this was only in case someone should challenge her accuracy—no one ever did. So far as can be determined, there is not even a minute error of fact in the novel. This stands as a testimonial to her integrity and scholarship; but so far as the average reader was concerned, it would not have mattered if small mistakes had crept into the historical part of the narrative. Character and drama were to make the book's universal appeal.

Though she possessed talent and self-discipline beyond most writers, Margaret shared with the meanest of them a tendency to underestimate the time revisions would require. On September 10, she was writing to Lois Cole that final copy might be ready early in the fall. Miss Cole was enthusiastic, but probably had private doubts that it could be done. There were still many things to settle; for instance, like all great novelists Margaret had a special touch with names; they were mostly "just the names the characters had," as she put it; but one or two did not ring properly. She changed the aristocratic Ellen O'Hara's family name from D'Antignac to Robillard—an instantaneous improvement. She worked on her second heroine's given name of Melanie; tried Permelia instead; it would not do, somehow it had a comic sound. She tried Melisande. That was better, but too rich, too regal. Then the tension relaxed: of course, Melanie was right. Let it stand, with the accent on the first syllable. Now she squared off at the problem of her first heroine's name. Pansy O'Hara was good, and they liked it at Macmillan. But still there was something wrong. She tried Storm: Storm O'Hara. Not bad, but it had the aura of conventional fiction. How about Robin? Good, except for its tomboyish flavor, and this was no tomboy. Kells? Irish but unfamiliar. How about Angel? Same objection as to Storm. Margaret kept this problem "on the back of the stove," and one afternoon late in September took a pencil and made her heroine Scarlett, to form one of the most striking and unforgettable names in prose fiction. The unanimous reaction at Macmillan was, "Three cheers for Scarlett O'Hara."

One problem was to avoid using the names of real people, since Margaret usually kept the name that first occurred to her when a character took shape. An embarrassment came from the coincidence that the newly appointed Bishop of the newly created Roman Catholic Diocese of Savannah-Atlanta was named Gerald P. O'Hara. Up to the time she wrote the book, the only O'Haras Margaret knew of were a group of traveling horse traders, the Clan O'Hara, that convened in Atlanta once a year. Her book was on the press when she first read in the papers about the new Bishop. After publication, she heard Bishop O'Hara was unhappy, and wrote to him:

"I regret the embarrassment you have suffered and I can say with all sincerity that I would have been happy to save you from all of it, and I tried my best to save you from it. If you had come to Savannah a few months, or even a few weeks, earlier than you did, there would have been no Gerald O'Hara in my book. I would have changed his name without any request from you and without your even knowing it. I went to endless pains to avoid using names that would cause embarrassment to anyone. Before I adopted the name of Gerald O'Hara, I made lengthy investigations to make certain that no person by that name had lived in Savannah, Atlanta or Clayton County during the period of my book. The same was true of all my other characters. Of course, I also avoided using the names of prominent living people. It required months of tedious research but I have been rewarded by the fact that none of the names of my many characters has caused embarrassment to anyone, excepting Gerald O'Hara alone. And that one name would have been changed if I could have foreseen that a strange quirk of fate would send a Bishop to Savannah with the exact name of Gerald O'Hara after it was too late for the change to be made.

"When I first read in the newspapers of your coming to Georgia, I was stunned. I had worked so hard to avoid using the wrong names, and here was an almost malicious turn of affairs to upset my well laid plans. My book had already been finished, it had been delivered to the publishers and it was far advanced in production. I wired my publishers explaining the situation and begging for time to change the name, but they said it was too late. Gerald's name appears so often in the book, it would have required a wholesale resetting of the type and there was not time to do that. And so Gerald O'Hara kept the name he had had for nearly ten years before you came to Georgia, to your embarrassment and mine."

What worried Bishop O'Hara was his namesake's addiction to drink, gambling, and profanity; he thought the notoriety could become unbearable for a man in his position if the book appeared on the moving picture screen. The fear seemed logical, and Margaret shared the anxiety until the coincidence of names had a happy ending: within a year, the Bishop reported that all it amounted to was a conversation piece, and one that gave people a cordial impression even before they met him. Bishop O'Hara had a distinguished career, becoming an Archbishop and Papal

Legate to the British Court. He was a friend of the Mitchell family until his death.

Names for the characters were not the only problems of that kind: Margaret was still uncomfortable about the title of the book. Though the publishers had accepted *Another Day,* she kept suggesting alternatives. Some of them were:

> *Tote the Weary Load*
> *Milestones*
> *Jettison*
> *Ba! Ba! Black Sheep*
> *None So Blind*
> *Not in Our Stars*
> *Bugles Sang True*

The last title came from a Civil War poem: "Our bugles sang true for the night cloud had lowered, And the sentinel stars set their watch in the sky; And thousands had sunk on the ground, overpowered, The weary to sleep, and the wounded to die." This was good of its kind; yet Margaret was not sure *Bugles Sang True* said what she wanted. However, she decided she might find the answer in some other quotation, and her subconscious stayed alert. Stephens offered help, making Margaret laugh with *Piccolos at Dusk,* though she said he bettered that suggestion with *At Home in a Hurrah's Nest.* The search ended during the last week in October, when Margaret picked up an anthology of English verse, and glanced at Ernest Dowson's poem, *Non sum qualis Eram bonae sub regno Cynarae,* an old favorite of hers. Dowson had taken *his* title from an ode of Horace, the Latin translating to: "I am not what I used to be in the days of the good Cynara." This was the best-known work of a romantic whose brief and mostly wretched life had ended in death from tuberculosis in 1900. Since then generations of young people had felt a piercing emotional reaction when they first read Dowson's opening, "Last night, ah, yesternight, betwixt her lips and mine, There fell thy shadow, Cynara! . . ." and the conclusion of each stanza, "I have been faithful to thee, Cynara! in my fashion." But the lines that now caught Margaret's eye were, "I have forgot

much, Cynara! gone with the wind, Flung roses, roses rio-
tously with the throng . . ."

Gone with the wind—these were the words she had
been hunting for. They made one of those titles that in
some magical way improve the books that bear them.
Though Margaret perhaps did not stop for detailed analysis at the time, there were many reasons why Dowson's
phrase was an ideal title. First, it sounded well: it had as-
sonance in "gone" and "wind" and alliteration in the first
letters of its second and last words. "With" and "wind"
also furnished a happy rhyming of vowels in the short i-
sounds. The first word began with a guttural consonant
that made a substantial base from which one could easily
enunciate the complete phrase. And it was a phrase whose
meaning linked hauntingly with the story; one could not
read more than a page without beginning to hear its echo
in the mind: these people were gone, the wind had blown
them away.

It is likely, of course, that Margaret's novel would have
succeeded if she had called it simply A Story. But the extra dimensions of success the book achieved may well be
due, more than to any other single factor, to its perfect
title. Dowson had used the words in a sense differing from
Margaret's. The poet was saying he had allowed himself to
be carried by the wind; Margaret, of course, used "gone"
in the sense of "departed." The phrase occurs in the text
of the novel on page 397 of the American edition, where
Scarlett is struggling home along the road from Atlanta,
and asks herself: "Was Tara still standing? Or was Tara
also gone with the wind which had swept through Georgia?" Did Margaret add this passage after deciding on the
title? She never said, and so we shall never know.

A list of twenty-four possible titles was sent to New
York. "Gone with the Wind" was number seventeen, with
a note "I really like this the best." The editors immediately agreed it was perfect.

Tara started out in life as Fontenoy Hall; an Irishman
would be likely enough to name his house after the Bel-
gian village where Maurice de Saxe defeated the Duke of
Cumberland in 1745 with the help of Irish brigades in the

service of France. But to Margaret it was a crime to slow up narrative for explanations of that sort. Almost every literate person remembered the reference to Tara's halls in Thomas Moore's ballad, and since there was a harp concerned with it, the flavor was high legendary Irish and exactly what Margaret wanted. The hill of Tara in County Meath was supposedly the seat of ancient kings; Tara in Georgia sounded as right as Scarlett O'Hara and the title of the novel itself.

Margaret and her helper John were talking about getting the manuscript to the production people "within six weeks." It took them nearly six months, and after this was to come their struggle with the galley proofs (so called from the long trays or "galleys" holding the type) with the page proofs to follow. All through October, they were optimistic. The perfection of the characters' names, and the finding of the apt and beautiful title had stimulated them. In his small neat handwriting John drew up a seventeen-page glossary of terms in Negro and frontier country speech to help keep the various kinds of dialect consistent; this expert aid no doubt held a warm memory of the time during their courtship when John had acted as volunteer copy editor. So far as big decisions went, she had no difficulty in selecting, for example, the more dramatic version of Frank Kennedy's death. Margaret used the episode which has Shantytown hoodlums kill Frank in a battle with the Ku Klux Klan caused by Scarlett's obtuseness and vanity.

"For the first time in my life," she wrote to Harold Latham, "working is comparatively easy . . . As John says, there's nothing like signing a contract, having a conscience about delivering the goods, and burning your britches behind you . . . There is still a lot to be done . . . loose ends to be hitched up and repetitions to be eliminated . . ."

But the manuscript took on a kind of stubborn life; Margaret began to feel she would never subdue it and get it out of the house. It was a physical struggle; she wrote that she "scratched at the manuscript, cut it with scissors, slashed it, pulled it apart and pasted it together again." When you got right down to it, Margaret realized, writing was manual labor. Perhaps because of the physical strain, boils broke out on her head. She wrote to Harold Latham in November that the doctors had shaved her scalp in spots the size of a fifty-cent piece in order to treat this ailment. She pressed on, took out two long chapters, wrote a "bridge" to cover the omission, then examined every remaining page from what she called the reader's point of view. So far as the reader was concerned, Margaret wanted her story to stand without mannerism, in absolute simplicity and clarity.

As Margaret saw it, such efforts to communicate with readers had nothing to do with form or style. If there should be any style, she wanted readers unaware of it. In a letter to a friend she wrote, "Perhaps it's a hangover from newspaper days, but I always felt that if your story and characters weren't strong enough to stand up against stripped and bare prose, then those characters and that story had better be abandoned. I'm not a stylist, God knows, and couldn't be if I tried. Moreover, I sweat blood to keep my writing as bare as a law report, as uncolored as the newspaper versions of a hit-and-run accident." But Margaret's text was neither intrusively nor affectedly stripped and bare. When it suited her purpose, she turned a desciptive phrase as in setting a north Georgia landscape "amid the dismal dark beauty of the pines on the rolling hills" or saying that an untidy old gentleman's clothes "looked as though they had been blown on him by a hurricane."

Margaret was discreet in not talking about her prospective debut among contemporary novelists. She wanted no official announcement until she had finished the revisions. Nevertheless, news was circulating in the trade that Macmillan had something on the fire. Harold Latham talked to the Macmillan salesmen in December, telling them he brought tidings of great joy: a best seller, as certain as anything in their hazardous trade could be. Dispersing to the former speakeasies in midtown Manhattan where book travelers, literary columnists, and publicity men gathered for lunch and cocktails, the Macmillan people heard congratulations from their colleagues. The word was out, the excitement of a big hit was in the air. Some of the promoters from rival firms were sincere in their good wishes; others were not, and men in two big New York publishing houses said their editors had turned the book down because it was not much good. But even as they uttered this lie, they knew that if the book sold as Macmillan expected, it would help the entire industry.

Meanwhile, Margaret continued to struggle with her "seven or eight bushels of typed pages" through days that reminded her of the ordeal Zeus inflicted on King Sisyphus of Corinth by condemning him to push a heavy rock up a hill for all eternity. But Sales Manager Alec Blanton frequently asked when he could make firm commitments to deliver Mrs. Marsh's book. He said he planned to give dealers "a real Macmillan promotion." The sooner he started, the better for all. Nevertheless, the editors refrained from telling Margaret their special publishers' fear that somewhere in the United States an unknown man or woman might at that moment be putting the last touches on a long romance, based on the Civil War and full of the elements that sell fiction. Nothing could shake their faith in Margaret and her novel, but even a great book will benefit from a clear field.

That was an easy decision, but Margaret was finding it progressively harder to rewrite while at the same time hunting for authorities on architecture, decoration, costume, language, geography, agriculture, and the history of the Southern blockades. Just before Christmas, Lois Cole wrote to John that she feared there might be "too much pressure on Peggy." It was true that sitting at a desk nine and ten hours a day was not the treatment of choice for a spine that had suffered injury in an automobile accident; but there was no such thing as "too much pressure" for Margaret. The work was agonizingly hard, but she let off steam by laughing at herself, or making some humorous exaggeration like the claim that she had re-done the opening chapter forty times. She did write it with scrupulous care; and, according to her custom from childhood on, gave her first sentence an arresting quality: "Scarlett O'Hara was not beautiful, but men seldom realized it when caught by her charm as the Tarleton twins were." To make sure no reader went away, Margaret then gave an exact picture of Scarlett, like one of those miniatures by Rembrandt Peale, itemizing a pointed chin, pale green eyes, and black brows slanting upward to cut a startling oblique line in the magnolia-white skin. The Tarleton twins were not the only ones to be fascinated by Scarlett O'Hara; her creator saw to that. Margaret wrote this curtain-raising passage in December; and during the holiday season, took only Christmas Day off, for the traditional Marsh "brawl" with so many guests that "some of them had to squat in the hallway." Margaret worked through New Year's Eve; on the following day she told John it was faintly conceivable she would finish the editing and revision "in 1936." Three weeks went by in a closing sprint of work, and on January 22 the typists brought back the last page. In New York, the Macmillan people rejoiced to hear the typescript was ready at last. But now there must be delay: Margaret would not release the final manuscript until Eugene Mitchell had read every word. However, since he had already approved the rough draft, this did not hold up proceedings to the extent the editors feared. Mr. Mitchell understood their needs and gave his imprimatur in less than a week. On January 27, John Marsh telegraphed Lois Cole, "COPY ON WAY." On the 31st, he wrote that he assumed the manuscript had arrived at the Macmillan office, and shortly received a wire that copy was in hand. In the Seventeenth Street apartment, Margaret and John sank back in their favorite chairs, looking at each other with affectionate congratulation and hilarity. They thought the work was over; they thought there would be no more trouble; they thought it would be interesting to see what the reviewers had to say about the novel, and pleasant to collect a few royalty checks. But Margaret told John she felt like the man whose neighbors had ridden him out of town on a rail, who reported that if it wasn't for the honor of the thing, he wouldn't care about it at all.

The honor of the thing began to manifest itself within a week, when *Gone with the Wind* received its first notice in print. An Atlanta newspaperwoman named Yolande Gwin broke the story in the society feature she wrote for the *Constitution* under the byline of "Sally Forth." She had telephoned Margaret on the chance of picking up some routine item, and struck gold. On February 6, the following morning, Miss Gwin headed her column: "MARGARET MITCHELL'S NOVEL DEPICTS THREE MAJOR PERIODS" and went on to report that "Sally takes pride in adding the name of Margaret Mitchell to the list of Atlanta authors. Her book, *Gone with the Wind*, is scheduled for spring publication." The story explained that the three periods of the book were prewar, the siege and fall of Atlanta, and the Reconstruction years.

Margaret told Yolande Gwin her column brought on a case of author's feet, an ailment which came from "standing on hard sidewalks explaining to everyone who stops you that you really have written a book, and it will be out in a few months." The new author could not give the date of publication, nor did she care, for she was feeling the exhilaration that comes to writers who have mailed their editors the last pages of a long piece of work. This euphoria continued until February 6, when the Macmillan Company sent a letter asking Margaret to accept a flat 10 per cent royalty, with *no* increase to 15 per cent after the sale of ten thousand copies. The publishers explained that the length of the book compelled them to ask this adjustment. Margaret agreed, though along with her brother and husband she thought the publishers might have made this calculation when they first saw the manuscript and offered their contract. John Marsh later took occasion to point out that Margaret had said the novel was too long, and in the face of Macmillan's advice not to cut, had sent them a shorter manuscript in the final version; yet *they* were the people who supposedly knew all about publishing, of which Margaret knew nothing. Late in May, the Macmillan Company restored the 15 per cent royalty on all sales over twenty-five thousand, adding a provision that they would pay only 10 per cent in any year when sales were less than five thousand. Margaret realized the publishers were spending an unusual amount for advertising and promotion; but the request for reduction had been a cloud on her relationship with the Macmillan Company. In spite of the improvement in terms, and the prosperity that rewarded the combined efforts of author and publishers, the relationship was never again a completely happy one; before the year 1936 was over, the partnership was to be called on to withstand a further and almost unbearable strain.

This unfortunate affair still lay in the future when four days after the bad news about the royalties, a parcel arrived at the Seventeenth Street flat. The package came from Susan Prink, the Macmillan copy editor in charge of typography, usage, and uniformity of style. It contained the first thirty-five galleys of proof; and as Margaret examined these proof sheets, with their impersonal queries and corrections, the latter often destroying carefully planned effects, she felt the hopelessness that had beset her in the depths of rewriting. Indeed, she began to look on *Gone with the Wind* in the way Br'er Rabbit regarded Tar-Baby—as a clinging nuisance she would never be rid of. Margaret and Miss Prink started an extensive correspondence. They had to reach agreement on many matters, perhaps the most crucial being the treatment of words by which Margaret proposed to show what was going through Scarlett's head while the story unfolded. Because these words were parts of conversations in the heroine's mind, Miss Prink strongly recommended quotation marks around the passages. Margaret disagreed, and after spirited discussion gained her point when Miss Prink came to realize how the author was using Scarlett in the book as a whole. Scarlett exemplified the point-of-view character that students admired in the work of Henry James, and this had not happened by accident; Margaret planned it so, and wanted no redundant punctuation marks to distract the reader's eye.

Another discussion concerned the handling of dialect. Margaret wished to indicate several varieties of regional speech, and was especially anxious for accuracy in the talk of her Negro characters. A letter to a Northern friend shortly after publication showed her painstaking care, and her instinct for using the simplest methods of indicating non-literary speech. Margaret wrote: "And about the dialect which you didn't think Uncle Remus would have liked. No, I don't guess he would. And I sweat blood to keep it from being like Uncle Remus. Uncle Remus is tough reading as I know from having had to read him to many children. It sounds grand but it's tough reading. So is most dialect and I, a Southerner, usually refuse to read any dialect stuff that's like Uncle Remus. And so do most Southerners. I wanted it easily readable, accurate and phonetic. And I scoured the back country of this section routing out aged darkies, speaking Geechee, who might just as well be speaking Sanscrit for all they mean to me. The middle Georgia darkies (around Macon) have constructions that are practically Elizabethan. When you get into such tangles as the word 'if' which in some localities is 'ef' and in others is 'effen' and in still others is 'did' (for instance, 'Did I picks up a snake I'd be a fool'), it is enough to drive one mad. No, I'm not a dialectician (if there is such a word). Latin is far easier ... If you ever get down to Charleston, I wish you'd go out to Magnolia Gardens and listen to *their* combination of English accent and Gullah. 'Get' for 'gate,' 'race' for 'rice' etc. I can never understand half what they say."

Although Miss Prink sometimes needed instruction on the fine points of regional speech like those Margaret discussed in this letter, both editor and author were agreed on their common objective—quickness in final correcting of the proofs. What they achieved is astonishing. The average educated person today may scrutinize *Gone with the Wind* from the first page to last without spotting a single typographical error, inconsistency of style, or confusion in the names of characters. This is due primarily to the conscientious labor of Margaret, John, and Susan Prink, but the typesetters and proofreaders also deserve credit, for it was their responsibility that final corrections appeared in the published work. All concerned performed so well that there are less than half a dozen typographical errors in the entire book, about as close to perfection as human printers can come.

Another striking achievement was the speed with which Macmillan's production department operated; these people said if they could get final proofs on March 15 they could promise publication on May 5. That was only a little more than three months after the copy came in; nowadays publishers need from six to nine months after receipt of copy to bring out books one-fifth the length of Margaret's novel. She sent in most of the proofs well ahead of the deadline, mailing a final batch on March 16. There was a flurry of telegrams concerning Scarlett's age and the ages of her children by three husbands; someone suspected inconsistency here, John Marsh settled it with a telegram on March 19, and the printers locked the forms. For better or worse, *Gone with the Wind* would stand as they had it.

Exuberantly she sent off a letter to Professor Everett: "I am writing to thank you for the part you played in the acceptance and publication of my book, now titled 'Gone With The Wind,' which Macmillan Co., is bringing out some time in the near future . . . But for you and the fine things you said about it, I'm sure the book would never have been sold and now that the last corrected proof has gone out of this house, I am so very grateful to you for your kindness and the pains you took over a hard job. Your kindness and enthusiasm rather dazzled me for it had never occurred to me that anyone except my husband could possibly find it interesting or readable.

"In particular was I charmed by your remark about my 'tempo.' I'm sure you've forgotten the remark but you said I had it and I was completely dumbfounded as I was no more conscious of having tempo than I was of having a gall bladder. I nursed your remark to me in silence until one day when my husband was reading the manuscript which had just been returned. My husband, I should add, used to teach English at the University of Kentucky and has a reverence for the English language which I do not share. He was reading along and suddenly rushed out onto the porch with a double handful of dangling participial clauses and dubious subjunctives, crying, 'In the name of God, what are these?' I said with as much dignity as I could muster that they were tempo and let no dog bark. From then on, I heard about my tempo from all members of the family, including the colored cook. When she made her first, and only, failure on a lemon pie and I asked her what had happened she said gloomily that she guessed something had went wrong with her tempo.

... "I wanted you to know that a few words of yours had a far reaching influence. You made an utter stranger work like a field hand from last September until yesterday when the last blasted galley proofs slipped through the air mail slot and I shook hands with a man I'd never seen before in my life who was loafing in the post office. Thank you again."

The cheerful mood of the Everett letter soon faded, as Margaret began to fear they had overlooked some egregious error that would expose her to the scorn of scholars and the adverse judgment of those indescribably austere personages, the professional historians. She also had sudden and heavy doubts of the book's reception in its home town; she had, indeed, described that city as a pushy place where more than one carpetbagger had made a fortune. She wrote a friend, "God knows what the old-line Atlantans will think of this thing." Had it been possible, Margaret would have called the book back; instead, she went to a doctor for removal of the callus that had developed on the middle finger of her right hand from clutching a pencil while laboring over the proofs. She had also strained her eyesight, how badly they did not realize. She was exhausted. Margaret remembered interviewing authors for the *Journal*, and recalled her impression that they were on the whole a tired, harried sort of people. Now she understood why.

Many authors are vain, though some of them have sufficient cunning to hide this unattractive trait under a modest manner. But Margaret had genuine humility, as she showed in a speech before the book appeared. As Margaret apparently saw it, she had nothing even to be modest about, early in April, when she addressed the Writers' Club of Macon, Georgia. Here is how she reported this, her first speech, to Lois Cole:

"Now, about that Macon Writers affair—it was the most dreadful ordeal I ever underwent and untold wealth would not make me repeat it. As to why I didn't tell yall—first place, I didn't know you'd be interested and in the second place I didn't have the time. I had only thirty six hours notice. I was in bed and the paper hangers were going through the apartment like Attila and his Huns and the long distance rang and it was a strange lady from Macon. She said that Edison Marshall, their speaker, had illness in the family and couldn't come and would I come and speak? I said no, I would not and thanked her, explaining that I wasn't yet published and that I was sick. And hung up. In about thirty minutes, Macon had me again, this time it was the gang on the *Telegraph,* Susan Myrick, the feature writer, and Aaron Bernd the book reviewer and Ben Johnston the city editor. Sue, in her hoarse baritone, told me that the Literary ladies had learned that she knew me and they had brought pressure on her to bring pressure on me to come. I repeated that I hadn't been published, that I loathed meeting strangers, that I had never made a speech and, God willing, never intended to and, moreover that I had glands.

" 'You and your goldarned glands,' said Sue. 'If your glands would hold up under writing such a long book, they will hold up as far as Macon. The UDC* as well as the Literary ladies are on my neck so get yourself over here.' I refused and heard a muffled argument with Aaron. 'Appeal to her better nature.' 'Bah,' said Sue. 'Try bribery, then.' Sue said, 'We've got Sherwood Anderson hid out at Aaron's country place and if you'll come, we'll let you associate with him.' I said that not even James Branch Cabell would be bribe enough for making a speech. 'Try intimidation,' said Aaron. 'If you don't come,' said Sue in a sinister voice, 'I will review you in the *Telegraph* and compare you favorably with Ethel M. Dell and Temple Bailey and Aaron will review you in the *News* and compare you with 'Diddie, Dumps and Tot' and moreover he will use the word 'poignant' seven times and the word

* United Daughters of the Confederacy.

141

'nostalgic' eight times and he will refer to your opus as 'Adequate.' So I said, 'Alright you so-and-sos, I'll come.'

"It took me from that moment till I got on the train to buy a dress and a hat. I've fallen off to size eleven and there was not an eleven year old dress in town that looked dignified and authorish. Desperate, I finally got a green affair that was unendurably juvenile. I didn't have time to think of what I'd talk about, I thought I'd think of something on the train. But there were people I knew on the train and I didn't get the chance. And Sherwood Anderson met the train and we went to Aaron's house and I never got the chance to think about the speech that night. And Sue let me oversleep till I barely had time to make the luncheon. And when I got to my seat and saw that enormous room jammed with something over two hundred people, I ardently wished I was dead for by that time I was incapable of connected thought as far as a speech was concerned. While the president was introducing me I sat like a newly gigged frog and tried to think of what I would say and I couldn't think of a thing. Life will never hold as dreadful a moment as that. Never having made a speech I didn't even know how well my voice would carry and the hall looked every bit as big as the Grand Central Station.

"When I rose trembling I had a vague memory of how horses 'lock' their knee joints when they go to sleep standing up and fearing that I'd fall on the floor, I locked my knee joints and took a good grip on the table and also on some whipped cream on the table cloth. Don't ask me what I said. I haven't much idea. I only know that I hadn't said five words when the crowd began to bellow which so disconcerted me that I couldn't get a word out for a minute. And from them on it was a riot. I don't know what was funny but they laughed till they wept and two UDC ladies fell off their chairs and were replaced with great difficulty. The *Telegraph* reporter who was covering the debacle got the hiccups and had to be led out so she didn't get to cover it all. Long about midway, vague consciousness came to me and I found I was talking about Mr. Latham and the conversation we had when we were ambling about Atlanta looking at the dogwood. He had asked what my story was about and I had said vaguely, 'The south.' I know that sounded feeble minded but I ask you how would you describe such a book? And he smiled and said proddingly, 'Like Tobacco Road? Any degenerates in it?' And I said 'No' and explained something about the characters. Then he said that if Southerners felt that they were maligned by such books as 'Tobacco Road' why didn't they write books to show themselves as they truly were? Editors would just as soon publish books about decent people as Jeeter Lesters—if the decent books were as interesting as the others. Now this did not seem a remarkable statement to me, but dearie, it brought down the house. (Afterwards everybody spoke so highly of the Macmillan Company and said they could *always* trust Macmillan books not to be full of garbage and Mr. Latham must be a perfectly wonderful editor and was he ever coming to Macon?)—The applause shattered my nerve far more than the laughter and I went on to tell about how Mr. Latham asked why I hadn't ever submitted the book to any one and I had told him that I didn't think it would sell because there were only four Goddams in it and only one dirty word. Some kind friend in the back of the hall yelled, 'Come on! What was the dirty word?' and, cornered, I refused to tell and hastened on with my saga that I didn't think the book would sell because the heroine was in love with another woman's husband for years and they never did anything about it. This was where the UDC's fell on the floor.

"After they had been retrieved I had forgotten what I was talking about and plunged into the horrors of galley proofs. I admitted that I could either take subjunctives or leave them, was partial to split infinitives and would not know a dangling participle if it rose up and gave me the Bronx cheer but that Miss Prink was, unfortunately for me, well informed on these subjects and that Macmillan, alas, had a high standard of English. I forget what came next. I had only flashes of consciousness. I recall sitting down and rising with violent abruptness because the waiter had brought some corsages for me and put them in my

143

chair and I sat down on them and the pins were right up. This seemed to complete the disorganization of the meeting ... I asked afterward how long I talked and they said forty minutes and at that they had to bear me off and revive me with Bibb County corn. So help me, I'll never get cornered again, come what may or make another speech. I never went through such a horrible experience in my life (except when I dropped my drawers in the church aisle when I was six or seven). As I said before, I can't tell you much of what I said in that forty minutes. Blythe MacKay covered what she could hear above the bellows but I haven't a copy as I gave it to Mr. Berg who intends to use it for his own dark purposes. . . .I will try to get you a clipping from Macon. . . .However I found to my distress that everyone had gotten the impression that *Gone with the Wind* was a sweet lavender and old lace, Thomas Nelson Pagish story of the old South as it never was. The newspapers all over the state picked up the story, commending me for writing a book that put the South in its true light. Alas, what shall I do about Rhett the speculator and Scarlett the Scallawag? I can never visit in Macon after publication."

Good fortune was brewing even while Margaret was having her finger operated on, and was peering at oculists' charts. For one thing, editors at Macmillan & Co. Ltd. of London were reading the proofs in a mood of interest and optimism. The managing director was Harold Macmillan, the future prime minister, an ex-Guards officer who had fought in the 1914 war and survived a bad wound. He thought the passages of violence and war in the American story rang true, but he had no way of deciding about the national authenticity of the characters. However, like his friend Winston Leonard Spencer Churchill, Harold Macmillan had an American mother, and at his request she read the story. Mrs. Macmillan was no Southerner, having been born in Indiana, but that did not keep her from recognizing the soundness of Margaret's characterizations. His mother's favorable report was all Harold Macmillan needed, and he asked for the privilege of bringing out the British edition of *Gone with the Wind*.

At the same time the moving picture companies were becoming interested in the book. Already Macmillan had received inquiries from agents who believed the story had motion picture possibilities simply from what they had heard about it. In early April, Harold Latham suggested that Margaret appoint The Macmillan Company her agent for selling the picture rights. He used the tone of one who was sure there would be a sale: Margaret's book was a hot property. On April 15 news came that the Book-of-the-Month Club was going to make *Gone with the Wind* an "early selection." In two weeks the club made it definite: Miss Mitchell's novel would be its selection for July. This caused Macmillan to postpone the trade release date from May 31 to June 30. There was rejoicing, for it meant a special extra edition of forty thousand copies to be distributed to club subscribers; in addition, the fact that the novel was a Book-of-the-Month would stimulate general sales. It looked as though there would be nearly one hundred thousand copies in print before the book appeared in the stores; and this was the sort of advance activity that impressed moving picture companies.

One scout for a movie company who took quick action was Katharine Brown, Eastern representative for the independent producer David O. Selznick. When not yet halfway through a set of proofs, she telephoned Ronald Colman in Hollywood and began reading him passages in which Rhett Butler appeared. Colman thought it wonderful stuff, for his actor's ear noted that Margaret's dialogue would "play." "Ripping!" Colman cried at intervals over the long line. "It's topping, simply topping," he would go on whenever Kay Brown paused for breath, and when she finished, he said he would certainly read the book. Apparently Miss Brown was the first to engage in what was to become the great American game of casting *Gone with the Wind*. But Kay Brown could do something about actually bringing the book to the screen. On May 20 she sent a synopsis and a copy of the novel to Selznick in Hollywood, together with a telegram urging him to read the book as well as the outline. Her message concluded: "ɪ

KNOW THAT AFTER YOU READ THE BOOK YOU WILL DROP
EVERYTHING AND BUY IT."

On the following day, Harold Latham wrote to Margaret suggesting the time had come to "make some move in connection with the possible motion picture sale." Mr. Latham sent the letter in duplicate, asking Margaret to sign one copy if she wished to have Macmillan assume the role of agent and make the sale for her. Margaret signed. As a result, unfortunate and irritating events took place shortly after the publication of the novel. In the long run it would become evident that this was nobody's fault: everyone concerned tried to do the right thing, but it was to be a demonstration of the maddening difficulties that arise when too many cooks are hovering around the broth and getting in each other's way.

The publishers' good intentions were beyond question: prior to the formal release date of June 30 they distributed advance copies of *Gone with the Wind* not merely to the literary journalists and critics of the syndicates and metropolitan papers, but to each editor and book reviewer on the remotest weeklies and smallest regional magazines. Copies also went to buyers and sales people in book stores across the country. The distribution included 1000 books for which Margaret had autographed the end papers. All told, the copies Macmillan gave away numbered in the thousands—more than the sale of many a book. The price was to be $2.75 before publication, $3.00 thereafter, a low price even then for 1037 pages and nearly five hundred thousand words. Alec Blanton knew there would be a considerable selling of review copies from which neither publishers nor author would profit, but it made no difference; he also knew the reviews and mentions in book columns would be the kind of publicity money could not buy.

Though they expected a great deal of free publicity, the officials at Macmillan were far from niggardly in contracting for paid space. They scheduled advertisements for July in the literary weeklies and in such monthly magazines as *The Atlantic, Harper's,* and *Scribner's.* They took generous space in fourteen newspapers of the five biggest cities, and ordered advertising for August in the newspapers of all cities having large bookshops. Lois Cole wrote that she had not seen anything like it in her experience; Margaret answered by saying it was simply beyond belief. She was afraid the novel might collapse under this investment in advance copies and paid space, in spite of the book club selection.

Margaret might have relaxed when Harold Latham himself passed through Atlanta in April, for he had nothing but good news to report. The influential syndicated literary commentator May Lamberton Becker had accepted an advance copy under pledge of not violating the publication deadline with a full-dress review. And Mrs. Becker had written for her national audience: "The Civil War and Sherman's march to the sea crash right through the middle of this book and leave you quite breathless. I meant to save my advance copy for steamer reading; I dipped into it before dinner, and it cost me the rest of the night, and now I can't forget the thing. It is the shortest long novel I have read in a good while." But Margaret did not realize Harold Latham's visit meant she was already a star Macmillan author. She was incredulous when he told her it looked almost certain that both the *New York Times* and the *Herald Tribune* would give her front-page treatment in the weekly literary sections on July 5, the first Sunday after publication. And she was almost in a panic on hearing that Stephen Vincent Benét would write the criticism of *Gone with the Wind* for the *Saturday Review*.

It might seem that these preparations to review the book were unnecessary, in view of the flat statement in the *New York World Telegram* that "The forthcoming Civil War novel, *Gone with the Wind*, will undoubtedly be leading the best seller lists as soon as it appears." But even more breath-taking was the statement in *Publisher's Weekly: "Gone with the Wind* is very possibly the greatest American novel."

VIII

Impact

There was a dreamlike quality in the advance notices stating so flatly that *Gone with the Wind* was already a success. As a newspaperwoman, Margaret had written of nine days' wonders herself, but she could not deny the reality of the check for $5,000 that arrived on May 21. It was, in fact, something like a miracle, for the contract did not require Macmillan to pay anything at this time, and most novelists waited from six to ten months after publication—in England, up to fifteen months—before payment. And even then, there was nothing to pay unless the book had earned more than whatever advance the writer received on acceptance. Margaret did not know it at the time, but one of the greatest assets a woman novelist can have is a husband with a job bringing in a regular check. She was fortunate also in her publishers; The Macmillan Company was a leader among the old-fashioned family firms, as solid as good banks, that dominated the book trade in England and America. Its chairman's father had been the first American agent of the British house the brothers David and Alexander Macmillan had built from a bookstore they bought in Cambridge in 1843. In 1869, Mr. Brett started The Macmillan Company of New York as an independent business, but with close ties to the parent organization. There had been successes, such as the publication in 1899 of *Richard Carvel*, by the American novelist Winston Churchill. The tale of Richard Carvel's adventures sold 200,000 copies its first year in print. Three years later came Owen Wister's *The Virginian*, to be followed by the novels of F. Marion Crawford, Jack London's *The Call of the Wild*, and James Lane Allen's *The Choir Invisible*—all best sellers. From these titles alone, one can see Macmillan was no stranger to big sales; but, in 1936, the publishing trade still suffered from the bad times that followed the panic of 1929, and Mr. Brett was ready for another successful book, even if it did not approach the performance of *Richard Carvel*.

After the first of June, the telegrams and long distance calls from New York to Margaret's apartment were mostly appeals for biographical material to satisfy the newspaper and magazine writers who were already besieging the publishers for information about the new author. Lois Cole asked for just 350 words by Margaret on her past career and future plans, with perhaps a paragraph on her novel's aim. Margaret answered that it would take her three weeks to write 350 words. "I would write 100,000 and then put in weeks boiling it down," she said. "I don't see any reason for personal publicity and never have. I just throw up when I think of it. I haven't anything of vital importance to tell the world. The truth is, I can't write my own publicity and my book hasn't got any aim. Thank God." A trip to Savannah was John Marsh's prescription for his wife's jitters over publicity. They spent a few days there, and one calm evening drove with two friends through the coastal cotton fields, with glimpses of Greek revival houses in the distance and Margaret reciting long passages of *John Brown's Body* from her capacious and accurate memory.

Back in Atlanta, Margaret found the first of the many overtures from magazines that were to solicit contributions from her, always unsuccessfully, for the rest of her life. The enterprising publication was *Pictorial Review,* then at the height of its influence. Margaret wrote a brief but appreciative note of refusal; on the same day she replied at length to a Southern bookseller who had sent her a fan letter after reading an advance copy of *Gone with the Wind.* This was the first indication of what the pattern would be: a tremendous correspondence with strangers, kept up because of Margaret's inbred courtesy, and a nature at the same time reticent and cordially friendly that made her love to chat with a sympathetic person, either directly or on paper.

Margaret sometimes would discuss herself with these unknown correspondents in a way that seemed at first glance exceedingly open and revealing; yet she never wrote anything really intimate. This passage from the reply to the bookseller is typical of thousands: "I don't like parties and I never go to them when it is humanly possible to avoid them. I'm not really rude. I'm always wearing myself out doing things I don't want to do, just to keep from appearing rude." One of the things she did not want to do was address a meeting of librarians in Atlanta. But she felt that her friends at the public library had done so much extra work for her during the time she had been checking her manuscript that she was obliged to accept their invitation and deliver a talk. Before making her speech, Margaret withdrew for a moment. Later she told John, "Everything I had eaten came up." Her remark about the nauseating effect of publicity was strict truth.

In the same week, Margaret began her long friendship by correspondence with Father J. M. Lelen, a priest who was a Doctor of Philosophy living in Falmouth, Kentucky. Father Lelen was another in the army of readers with advance copies of the novel; he had written, in care of the *Atlanta Journal,* to tell her he thought Scarlett resembled Becky Sharp, and that Melanie Wilkes reminded him of Amelia Sedley. Margaret answered that she had not read *Vanity Fair,* and trembled at the thought of having any of her characters mentioned with Thackeray's. She continued in her ingratiating, dinner-partner tone that Thackeray had not been among the authors her mother had paid her to read when she was a little girl. The fees were five cents for a play of Shakespeare, with Dickens at ten cents per novel. Perhaps if there had been special rates for Thackeray, she would now understand how her Scarlett could resemble the heroine of *Vanity Fair*. In this courteously indirect way, Margaret's chatting letter to Father Lelen served to deny his implication that she had lifted two characters from a classic. That she was one of the numerous well-read people who had not gotten around to Thackeray is borne out, also, by the testimony of Stephens Mitchell.

What amounted to advance reviews now began to appear in the newspapers of Atlanta and other cities. Mildred Seydell of the *Atlanta Georgian* was among the journalists who gave readers a preview of the book. Along with various favorable comments, Mrs. Seydell wrote: "There ought to be a law that hangs anyone who writes a novel over 350 pages long. But I fell into this one as into a swimming pool. I don't know whether *Gone with the Wind* is a true picture of the South in those days. But I do know it is a true picture of the picture of those days that I got as a child from listening to aging, graying relations and friends of their youth." In the same paper, "Polly Peachtree" reported that "Peggy Marsh is a homeloving soul who does not want to become a celebrity. But she has already become one whether she wants to or not." The perspicacious Professor Everett had a similar impression. On June 19 he wrote: "Now you are a successful author and will come in for a crossfire of envy, malicious gossip, and hatred that will make your hair curl. Those are the penalties of success. Whether you can ignore it I don't know. I suspect that you can, for I rather think I recognized you in one of your characters—Rhett Butler. It is not too good to see too clearly into the illusions by which people live—that is, it isn't good for a person. It's absolutely necessary for the literary artist." Professor Everett then repeated his prediction for a sale of 200,000 copies, adding that when this was achieved, it would be "a pleasant confirmation of a sentimental belief I have that good work is far more likely to achieve success than the literary racketeers believe possible."

A few days before Professor Everett's letter there had come a note from Oscar Graeve, editor of *The Delineator*, a woman's magazine, now extinct, that ranked among the great ones of its day. Like his colleagues on all the other national magazines, Mr. Graeve wanted a contribution from Mrs. Marsh: whatever she cared to write, or anything she had lying around. In a letter characteristic of her attitude during these first days of prominence, Margaret replied that she appreciated kind words, because "as my publication date (June 30) approaches, my knees wilt like boiled custard and it takes all my courage not to take cover in a swamp, like a rabbit. All this author business is practically the only thing that has ever happened to me that has thoroughly frightened me. As you can gather from my novel, I'm a verbose creature, but I feel that nothing short of insanity will ever make me write another line. And even if I wanted to I personally am now too busy sending back manuscripts from perfect strangers who want me to rewrite them to get down to any work of my own."

Not only magazines of general circulation were begging her to write for them, even though her book was not yet officially on sale in the stores, but all kinds of esoteric and special publications were crowding the mail with letters requesting and sometimes demanding that Margaret work for them, often without mention of pay. For example, *The American Hebrew* asked for help in combatting "furtive forces" and said that "while on the surface there seems to be a lull in attempts to incite racial and religious prejudice, there is evidence to indicate that sinister un-American propagandists, bent on breeding antagonism between Christian and Jew, are busily at work in many parts of the country." Margaret replied that she was not able to write magazine material, and added, with the candor that brightened her letters to inquirers of every kind, "I do not want to ever write anything again, as I dislike writing above all things in the world."

Near the end of June, Margaret saw proof that Harold

Latham had been right about the *Times* and *Herald Tribune*. Each paper announced that the subject of its principal review on Sunday July 5 would be *Gone with the Wind*. In the *Times* the reviewer would be the chief staff critic, J. Donald Adams. In the *Herald Tribune* Margaret's novel was to come under scrutiny by one of those people she claimed to dread most of all—a famous historian, the distinguished professor at Columbia University, Henry Steele Commager. With this on her mind, the last days before publication now shot past like speeded motion picture film for Margaret. She attended several parties as guest of honor, wearing a new light-aqua suit with a bolero and a white organdy blouse and with her hair trimmed short because of the damage done to her usual coiffure by the doctors treating her scalp trouble. Her eyes felt strange and she shielded them from direct light.

In another sense, the full and complete light of criticism and unmanaged publicity flashed on, and immediately mounted to a steady glare, when the official trade release date at last arrived: Monday, June 30, 1936. Friends in the Macmillan office sent telegrams, Miss Cole adding to her congratulations the news that dealers had sold 50,000 copies and were reordering, Mr. Latham with characteristic phrases about "this important book" which was "already an assured success" and his gratification at having taken part in bringing it out. George P. Brett, Sr. was not a man to use telegrams. He was dictating a letter to accompany another check for $5000. Mr. Brett also approved expenditure of an additional $10,000 in advertising *Gone with the Wind*—these sums a partial measure of the extraordinary achievement by the author who had started pecking at a typewriter on a sewing table ten years before. The day following publication, her book had brought her a total advance of $10,500, and there were over one hundred thousand copies in print, counting the book club edition, with the British edition yet to appear. Many a writer has a respectable career and sells less than that number of copies with a dozen different works. Also her publishers were confident of selling the story to the moving pictures. All this added up to certainty that the book would roll on to the sales predicted by Professor Everett, or even more, under its present momentum. So far as material success was concerned, it did not matter now whether the critics gave it good notices or not. But it mattered to Margaret, and she waited for the reviews like a playwright on opening night. Reviews would be coming out, to be sure, for many ensuing days, weeks, and months. But Margaret's instinct told her what publishers had learned from experience: to help sell a book, reviews must not only be favorable, but must appear close to publication. A notion has grown in the passing years that *Gone with the Wind* had an unfavorable press, and that it won public approval even though most of the influential papers and reviewers either ignored or attacked it. Nothing could be further from the truth. The number of reviews was prodigious, and few books in the history of publishing ever drew so high a proportion of wildly enthusiastic approval, as against neutral or unfavorable reviews.

In the brief time between publication and the appearance of the Sunday papers, the dailies let go with a cannonade of praise. Edwin Granberry wrote in the *New York Sun*: "The history of criticism is strewn with the wrecks of commentators who have spoken out too largely, but we are ready to stand or fall by the assertion that this novel has the strongest claim of any novel on the American scene to be bracketed with the work of the great from abroad—Tolstoi, Hardy, Dickens, and the modern Undset." Mr. Granberry went on to say that Miss Mitchell's book was "a great panoramic novel such as the English and the Russians and the Scandinavians have known how to produce." And he put Margaret's novel into favorable comparison with what many believed to be the highest revealed word in fiction when he said, "In its picture of a vast and complex social system in time of war, *Gone with the Wind* is most closely allied to Tolstoi's *War and Peace*. To be sure *War and Peace* overshadows Miss Mitchell's novel in many respects, but the American also has her points to offer against the Russian's. The uncertainty of subject in *War and Peace* long pointed out by critics—Tolstoi's seeming indecision as to just what his novel was to be about—is not a fault of the Civil War novel. *Gone with the Wind* has a center if ever a novel had it, which in great part accounts for its superb climactic tension."

The *New York Sun* was written for educated people; such a notice on its book page was as much fine gold. Another respected literary page was that in the *New York Evening Post* conducted by Herschel Brickell, who had come from Mississippi to work in publishers' offices and then turned to reviewing. He was one of those newspaper critics, now found more often in England than in the United States, who gave a performance of his own while reviewing a book, and he had a large following. "Great" and "superb" were among the adjectives he summoned to describe this book which he said would pass into the permanent body of American literature. There might be minor flaws, Mr. Brickell reported, for every tremendous work of fiction had a few; but, "Faults dwindle into nothingness when they are considered against the merits of the book, and the most profound merit of all is the simple and elemental truthfulness of the pictures." Visual metaphor occurred also to at least two other influential New York reviewers: in the *World Telegram*, Harry Hansen spoke of "an unforgettable picture ... a torrent of narrative ... an extraordinary book . . ." And Charles Hanson Towne, writing in the *American*, said, "It is an overwhelmingly fine novel . . . a broad canvas that throbs with color and life."

When words of praise like these were on record, Sunday reviews might seem an anti-climax. However, the *Times* and *Herald Tribune* weekly literary supplements had, on the whole, the greatest significance of any reviewing media in 1936, just as they do today. That they chose the same book for their leading articles on July 5 gave added importance to the verdicts. Experienced literary people might have predicted that in this case all would be well, but one never knew for certain until the reviews were in hand. As it turned out, Mr. Adams had the same opinion as his weekday colleagues: *Gone with the Wind* was a splendid book. He said it seemed to him "the best Civil War novel that has yet been written." This left only the frightening

Mr. Commager to be heard from—and he proved to be one of the book's most enthusiastic professional readers. Among other good things, he said, "The story, told with such sincerity and passion, illuminated by such understanding, woven of the stuff of history and of disciplined imagination, is endlessly interesting." Woven of the stuff of history! At this, Margaret felt like a student who had passed a difficult examination with an honorable mark.

After digesting the New York newspaper reviews, and equally laudatory notices in most of the big papers throughout the country, Margaret never again apologized for her book. It is true, however, that the chorus of praise was not unanimous. The reviewer in *The New Yorker*, for example, led off the magazine's literary section with *Gone with the Wind*, but before he was done made it clear that he did not take the book seriously. Louis Kronenberger was a brilliant young writer with almost faultless taste, and if he had a weakness as a critic, it might lie in treating popular work with suspicion. Yet he started his review with high praise: "For sheer readability I can think of nothing it must give way before; with her first novel, Miss Mitchell proves herself to be a staggeringly gifted storyteller, empowered, as it were, with some secretion in the blood for effortlessly inventing and prolonging excitement ... Miss Mitchell has dug out Scarlett O'Hara bit by bit with a daggerlike pen, creating in the midst of Confederate heroics a thoroughly heartless, calculating, and unscrupulous woman, no lady, but still, with her superb gumption, a kind of thoroughbred. She is not entirely real, but she makes glorious theatre . . ." Then Mr. Kronenberger considered the character of Melanie Wilkes. Here, he found, the author "offers us one of the really great impossible characters in all fiction—perhaps the greatest since Elsie Dinsmore." Summing up, Mr. Kronenberger said that *Gone with the Wind* deserved to be "extravagantly praised as a masterpiece of pure escapism." And in conclusion, "It provides a kind of catharsis, not, to be sure, of pity and terror, but rather of all the false sentiment and heady goo that even the austerest mind somehow accumulates." This austere verdict appealed to Bernard DeVoto, an editor and writer of popular history, who detested *Gone with the Wind* and never could see anything in it. He was still hammering at the novel a year later; "It has too little thought and no philosophical overtones ... The size of its public is significant; the book is not."

That put Margaret in her place so far as Bernard De-Voto was concerned. And Evelyn Scott in *The Nation* maintained that Margaret had failed "to master the wide significances implicit in her own material," while Malcolm Cowley reprimanded her in *The New Republic* for promulgating "the plantation legend." The novelist and dramatic critic Stark Young, an editor of *The New Republic* like Mr. Cowley, wrote Margaret to assure her he disagreed with his colleague's findings. She replied: "About the review ... I sent out and bought it as soon as I got your letter. It was a joy, wasn't it? I had had a cheerless day and that review brought cries of joy from me. A number of friends called during the day and each one read it aloud with joy equal to mine. When they'd read the part about the legend of the old South being 'false in part and silly in part and vicious in its general effect on Southern life today' they'd throw themselves on the sofa and laugh till they cried.

"I suppose I must lack the exquisite sensitivity an author should have. Otherwise, I should be upset by such criticism. But the truth of the matter is that I would be upset and mortified if the Left Wingers liked the book. I'd have to do so much explaining to family and friends if the aesthetes and radicals of literature liked it. Why should they like it or like the type of mind behind the writing of it? Everything about the book and the mind are abhorrent to all they believe. One and all they have savaged me and given me great pleasure. However, I wish some of them would actually read the book and review the book I wrote—not the book they imagine I've written or the book they think I should have written. They have reviewed ideas in their own heads—not ideas I wrote."

On the far left, the American Communist press assailed the book with the worst epithet in its vocabulary: fascist.

But even the comrades admitted that Miss Mitchell knew how to tell a tale.

With or without *The Nation, The New Republic, The New Yorker,* and the daily *New York Times,* or any other publication or combination of them, Margaret's novel was now much more than publisher's merchandise—it was a social phenomenon. Do we live by fashion? Some acute persons think so; and within a few days of publication, *Gone with the Wind* became a national fashion unlike anything of its kind this country had ever seen. Unique in that it was the only novel of presentable literary quality to achieve a like success, *Gone with the Wind* penetrated the national consciousness as though broadcast by waves of extra-sensory perception. The Macmillan Company recorded the public's extraordinary interest during the first six months in the life of *Gone with the Wind* in publicity releases which read:

July 13—A sixth printing, making a total of 140,000 copies to date, is being rushed through the press. It will be ready this week, and orders now on hand can then be taken care of.

July 20—176,000 copies of Margaret Mitchell's *Gone with the Wind* have now been printed in an attempt to cope with the steady inrush of orders.

July 23—What is believed to be a record in recent years has been established by Margaret Mitchell's *Gone with the Wind.* Although it has been published less than a month, printings already total 201,000 copies.

July 24—New orders booked yesterday totalled 10,753 copies.

August 5—*Gone with the Wind* is now going into its ninth printing, bringing the total number of copies to 226,000.

August 17—Two printing plants are working on the book in three eight-hour shifts and two binderies are fastening the sheets together.

September 3—330,000 copies have been printed up to August 30, two months after publication.

September 8—Another large printing of *Gone with the Wind* is in progress, bringing the total to 370,000.

Up rushed the rocket, faster and faster, higher and higher: a salesman took a single order for 50,000 copies from one New York store; by the end of October, the total was 700,000 copies. And in December 1936, half a year after publication, 1,000,000 copies had come off the presses. The books went out in carload lots, and carloads of paper halted in the sidings by the printing plants. At the one millionth copy, statisticians calculated the novel had so far used up 33 tons of ink, and 150,000 pounds of boards for the covers. Looking at the book's performance this early in its life, from the point of view of all-time records, the publishers found that there had been books that had sold more than a million, but, in the history of printing, no book had sold at so rapid a rate. This caused the experts to predict that the end was not yet; but their most sanguine estimates fell short of the stupendous achievements still to come.

Benefits flowed through The Macmillan Company from top to bottom; in December, Christmas bonuses appeared for the first time in recent memory. Outside New York and beyond the Macmillan office, and into every suburb and village where anyone struggled for three meals a day by selling books along with gifts and greeting cards, Margaret's novel brought the grateful warmth of ready money to the trade. It was timely help; the country's independent retail book-sellers were in trouble, many still feeling the effects of the 1929 depression. Though they worked long hours, these people saw their profits shrinking year by year, and in 1936 had come on very hard times. Many were living on credit extended by publishers who, in their turn, found the burden increasingly hard to bear. Book shops were failing right and left, but when news of the great best seller came, hundreds of small proprietors decided to keep their doors open somehow in the hope of making two or three months' rent from "that new Civil War book." They did better than that—with the price at $3, the million copies of *Gone with the Wind* the public bought by Christmas of 1936 caused $3,000,000 to go through the retailers' cash registers. On that sum they retained their discount of around $1,200,000, a substantial part of which went back into the general book industry as dealers settled their back bills with publishers in New York, Philadelphia and Boston out of the profits from *Gone with the Wind.*

The fashion industry also benefited from the explosive acceptance of Margaret's book. *Women's Wear Daily,* a trade paper with a large staff of domestic and international style scouts, correctly predicted profitable wholesale activity in silk taffeta and checked gingham, materials mentioned in the book as fashionable with planters' ladies before the war—and, a few years after it, among prospering carpetbaggers. However, one dress material used with much effect in the story did not become popular; this was the velvet of the parlor curtains at Tara Hall, from which Scarlett made a seductive gown for the purpose of charming money from Rhett Butler. But there was compensation for this single oversight in what the *World Telegram* saw as "a flurry of heaped petticoats, nosegays, billowing taffeta and puffed sleeves" that would last longer than most fashions, in colors such as Scarlett Green and Melanie Blue. Bags, dresses, hats, blouses, stockings, lace mittens, underwear, handkerchiefs, and gloves appeared in advertisements stating that they drew their inspiration from Miss Mitchell's book, though this exploitation, contrary to popular belief, did not put a penny into her bank account. Promoters linked even such insubstantial items as powder puffs, a brand of cologne, and a costume-jewelry necklace to *Gone with the Wind.* And the novelty counters offered a box made to resemble a copy of the novel that opened to reveal a manicure set.

Perhaps the items of dress, which became popular because of the mood that *Gone with the Wind* conjured up, were answering a childhood need that remains in maturity—the instinct to raid the attic, open the trunks, and put on the garments that lie folded away there. Men felt it as well as women, and although no beaver hats and longtailed coats appeared in the store windows, the nation's

Margaret at three (above).

With her mother and brother Stephens, about 1905 (bottom).

Margaret as Steve Hoyle in *The Traitor*.

Dressed for a hike during her nineteenth summer.

Margaret at twenty.

Stephens Mitchell standing before the door of the big house on Peachtree Street in 1922.

John Marsh at about the same time.

Margaret interviewing Rudolph Valentino for the *Journal Sunday Magazine*.

(credit: *The Atlanta Journal*)

On East Seventeenth Street, the author holds an advance copy of her novel.

On the Selznick lot at Culver City.

(credit: *Wilbur G. Kurtz*)

(credit: *Wilbur G. Kurtz*)

Vivian Leigh as Scarlett O'Hara awaits her cue (top).

The stars in costume showing the characters' post-war prosperity (left).

(credit: *Metro-Goldwyn-Mayer*)

Clark Gable meets the author.

Clark Gable and Vivian Leigh as Rhett Butler and Scarlett O'Hara in the Atlanta mansion where they notably failed to find happiness.

At Culver City, the stars of *Gone with the Wind* honor the
veteran Harry Davenport, who plays Dr. Mead.

(credit: *Metro-Goldwyn-Mayer*)

Selznick's vast and authentic blaze for the burning of Atlanta.

Tara Hall as David Selznick's designers imagined it, and not too far, according to the author, from the plain "up-country functional" she had in mind.

(credit: *Metro-Goldwyn-Mayer*)

(credit: *Leonid Skvirsky, A.R.P.S.*)

Margaret in the early 1940's.

Stephens Mitchell as he is today.

(credit: *Ludi, Atlanta*)

John Marsh in his office at the Georgia Power Company.

Margaret with her friend and newspaper colleague, Medora
Field Perkerson—October, 1940.

A publicity pose to help the Red Cross.

Margaret's last picture, taken in the summer of 1949.

costumers called on manufacturers for extra supplies of these articles to outfit thousands of clients who went as Rhett Butler or Ashley Wilkes to innumerable *"Gone with the Wind"* garden parties, dances, and balls that occurred all over the country.

The decorating trades also were stimulated. Wallpaper and pictorial chintz showing scenes from the story were designed, along with other drapery fabrics inspired by the description of Twelve Oaks, the mansion of the aristocratic Wilkes family. A social historian, however, would not have needed to visit decorating establishments to realize the permeating ubiquity of *Gone with the Wind*. He need only have picked up a newspaper and read the advertising columns, for the nation's copywriters, alert as always to whatever occupies the public mind, had recognized, the moment the book appeared, that they could use its characters and title in extolling almost any product or service in the world. There were thousands of examples, some ingenious, some merely hitchhiking on the title, as in the Pittsburgh advertisement headed "GONE WITH THE WASH" which explained that the troubles of home laundering would disappear for those who sent their laundry out. More adroit was the copy in a Los Angeles paper that announced: "IF SCARLETT O'HARA HAD WORN GLASSES SHE COULD HAVE MARRIED ASHLEY WILKES." This advertisement took the public's reading of the book for granted in explaining that with her near-sightedness corrected by glasses, Scarlett could have become a well-informed young lady whom the cultured Ashley would have regarded as an ideal mate. A publisher of Bibles announced that Second Kings was "even more breathtaking than *Gone with the Wind*." In Florida, the Power and Light Company urged its customers to read the novel by the light of an improved lamp it was ready to supply. The advertising of the book itself was not always in the expert copy and layout prepared by Macmillan. Local dealers were free to phrase and present additional promotion as they say fit. Many simply ran the line: "Fast delivery of *Gone with the Wind*—order by telephone." And in Maysville, Kentucky, John Marsh's home town, the bookstore concluded its advertising with the statement, "The author married a local boy."

As important as advertising and probably more effective than the reviews, except those in the *Times* and *Herald Tribune,* were the writings of the newspaper columnists, taste makers for the general public in those days before television. The newspaper writers recognized *Gone with the Wind* as a prime source of copy the moment it appeared, and were almost unanimous in enthusiastic approval. Among the columnists with national influence, Heywood Broun stood alone in failing to report an even remotely favorable reaction. He placed the book among the year's unimportant works of fiction, and thought it would soon vanish into well-deserved oblivion. Broun was usually right in such predictions, and not often disposed to condemn a book or play merely because it was popular. In those days, however, the columnist whose literary judgments had most weight was F.P.A. (Franklin Pierce Adams), who ruled on questions of taste and usage in "The Conning Tower" of the *Herald Tribune.* Adams gave *Gone with the Wind* the seal of sophisticated metropolitan approval shortly after publication when he wrote, "You start that book, and unless you neglect everything else, the first thing you know it's day after tomorrow." Two weeks later, he resorted to rhyme in telling his readers "A book at which I've wept and grinned, Is Margaret Mitchell's *Gone with the Wind.*" Next day, in his "Diary of a Modern Samuel Pepys" Adams wrote, "Up early and began to work at eight, but fell to reading again in *Gone with the Wind* and could not put it down until I finished it, and it was a marvel to me how the interest could continue so unflaggingly." Another columnist who liked Margaret's book was Damon Runyon, the Hearst star reporter and feature man. Runyon also wrote short stories that were popular in the United States and had become a cult in England. The claims of some now forgotten rivals to Margaret's novel prompted Runyon's tribute: "Certain publishers say their wares are better than *Gone with the Wind.* We are no literary critic, and we would not know about that, but it sounds to us like trying to knock down the 1-

to-4 favorite in a horse race. It can be done, occasionally, to be sure, but it is not sound judgment to attempt it."

Mrs. Franklin D. Roosevelt was an amateur columnist; indeed, her syndicated "My Day" had more resemblance to a letter from a conscientious aunt than to the expert journalism of Adams, Runyon, or Broun. Nevertheless, her word had weight, and her report on *Gone with the Wind* was one of the most valuable notices Margaret received. For one thing, it showed that Mrs. Roosevelt had read the novel, a final accolade in itself to millions of people. Mrs. Roosevelt reported the fascination of the story, and told her readers, "I can assure you that you will find Scarlett O'Hara an interesting character." From Mrs. R., that was enough.

Several years before her book appeared Margaret had had a lively exchange about country-wide folk legends with Alexander Woollcott, then a columnist on *The New Yorker* and famous as wit and commentator, a member of the Round Table of the Algonquin Hotel, and a receiver who had a wide influence on devoted readers. In one column he had referred to her as "my cherished correspondent in Atlanta." Not long after publication came a letter from him.

"I have just finished reading 'Gone with the Wind' and found it completely absorbing. Its narrative has the directness and gusto of Dumas. I enjoyed it enormously. I was almost through it when I said to myself: 'God's nightgown! This must be the Peg Mitchell who wrote me about the little girl who swallowed a water moccasin and the tall man in the wrinkled nurse's uniform who thronged the road from Atlanta to Miami.' Is it?"

In addition to recommendations from newspaper writers came those of important and impressive people in every line of work, unsolicited testimonials that piled up by scores and hundreds. The President of the United States let it be known that he had found refreshment in the story; it had seen him through several evenings of his reading in bed, a habit he shared with other middle-aged Americans. Traveling in Europe, the author and scholar Mary Ellen Chase confessed she had "forgone the sights of

Paris for three days and two nights to read it." In Richmond, the distinguished novelist Ellen Glasgow gave the book warm praise. In Detroit, Mrs. Henry Ford read the story aloud to her husband, and in New York a former Democratic presidential candidate, the eminent corporation lawyer John W. Davis, reported "The characters come alive." And the emotional reward *Gone with the Wind* could give a whole-hearted reader was summed up by the London and Broadway star Gertrude Lawrence when she said, "I loved it and I lived in it."

It was reality rather than romance that made these deep impressions. Except for television, there were as many avenues of emotional release and day-dreaming available to Americans at the time Margaret's book was published as there are today. There were, for example, the heroes of sports who stood in the public imagination at more than life size; both men and women turned from reality in contemplation of Babe Ruth, Bill Tilden, and Bobby Jones, the fabulous Atlanta golfer whom Margaret had never met. But *Gone with the Wind* had a quality that went further than merely providing entertainment. It had a life outside its covers, and its heroine was a creation with the kind of undeniable vitality that animated Captain Ahab and Huckleberry Finn. The *London Observer*, taking inventory of characters created in the past fifty years, put Scarlett on a level with Sherlock Holmes, Jeeves, George F. Babbitt, and Peter Pan. And it was not only Scarlett who walked from the pages into an existence as someone known and thought of as a person in millions of minds; the three other leading characters, and a number of minor ones, also were accepted as real people. This came not only from deft characterization, but from the total effort of solid structure. Here was one novel that did not disintegrate, that hung together, greater in sum than in any part; and, taken as a whole, it achieved greatness.

This feeling of unified experience was what stayed with readers; and this was what gave *Gone with the Wind* a pervasiveness of influence that caused references to characters and story to appear time and again in the sermons of ministers, priests, and rabbis, in the writings of editorialists, and in the drawings of cartoonists, including Rube Goldberg's picture of Franklin Roosevelt as Rhett Butler, with Scarlett as "The Third Term" asking "Does he love me?" The book figured in an unprecedented legal stratagem when the lawyer defending a girl charged with infanticide read to court and jury the pages describing the birth of Melanie's baby. Margaret's characters even worked their way into the books of other authors: the high school teachers of New York City reported that in writing essays about Hawthorne, their students now invariably referred to the story of Hester Prynne as *The Scarlett Letter*.

Such were some of the manifestations of the power in Margaret's story that caused the *Herald Tribune* to remark, a few weeks after publication, that *"Gone with the Wind* has come to be more than a novel. It is a national event, a proverbial expression of deep instincts, a story that promises to found a kind of legend." So multitudinous were the individual effects of the story that no social scientist would dare attempt to count or classify them all. These effects touched every human activity that can be influenced by observed reality, including, for example, the matter of naming: flowers, streets, schools, theaters, restaurants, houses, animals, and babies all drew names from places and people in Margaret's book. The four lion cubs at the Atlanta Zoo were named Scarlett, Melanie, Ashley, and Rhett. An appropriate idea struck both the president of the New York Junior League and a professor at Smith: each named a small dog Scarlett O'Hara, and each explained this was because the animal was a little bitch—anyone they met would also have read the book and get the point.

Readers stayed with Scarlett. Some tried to read the book at a sitting, and some may have succeeded, although of those who wrote to the author, the closest to finishing in one reading seems to have been a woman who kept at it from eight in the morning until 2:30 the following morning, subsisting on crackers, putting the book down for the first time about a hundred pages from the end, and finishing after a few hours' sleep. Several persons wrote to say they had read thirteen hours at a stretch, like Dr. William Pennypacker Stauffer of Philadelphia, who added that he was proud to have read the book seven times. Others regarded *Gone with the Wind* as a temptation. One of many who could not resist was the young mother who wrote to Margaret, "I get up to give the baby his two o'clock bottle, and there's your book on the table, and there I am three hours later still reading." People carried the book to work, they read it in subway and commuter trains and perched on stools in lunchrooms, they read it in prison cells and farmhouse kitchens, and in penthouses overlooking Park Avenue and Lake Shore Drive. A woman in Nashville wrote, "I finished the book last night, and when I tried to read the morning paper I couldn't—it seemed not to matter, to be unreal." The star aerialist of the Ringling Brothers–Barnum & Bailey circus put a sign on his dressing room door that read, "DO NOT DISTURB—READING GWTW," using an abbreviation understood throughout the country. The novel was a favorite item of loot with the stateroom thieves who worked outgoing ocean liners; they easily disposed of stolen copies in the underworld of the book trade, for all dealers were behind on orders for *Gone with the Wind,* and some few were none too scrupulous as to who supplied them. The thieves had ample opportunity on the big ships, for the smart Manhattan bookstores (whose sources of supply were legitimate) would deliver as many as 1,000 gift orders to the piers on sailing days. Not only stateroom thieves, but the entire community of robbers, crooks, and dubious persons in general were just as great readers of *Gone with the Wind* as everyone else. New York reporters saw an agent of the numbers racket running from the police and still clutching the copy he had been reading when the officers surprised him.

In those times, when publishers seldom issued a book of more than five hundred pages, *Gone with the Wind* made an impression for its weight of nearly three pounds if for nothing else. The weight was a problem for old people; it tired their wrists and hands to hold the book as they read it hour after hour. A helpful woman wrote to the *New*

York Daily News to say she had solved the difficulty for her mother by rebinding the novel in five sections. The idea spread and other elderly persons wrote to tell Margaret about it. Mostly, people liked the idea of such a big, thick book; but its weight figured in a domestic crisis. In Birmingham, Alabama, a husband ended an argument with his wife by picking up their copy of *Gone with the Wind* and throwing it at her. The court accepted this as cruelty and granted the woman a divorce.

Few people had to dodge Margaret's novel flying through the air, but it was hard to avoid reading it if one read anything at all. There were some literate persons, nevertheless, who refused to read the book, in some cases perhaps with the harmless desire to attract attention by going against a ruling fashion. One abstainer was Edward J. O'Brien, a lecturer and editor who published an annual selection of short stories. Mr. O'Brien said he was preparing to go on a four-month lecture tour by *not* reading *Gone with the Wind* so that he would not have to answer questions on it. He told reporters, "This puts me in a strong position." Be that as it may, most literary lecturers avoided Mr. O'Brien's position, and the king of them all, Professor William Lyon Phelps, named *Gone with the Wind* best novel of the year. Billy Phelps, an institution at Yale and popular throughout the country, had made the annual announcement of his choice of best books an important event. Although *Gone with the Wind* had been out only two months at the time of his announcement for 1936, he unhesitatingly put it in first place—and on the country's front pages. In so doing, the professor ran the risk that before the year ended another big novel might come along and surpass Margaret's book; but it was a small risk. An uncharted comet would be more likely to appear in the sky than a book to supercede *Gone with the Wind* in the literary market.

The sale of the millionth copy in December showed that Professor Phelps was right. Indeed, from many points of view Margaret's work might be the greatest novel of *any* year. There was magic in the huge round number, and Macmillan happily sensed a bandwagon element in the continuing rise of sales: no one could now predict where the end might be. Alec Blanton plastered American Express vans with posters blaring, "ONE MILLION AMERICANS CAN'T BE WRONG—READ GONE WITH THE WIND."

These six cyclonic months put *Gone with the Wind* and Margaret as author in a special classification that it seems unlikely they will ever have to share. For rapidity of public acceptance and instantaneous achievement of fame, there had been nothing like it prior to 1936, nor will there be until future history duplicates the circumstances in exact detail—which is at best only a remote and theoretical possibility, on the order of the apes at typewriters hammering out the works of Carlyle as a mathematical chance. This is not to say that Margaret had the field to herself in 1936. On the contrary, she encountered hard competition from experienced writers, and books of popular appeal. In that year Walter D. Edmonds published *Drums Along the Mohawk*, and Pearl Buck brought out *The Exile*. Buyers had their choice of *Jamaica Inn*, by Daphne du Maurier; *My Ten Years in a Quandary*, by Corey Ford; *Inside Europe*, by John Gunther; *Arouse and Beware*, a Civil War novel by MacKinlay Kantor; *John Reed*, by Granville Hicks; *Wake Up and Live*, by Dorothea Brande; *Eyeless in Gaza*, by Aldous Huxley; and *The Big Money*, by John Dos Passos;—these among scores of titles that sold well, but far behind Margaret's novel. By ordinary standards, Margaret should have been happy in the last half of 1936, with the success of *Gone with the Wind* and the incredibly varied opportunities it brought.

However, the novel's fame did not strike Margaret altogether as success, in a way one usually interprets the term. She was inclined to regard it as notoriety, and as something she could never welcome, for it meant a change in the Marshes' completely satisfactory way of living. Reasonable enough: but Margaret's sense of self-criticism told her this attitude might look like insufferable posing. Even before the publication date she was trying to explain her reluctance to become a celebrity, as in her letter to Julia Collier Harris of Chattanooga, Tennessee. This lady, daughter-in-law and biographer of Joel Chandler Harris, conducted a column on the *Chattanooga Times*, and had received an advance copy of *Gone with the Wind*. Like most of the readers in advance, Mrs. Harris thought the book would be a huge success, and she wrote to advise the author to conserve privacy, energy, and time when the storm of publicity broke. The day before publication, Margaret answered:

"I did not know that being an author meant this sort of thing, autographing in book stores, being invited here and there about the country to speak, to attend summer schools, to address this and that group at luncheon. It all comes as a shock to me and not a pleasant shock. I have led, by choice, so quiet and cloistered a life for many years. John likes that sort of life and so do I. Being in the public's eye is something neither John nor I care about but what good does it do to say it? No one believes a word of it or if they do believe it they get indignant. I have been caught between two equally distasteful positions, that of the girlishly shy creature who keeps protesting her lack of desire for the lime light but who only wants to be urged —and that of a graceless, ungracious, blunt spoken ingrate who refuses to let people do her honor. It has all been very distressing to me. I was brought up to consider it better to commit murder than to be rude and it is hard to depart from Mother's teachings. I'd rather never sell a book than autograph in department stores—other than those in Atlanta. I see no way of escaping these. This is my home town. Everyone has been so kind and helpful that I can never repay them enough. And I *would* seem an eccentric and ungracious person if I refused, here in Atlanta. But it has made me very unhappy. It is not that I think myself such a wonderful and precious vessel of genius that I do not wish to expose myself to the public gaze. Mrs. Harris, I did not intend to inflict all this incoherence upon you, but your letter with its common sense attitude tapped the spring. How comforting it was to read your words—how pleasant to know that someone like you felt as John and I do upon this subject. I felt that I had a strong rock on which to stand for if someone of your stature refuses them, I, too, can refuse."

Writing such a letter must have relieved Margaret's mind; but what she had to say was based on advance publicity and the intrusions it had brought. The moment the book made its official appearance, an additional turmoil broke out. Margaret described it by simply saying, "Hell broke loose." Postmen bringing special delivery letters to the door at six in the morning; bales of ordinary letters; and above all, personal visitations—these were phenomena of fame such as Margaret had not imagined. One of the most astonishing of all the uninvited visitors rang the doorbell of Margaret's apartment four days after the appearance of her book. A lank young man, dishevelled, and with an odd look in his eye, he demanded to be told the truth: was or was not Rhett Butler the father of Melanie's baby? The members of his wife's bridge club in North Carolina had told him to find out, and he could not go home without the answer. Was this young man insane, drunk, or merely a conspicuously insensitive ass? Margaret made no effort to classify him, and sent him on his way with the assurance that Melanie's lawful husband was the baby's father.

Other inane and impertinent questions kept pouring in by mail and telephone, and three days later, Margaret got in her car and turned its nose toward open country. Stopping in the small city of Gainesville, she thought of Herschel Brickell, established in her mind as a man of generosity and kindness. Since he was a fellow Southerner, Brickell might be expected to understand how Margaret felt about privacy and decency. She decided to get in touch with him, went into the hotel, and wrote him a letter. After introducing herself and thanking Brickell for the good things he had written about her novel, Margaret went on:

"As you may observe from this postmark, I'm not at home in Atlanta. I'm on the run. I'm sure Scarlett O'Hara never struggled harder to get out of Atlanta or suffered more during her siege of Atlanta than I have suffered during the siege that has been on since publication day. If I had known being an author was like this I'd have thought several times before I let Harold Latham go off with my dogeared manuscript. I've lost ten pounds in a week, leap when phones ring and scurry like a rabbit at the sight of a familiar face on the street. The phone has screamed every three minutes for a week and utter strangers collar me in public and ask the most remarkable questions and photographers pop up out of drains, always in the hope, poor things, that they can get a picture of me that doesn't look like Margot Asquith. This morning three boys from the A.P. gave me a brisk workout that lasted three hours and when they left I got in the car and left town, without a change of underwear or a tooth brush. And I got as far as here. Being anti-social by nature and accustomed to a very quiet life, it has all been too much for me . . ."

Having mailed that letter, Margaret turned back to Atlanta. Waiting for her there was an invitation to attend a writers' summer school at Blowing Rock, North Carolina, a place she knew to be a tiny and quiet resort town at one of the highest points in the Appalachians. Moreover, the school's announcement listed Edwin Granberry and Herschel Brickell as consultants and lecturers. Margaret sent a note saying she could never get away for such a meeting, much as she would like to. Then she wrote another note, accepting the invitation and requesting a room reservation.

John sent her off with his blessing; he thought it imperative that she have a change of scene, and promised to look after the telephone, the telegrams, and the mail. At Blowing Rock, Margaret met the Granberrys and Brickell, liking them on sight, sat through a few lectures at the back of the room, and obliged the autograph hunters at the village store. But something was wrong. Margaret suffered from an increasing nervousness, anxiety, and physical uneasiness. Even the tremendous blue views from every part of the village failed to give her comfort, for she found it hard to look at either the near or distant mountains. Perhaps what caused the trouble was the altitude; in any event, Margaret cut her visit short, came down from Blowing Rock, and went home.

Here she cringed at the sight of letters stacked by hundreds on chairs and sofas in the Seventeenth Street apartment, and at the screaming of the telephone which seemed to have gone mad during her absence. Before leaving for the mountains, Margaret had written to Harold Latham, expressing hope that she would be off the best seller lists by September. His reply had come in while she was gone, and it counseled her to make up her mind that big sales might continue through the Christmas shopping season. This may be the only case on record in which an author hopefully asked a publisher if sales might not be coming down. But Latham made no reference to this curious aspect of the matter, for he had by now recognized that, to say the least, Margaret was no ordinary author.

In a few days Herschel Brinkell returned to his home in Connecticut, where he told his wife Norma about Margaret and her need for privacy and rest. Mrs. Brickell immediately wrote to Margaret and urged her to come at any time for a stay of any length. The Brickells lived near Ridgefield in a part of Connecticut settled by editors and writers; Norma Brickell said this made it especially advisable for Margaret to come to their house—not for an intellectual atmosphere, but because "These people up here are always so tired and that makes them restful." Margaret accepted this invitation with gratitude, but with some embarrassment because she could not set a definite date. She thought it would be better if the Brickells could come to Atlanta; though too polite to write it to Norma Brickell, Margaret had at that time something of a phobia against New York. And now that the book was out, the New York friends and relatives she did not have time to call on might see a mention of her visit in the papers and take offense. Nevertheless, business connected with the book compelled Margaret and Stephens to take the overnight train to New York on July 29.

Before leaving Atlanta, Margaret wrote to Herschel Brickell, "I will stay in New York no longer than is necessary for me and brother Steve to clear up this damned moving picture contract. We've been trying to handle it by letter and long distance and not getting very far. It seems sensible to us to go up and polish the matter off, one way or the other. I do not want to go. I have no clothes and no time to buy any. I have been sick in bed for the last three days and do not feel like tackling a hot trip. But I will lose my mind certainly if this thing isn't settled soon. Just now I don't care which way it is settled."

What bothered Margaret then and later about the sale of the moving picture rights was the interpretation of her agreement with Macmillan that the publishers would act as her agent in the deal. To handle the actual sale, the Macmillan officials retained Annie Laurie Williams, an established and well-known literary agent who had wide experience with theater and motion picture contracts. From Macmillan's point of view, this was good business, appointing a specialist who knew the producers and had the feel of the market. However, Margaret wrote to Macmillan "Annie Laurie Williams is not *my* agent. The Macmillan Company is my agent. Please read the letter of agreement. In our family, we take written agreements seriously." Indeed she had the right conception of an author's agent as someone more than a salesman. It seemed to Margaret that a writer's agent should take the role of counselor, and watchdog of the client's rights, and it seemed to her that Macmillan had complicated negotiations for which the publishers themselves had accepted a direct responsibility. In any event, on July 8 Macmillan informed her that Miss Williams had closed for $50,000 with the well-known producer David O. Selznick.

It seemed likely that Selznick was the best qualified of all movie makers then in business to put Margaret's novel on the screen. Born to the trade as the son of Lewis J. Selznick, a silent picture pioneer, he had shown his idea of how to film long novels in *David Copperfield, Anna Karenina,* and *A Tale of Two Cities,* all of which Margaret had seen. "The trick in adapting novels," Selznick had said, "is to give the *illusion* of photographing the entire book. This is much more difficult than creating an original story directly for the screen." One could trust Selznick to make a good picture, and the money was not Margaret's primary concern. She did not want a job writing the screenplay, nor did she wish to get on Selznick's payroll as an advisor during the making of the picture. She wanted just the opposite: not to be bothered in any way about the script, or the shooting of the picture, or its promotion, and above all, not to have any connections with the casting. Few people at Macmillan, and no one in the Selznick organization, had the slightest understanding of how Margaret felt about these things. They were used to hard-driven authors struggling for money and recognition, who would have regarded a stay in a writer's bungalow on the Selznick lot, with a secretary, and a good salary, as the finest sort of paid vacation plus an opportunity for further exploitation of the movie industry. But none of this was for Margaret. She was the writer, after all, who would have been happy to sell 5,000 copies, please the Georgia kinfolk, and consider her next move in peace and quiet. Therefore, careful attention must go into the wording of her moving picture contract: accepting a price was only the beginning. In addition, Margaret wanted a thorough understanding of what she was selling, and what she was keeping back; her responsibilities to the producer must be clearly stated, and his to her. And Margaret's question was, what is so hard about that?

After the first day's discussion of the contract, Margaret and Stephens relaxed at dinner with the Taylors—Lois Cole and her husband Allan. They talked shop and Lois pointed out that the fine print in producers' contracts took away the author's radio, television, and dramatic rights, and suggested they make sure this did not happen to Margaret. On the following day Stephens and Margaret went into another meeting with all interested parties present, including Jacquelin Swords and Walbridge Taft of Cadwalader, Wickersham and Taft, lawyers for The Macmillan Company. On this second day of talk, Margaret's patience wore thin, although she did not show it, at the repeated emphasis of paragraphs in the contract designed to prevent the author from interfering with the producer or director.

Back at their hotel after an exhausting day, Margaret and Stephens telephoned John Marsh in Atlanta. John gave it as his opinion that if Margaret was not satisfied they should "come on home." But Margaret said they had made the trip to deal with the movie problem, and she was determined to settle it once for all. In his record of events, Stephens wrote:

"Margaret wanted to go on and finish the matter. She did not wish to say that Macmillan had not done its best; she saw that no one would offer more. It is difficult to realize it now, but $50,000 was a lot of money—the equivalent in the 1960s of $200,000. So on the following day, July 30, we signed the Selznick contract, and Margaret made one last comment. She said that she had sold the motion picture rights because she was worried by a great many things. The sale would get rid of one worry. She did not want another to take its place. She was happy to hear Hollywood did not want her and she was certain she did not want the worries which Hollywood could bring to her. She would not bother them, and they should not bother her. They had the movie rights; she had the $50,000 less commission; and we were all happy. With that, she went off to visit friends, and I came home."

The Brickells were the friends Margaret visited, and as Norma Brickell had promised, their house was quiet, with an atmosphere of relaxation and peace. Talk lasted late into the evening, and Margaret slept well. But, next day she had one of the most terrifying experiences that can befall a human being: an unmistakable failure of eyesight. Obviously she must go home at once. She was back on Seventeenth Street by August 2. Here, among the hundreds of letters that had arrived during her brief absence were two that had special significance. They showed that in a little more than a month, Margaret had reached the most exalted rank of universally recognized fame by becoming one of the few people to whom the Post Office can deliver mail with an abbreviated or eccentric address. On one envelope the correspondent had written simply "MM—GWTW—ATLANTA." The other envelope had nothing on it but a sketch of a cyclone carrying off a little figure from whose mouth issued a balloon containing the words "Good bye." When you can be reached through the mail by a pictograph, you have arrived. But Margaret could not see these remarkable envelopes. John had to tell her about them. The doctors had diagnosed extensive hemorrhages in both eyes, resulting from acute tension and fatigue after the continuous work on the manuscript and proofs. The most successful, famous and envied writer in the United States now lay in a darkened room, with a bandage over her eyes.

IX

Price of Fame

In the middle of August, John Marsh took stock of what he called "the six weeks that rocked the Marsh world." He wrote to a friend, "The news is that Peggy's eyes are quite a bit better but she still has some days of seclusion ahead of her. The doctor told her that she would have to give them a complete rest for 21 days, and this is the 12th day. He said that the broken blood vessels were only in the front part of the eye—the cornea, I believe—and that the retina wasn't involved, which would have been a much more serious condition, but even the less serious condition requires considerable time to heal. The first day or two in a darkened room with nothing to do, hour after hour, but twiddle her thumbs was pretty terrible, but after that she began to relax, some of the tightly wound springs inside her mind began to unwind from the steadily increasing tension of the past several months, and since then she has been able to get rest for her body, her mind, and her nerves, as well as her eyes, and I am convinced the enforced rest is doing her good. She has had plenty of practice in learning patience these past several years when she has had so much sickness, and the training is standing her in good stead now. She has even let me install a small radio by her bed—the first one ever permitted inside the Marsh home—and she is acquiring an education as to the cowboy ballads and hillbilly songs which seem to divert the American public. And also hearing quite a lot of very dull political speeches, Georgia now being in the midst of a heated primary campaign."

A rumor that Margaret was blind suddenly sprang up everywhere. Along with it went the persistent report that she was selecting the actors for the moving picture. This was maddening, for Margaret had worked hard at the contract table to make certain she should have no responsibility for any aspect of production. But that did not help her when Selznick announced his intention of making the picture, for the country immediately surrendered to an informal parlor game, the casting of *Gone with the Wind*, and the public's instinctive assumption was that the creator of the characters in the story would also create them on the screen, so to speak, by selecting each actor and actress.

There was, to be sure, a deep and unanimous agreement that no one should play Rhett Butler but Clark Gable. The other parts, however, offered a fascinating variety of interpretations, each suited to some popular player, at a time when the Hollywood moving picture was at the height of its glory, and the public admired favorite performers with an intensity that television seems unable to arouse. The movies were theater; there was magic in the stars and in the melodramas that framed them, absurd as some of the stories were. At these entertainments one sat for two hours with an audience, shared its reaction, and walked out at the end emotionally saturated with whatever had occupied the enormous screen. Therefore, as Mr. Selznick well knew, the assigning of parts in *Gone with the Wind* was an emotional question of national importance; and, as John Marsh observed, Margaret was feeling the insistent and obtrusive power of this emotion even before she recovered use of her eyes. She stated the case in dictating a letter to the syndicated moving picture columnist, Louella Parsons:

"Everybody in the world reads your column, and that is why I am appealing to you for assistance. I am appealing as an harassed and weary author, sadly in need of rest and unable to get it because of the mail and telegrams that flood in on me due to rumors which seem to be circulating all over the country. I am the author of 'Gone with the Wind.' When I sold the motion picture rights to Mr. Selznick it was on the understanding that I was to have nothing to do with the movie production. I was utterly weary from the hard labor of getting my large book to press, and it was understood that I would do no work on the adapting of the book for the screen, would have no voice in the casting and would not go to Hollywood. However, rumors are abroad that are very different from this. The story has even been printed that I am to select the entire cast! Mr. Selznick knows how to make movies and I most certainly do not, and I have nothing to do with picking the actors, but these stories and rumors have brought down on me a deluge of requests that I get people into the movies. A foolish story about a young lady said to be my niece being chosen by me for the part of Scarlett brought me endless trouble. . . . The truth is this young lady is not my niece and is not related to me in any way. I have never even seen her and I have certainly never chosen her for anything, but the flood of letters, telegrams and personal calls have so distracted me and made my work so heavy, that I have been unable to get any rest for weeks.

"On top of this, the persistent rumor that has appeared in many papers, and in your column too, that I am going blind, has caused me much work and worry. You see, I'm not going blind and have no intention of going blind. . . . But whenever such an item appears in a paper, my friends and relatives scattered all over the United States write and wire me in panic. I have so many wonderful friends and naturally such items alarm them. . . .

"I am begging you, if ever again the rumors come to your desk that I have something to do with the movie production of 'Gone with the Wind' or that I am going blind, that you will deny them. I know I am taking a lot upon myself in asking this of you.

"I also know you would laugh at some of the amusing things that have occurred. Several ladies have wired me that their little daughters tap dance beautifully and do the 'splits' most elegantly and can't I get them into 'Gone with the Wind'? No, they haven't read the book, they admit. People turn up with their colored cooks and butlers and demand that I send them to Hollywood to portray Mammy and Uncle Peter. If I can ever get a rest, I can probably laugh at such things, but not just now."

Margaret was no snob about movies or the people who wrote of them. She thought the Marx brothers hilarious, and John Marsh said when his wife was watching their pictures anybody in the theater could locate her by the sound of her "yells of joy." In fact, she did make one suggestion about the casting of *Gone with the Wind,* which was that the part of Rhett Butler be assigned to Groucho Marx. The report of this jocosity failed to halt the humorless persons who encamped before Margaret's doors to enlist her help in getting Mr. Selznick's ear. One of the most startling invasions was that of a woman calling herself an actress who gained entrance to the apartment, quickly covered her face with dark make-up, and put on a performance as Mammy in Margaret's living room.

This could happen because of the unpretentious way the Marshes lived. Four East Seventeenth Street had no doorman. Nor did it have a locked main door that tenants could open by pressing a button after callers identified themselves on a house telephone. Anyone could walk in and ring the bell at Margaret's door, the second on the right. If Bessie Berry was on duty, she would answer. If not, Margaret or John came to the door. In any case, automatic courtesy made it almost impossible for servant or employers to say anything other than "Won't you come in?" And so Margaret rented a secret room next door to use as an office. But this did nothing to keep uninvited callers from the apartment out of business hours, and for many of them that seemed the favorite time.

"Unbelievable things are happening in these unbelievable days," John Marsh wrote to Herschel Brickell in August. Among the incredible things were letters from Julia Peterkin and Marjorie Kinnan Rawlings, praising Margaret's book and warning her of encroachments. Hervey Allen wrote—Hervey Allen, author of *Anthony Adverse,* a famous novel that had sold 400,000 copies in eleven months. He said there was some mysterious element in sales of that size that made the readers act as though the author, as well as the book, was public property. And Stephen Vincent Benét wrote. He said *Gone with the Wind* was a fine book, and that he hoped Margaret would write many more of them. To him, the essence of fiction was the emotion that came when a book continued in mind after one had read it; then there was no need for anybody to say it was good. "It was that way with *Gone with the Wind,*" Mr. Benét concluded. "Thank you again." This, from the man whose work she could not listen to while writing, for fear its excellence would discourage her, was something that went to the depth of Margaret's heart.

But there were other letters, as John told the sympathetic and experienced Brickell, that had something sinister about them. Such communications are familiar to all who attach their names to published work, but they came as an especial unpleasantness to Margaret. These letters—from strangers, of course—start out with a sort of indefinable impertinence the practiced eye can recognize at once. The point is always "Please send me the secret of writing a book and getting rich. If *you* can do it, there must be some trick involved. Send me the secret method right away, as I am anxious to finish my book and get my money." These are not the letters of insane persons, but rather the expression of malicious envy combined with stupidity and greed. Even though she had seen some repellent human beings as a newspaper woman—Harry Thaw was no ornament to mankind—Margaret was unprepared for this kind of malice. It added to her discomfort, as though something unsanitary were deposited on her living-room rug. John Marsh continued in his letter to Brickell, "You have been extraordinarily thoughtful and understanding through this whole situation, and I feel that we have gained a real friend. Please don't worry about us. We have been through some pretty tough situations and we have come through them all so far. We have had plenty of experience with adversity and we'll come through. Incidentally, if Peggy were a professional writer, and not an amateur, she could have a steady income for the rest of her life, if we may judge from the rising demand that she go on with the story of Scarlett and Rhett. One letter after another is coming in, mostly from women, begging, pleading, demanding that she let the writers know whether Scarlett ever gets Rhett back or vice versa. She had no notion of giving the book a 'Lady or the Tiger' ending—in her mind the story ends where it ends—but unintentionally she has paved the way for a sequel if she should ever wish to write one—which she probably won't."

The paradox of Margaret's life is in that letter by John Marsh. And it does not seem possible that historians could find another example of a husband referring to a remarkable and very warmly praised achievement by his wife as a case of adversity that they must somehow survive. Even more extraordinary is Margaret's agreement with John's statement of affairs; she and her husband were as one, and he read her the letter to Brickell before mailing it. In this only she resembled Scarlett O'Hara: each was determined to come through a bad time. Scarlett's was ruin and starvation, Margaret's was exploding success. There was the quality of a folk tale in the Marshes' situation—the universal story in which a man and wife are given a certain number of wishes, and have to use the last wish to get things back the way they were before the good fairy came along. But Margaret and John were not granted the last wish.

By instinct the public realized that Margaret Mitchell was different from the usual celebrity, just as her book had elements of power that did not appear in the usual costume romance. But the public did not know all about her; it never would know all about her. In one sentence she told Herschel Brickell all she wanted known about herself: "Yes, I am a provincial lady and I know it and am proud of it." Comparing this with the show-business personalities who give interviews even on what they are discussing with psychoanalysts, one sees why a large section of the public was willing to believe fantastic things about Margaret. It was hard to understand a celebrity who sincerely wanted no publicity, and yet Margaret was right, from every point of view.

Already old-fashioned in 1936, Margaret began to pay the penalty of reticence before the bandages came off her eyes. The rumors sprang up like weeds, and were as uncountable. Many of them had to do with the writing of the book, all of these in one way or another detracting from Margaret's achievement. It was said that Macmillan had been in touch with Margaret for years, their editors coaching her while she wrote the novel; that she had tried numerous publishers who had turned the book down; and that she was not the author at all, but had paid Sinclair Lewis to write the book. People dined out on the story that Stephens was the author. Others said Eugene Mitchell had written the novel, and still others maintained Margaret had copied it out of her grandmother's diary. Over cocktails in New York it was said that Macmillan had committed the greatest robbery of the age in buying all rights from an unsophisticated Margaret for $250. Stories also were told making Margaret so wealthy that she had bought a large estate on Long Island, though it would have been of no use to her if another widely circulated rumor were true, which had her hopelessly insane. A variation of this told the tale that Margaret had paid $200,-000 to establish a mental sanitarium in Atlanta. There was no more truth in that yarn than in the New York gossip columnist's item that Margaret had been a notoriously dangerous automobile driver and was using her first royalties to pay claims rising from her traffic accidents in Atlanta.

So it went: Margaret found it exquisitely annoying to hear reports that she had a wooden leg; that she had written *Gone with the Wind* while immobilized in bed with plaster casts; that she was dying of leukemia; that she was saved from blindness by the surgeon who operated on the

King of Siam; and that she was going to give a lecture on the Civil War at New York's Town Hall.

Equally dismaying to Margaret were the tales that she had supplied Macmillan with an additional chapter revealing further adventures of Scarlett and Rhett, and that the publishers would mail it to anybody sending them one dollar; that she had never given permission to read the manuscript, and that Harold Latham had stolen it from her while taking tea; that she was planning to collaborate with Faith Baldwin on a Civil War play; and that she had signed a ten-year contract with *Cosmopolitan* magazine at $1,000,000 a year. Other canards tending to make Margaret look foolish or eccentric were those that had her refusing to write except by the light of an oil lamp; fainting at the sight of a royalty check, coming to, calling John and showing him the check, whereupon *he* fainted; and telling her publishers she could not think of a title, which inspired them to suggest *Gone with the Wind*.

There was no end to this legendry; and all of it got into print somewhere or other. This was because of the disregard for accuracy, or even for plausibility, that characterized the syndicated gossip columnists. These people seemed to believe that if they printed an item, that made it so. Nothing could be more disturbing to the methodical and conscientious Margaret. It was not only that the untruths offended her sense of order; when they touched her family or integrity as a person they gave keen anguish. An example of this was the report that she had gone to Reno to get a divorce. Another untruth that appeared in a New York column and then throughout the country had her saying she had written the book so she could support her invalid husband on the receipts. "I resent this with a bitterness I cannot even express," she wrote to Herschel Brickell. "I would rather have never written a book, never sold it, never made a cent or had what passes for fame in these parts than have one one-hundredth of such a lie published."

Almost equally offensive was the story that she refused to eat breakfast until John had decorated the table with two dozen American Beauty roses. But she was amused at the report that John had asked Wendell L. Willkie to recommend the book to the employees of Commonwealth & Southern, the holding company he headed, which included Georgia Power. And there was only annoyance, in hearing stories that she was in Hollywood directing *Gone with the Wind* before the cameras; in September, when this gossip emanated from the West Coast, there was not a page of script in existence. Another fantasy connected with the movie had it that Margaret had agreed to play the role of Scarlett. There was no more truth in it than in the tale that she had written the novel with Clark Gable in mind for the hero's part. During the time Margaret had been writing, Gable was trouping in obscure stock companies that played neither Atlanta nor New York.

With Margaret unable to read, an extra burden fell on John. His first concern was to review the moving picture contract, and after he had done so he raised some questions. Article 3 of the contract caught his eye: "The Owner [Margaret] will prevent the Property [the book] and all future arrangements, revisions, translations, and dramatizations or reissues thereof from vesting in the public domain, will affix, or cause to be affixed, to each copy or arrangement of any part of the property published or offered for sale by the Owner or any other person, firm or corporation any notice which may be necessary to protect the copyright or copyrights, or similar rights, in the Property and all arrangements, revisions, translations, dramatizations or reissues thereof for copyright or otherwise wherever its protection shall so require, will contract for the benefit of the Purchaser [Selznick] for the above protection, and will mention, except and reserve the rights herein granted, in any and all grants in the Property of rights not herein granted, which shall hereinafter be made to others."

This verbiage came close to Mark Twain's definition of chloroform in print, but John thought it best to tell Macmillan that he and his wife were wondering just how she could discharge her obligations as Article 3 appeared to set them down. The Marshes and Mitchells soon named this paragraph the "God Almighty clause," but on August

5, when John first questioned it, they thought the publishers' interests marched exactly, or nearly so, with theirs. "Our opinion in the beginning was that this clause did not belong in Peggy's contract," John wrote to James Putnam, a Macmillan official. "This was because it imposes obligations on her which she is unable to fulfill by reason of the fact that she has already conveyed the publication rights to Macmillan. However, Mr. Stephens Mitchell, my wife's attorney, consented to this clause remaining in Peggy's contract on the contention of Selznick's attorneys that, under the copyright laws, it is necessary for Peggy to be a party to the carrying out of these obligations. But it would be obvious to anyone that in this part of the contract, she has assumed certain obligations which she is unable to carry out except by and through Macmillan."

John went on to point out the extreme complexity of the obligation the contract had placed on Margaret to see that all copyrights were renewed according to the various laws governing such matters in all parts of the world, under laws then existing, and under any future laws that might be enacted. He also pointed out that keeping up with changing copyright laws throughout the world was not a normal or reasonable occupation for a writer in Atlanta, Georgia. He asked, "Couldn't we make an agreement that Macmillan will relieve her of the clerical and legal worries involved in this obligation? Peggy is in no position to do this, but Macmillan is. You do such things as a matter of routine. You have your bookkeeping systems to keep track of the time when copyrights should be renewed in this and foreign countries. You have your legal staff who know the intricacies of existing copyright laws and who make it their business to keep up with revisions of copyright laws in all countries. My understanding from Mr. Stephens Mitchell is that Macmillan has already given its verbal assent on these points, and in view of the fact that Macmillan was Peggy's agent in negotiating the Selznick contract, it seems obvious that these provisions are agreeable to you. But in order to bring this job to a workmanlike conclusion and also to relieve Peggy's mind of the worry of vague responsibilities hanging over her, we would appreciate a statement in writing from The Macmillan Company covering these points."

In a few days Macmillan replied that the Marshes were mistaken in thinking of the company as Margaret's agent. Annie Laurie Williams was Margaret's agent and the Macmillan lawyers at the negotiations had been representing the publishers only. Moreover, John had overestimated the size and reach of the Macmillan copyright department. The publishers would do anything in their power to help, but the protection of international copyrights would be primarily Mrs. Marsh's responsibility. Margaret could understand Selznick's need for assurance that no other producer would rush out a quick version of *Gone with the Wind* based on a pirated edition in some foreign country. Nevertheless, she found it impossible to see herself as an international businesswoman specializing in copyright procedure and running a worldwide enterprise from a small apartment. That this is what she finally did become is another example of what she called "my book taking off on its own and taking me with it."

Since the Macmillan letter showed such an unexpected and sharp division of interests, she put the matter in Stephens' hands. George P. Brett, Sr. had retired and it was to his son that Stephens wrote inquiring in detail about Macmillan's responsibility as agent. Mr. Brett, Jr. replied that his company had merely agreed to act as "broker," that The Macmillan Company did not want to contract for the benefit of David O. Selznick in situations where Selznick would have no cause for action against Margaret, and he repeated that he could not commit his company to the protection of the copyright throughout the world.

The letters passing between Atlanta and New York in discussion of these matters now grew increasingly crisp, making the situation of author and publisher strained and uncomfortable. Margaret felt she had been betrayed by those who should have made it their business to give her protection in unfamiliar territory, and her relations with the Macmillan front-office people—not the editorial or sales departments—remained cool for a long time. But after the exchange of disputatious letters, Margaret decided that although a breach was there, it must not be allowed to widen. Since she had not written any of the letters touching on the controversy, she could still address George Brett as though they were in perfect agreement on any topic that might concern them. The opportunity came when Mr. Brett sent her a fat envelope filled with clippings of the British reviews, to which she replied on October 29: "You were very kind to send me those English clippings. Naturally I was interested, and anxious to know how the book was going abroad and my clipping bureau was late. So yours were the first I had. The English reviews far exceeded anything I had expected for I did not dream the book would have such a good reception over there." George Brett immediately replied that he was happy to be of service and the truce was on. Aside from smoothing feathers, it had as a tangible result the placing in Margaret's hands by Macmillan of all rights to foreign translations. By 1965, of the nearly twelve million copies sold, more than five million were in various translations around the world.

During the time this discussion went on, there had been a certain amount of amusement in the daily mail. There were a number of marriage proposals, like the one from a poultry dealer who described himself as "An Emerson-like prose poet, a bachelor, 6 ft., rarely gifted, genuine idealist, greatest lover of fine and useful arts, simplicity and the beautiful, true and just. I have been seeking a REAL lady, rare, talented, original, experienced, wise, bighearted, ambitious, country life experienced; no church member, hypocrite, but Free Thought, Golden Rule, socialist; someone who prizes character, reputation, faithfulness, undying love far above riches. There are no such in my vicinity." Margaret did not answer this letter, but she did answer thousands that made only a little more sense. Many inconsequential letters that a few lines from a secretary might have answered courteously enough would draw two or three hundred carefully chosen words. To be sure, the letters were not all inconsequential, nor did all the replies come only from a sense of duty. Margaret enjoyed dictating an acknowledgment, on August 15, to Thomas Dixon,

who had written a fan letter about *Gone with the Wind*.
Mr. Dixon was the author of a novel called *The Clansman*, from which David Wark Griffith had made the first
great American feature picture, *The Birth of a Nation*.
Margaret was in good spirits when she told Dixon "For
many years I have had you on my conscience, and I suppose I might as well confess it now. When I was eleven
years old I decided that I would dramatize your book
'The Traitor'—and dramatize it I did in six acts. I played
the part of Steve because none of the little boys in the
neighborhood would lower themselves to play a part in
which they had to 'kiss any little ol' girl.' The clansmen
were recruited from the small-fry of the neighborhood,
their ages ranging from five to eight. They were dressed in
shirts of their fathers, with the shirttails bobbed off. I had
my troubles with the clansmen as, after Act 2, they went
on strike, demanding a ten cent wage in stead of a five
cent one. Then, too, just as I was about to be hanged, two
of the clansmen had to go to the bathroom, necessitating a
dreadful stage wait which made the audience scream with
delight, but which mortified me intensely. My mother was
out of town at the time. On her return, she and my father,
a lawyer, gave me a long lecture on the infringement of
copyrights. They gave me such a lecture that for years afterward, I expected Mr. Thomas Dixon to sue me for a
million dollars, and I have had a great respect for copyrights ever since then."

It was pleasant, too, to hear John reading a tribute to
Margaret that the cook Bessie Berry had asked Medora
Perkerson to publish in the *Journal*. "I wish I could tell
the many good things that Mr. & Mrs. Marsh have done
for me, but it would take the whole of Sunday's paper,"
Bessie had written. She went on to recall the time of her
illness at Grady Hospital when she despaired of getting
well, but "Every day about 2 o'clock I could look up in
the face of my dear Miss Mitchell and bid death stay thy
hand." Bessie was a member of the family; and it was the
family that Margaret thought of first and always. She was
particularly anxious about John's position as the husband
of a woman who had suddenly achieved fame. The gossip

item about his invalidism and Margaret's being forced to write to clear his debts had a sordid vitality; she continually heard echoes of it. Margaret was much disturbed when she wrote in mid-September to Herschel Brickell, "John is such a swell person, a positive genius in his own line, and he has held down a responsible, delicate job brilliantly for years. I just get in a killing rage at the very thought of anyone anywhere reflecting on his ability. I was asking for notoriety, I suppose, when I published a book and it is only right that I should take the consequences. And short of any reflection on my personal integrity, I intend to take it with as good a grace as is possible, hoping to God that this miserable period will end quickly. But I cannot take with any grace any lies about John or my family."

George Brett now wrote to Margaret urging that she come to New York and allow him to arrange a literary reception for her, and to see that she got standard celebrity treatment in the restaurants and nightclubs. He would put an office in the Macmillan Building at her disposal, and assign her the secretary who took care of John Masefield. Margaret replied that she could not come to New York until her eyes were better, and did not think Mr. Brett would wish to present her at a reception wearing dark glasses and an eyeshade.

As part of the process of recovering her nervous tone, Margaret decided to redecorate the Seventeenth Street apartment. This could be done—so she thought—while she was partially disabled by eye trouble. The painters came, dismantled the apartment and then disappeared. Margaret wrote to Lois Cole, "They come and tear your house to pieces, then go do the same to some other woman's house, and it takes a court order to get them back."

However, the Marshes could afford the decorators' charges plus a stay at the Atlanta Biltmore while the work was going on. Macmillan had sent in September a check for $43,500, and in October a check for $99,700 went into Margaret's account. Publishers often say there is no way of proving that advertising sells books, but it is to be noticed that they usually advertise a book that seems to be selling. In the case of *Gone with the Wind*, the advertising lagged behind sales; as fast as Alec Blanton advertised a new printing it sold out, and he had to revise his copy. No fault could be found with Macmillan's promotion of the book, and appreciative Margaret told them so over and over.

Another thing Margaret knew she need not worry about was the quality of script and direction for the moving picture version of her novel. In October, Katharine Brown sent word that Selznick had commissioned Sidney Howard to write the screenplay. A war hero and Pulitzer Prize winner, Howard had written the Broadway hits *They Knew What They Wanted*, *The Silver Cord*, and *Yellow Jack*. The director would be George Cukor, an expert costume-drama man who had staged *Little Women*, *Romeo and Juliet*, and *David Copperfield* for the films. He was now putting finishing touches on *Camille* with Greta Garbo and Robert Taylor. Katharine Brown also sent news that as soon as Cukor got through with Garbo and Taylor, he was coming to Atlanta where he and Miss Brown would start a great talent hunt for the right girl to play Scarlett O'Hara. Margaret's heart sank when she heard this, for she had a prevision of innumerable requests for introductions to George Cukor and Katharine Brown. She began to wonder if she would have to leave town and go into hiding while the movie people were in Atlanta.

It almost seemed she would have to leave before that time. Early in November she talked to an Atlanta reporter named Lamar Ball in one of her last efforts to make a direct appeal to the public. On this occasion Margaret said, "I know that the public interest in my book is inextricably tied up with its interest in me. There is no separating them, I suppose. I do believe, though, that my private life is my own. After all, I'm not trying to sell my own personality like a moving picture actress or a candidate for public office. I have merely sold the book I've written. I don't like to have women storming into a department store while I am standing there in my petticoat. They actually did this to me. They questioned me like a crowd of hard-hearted district attorneys. They wanted to know the sizes of my intimate wearing apparel. They screamed at each other about me as if I were an animal in a cage. One of them said, 'Ain't she skinny?' Still another said, ' expected her to look more middle-aged at the hips.' And I don't like them to comment that I have no lace on my petticoat. If I go down the street with my petticoat hanging a fraction of an inch below my skirt it becomes a city-wide scandal. If I make no excuses, I hear, 'With all this success, she's certainly got the swelled head!' or 'She certainly has gotten stuck up!' I want the quiet life I'm accustomed to."

Margaret was up and about again now, and able to talk to the callers who came with no discernible business other than to be able to go away saying they had seen her. But she could not yet read, nor pour out words at the typewriter, and she passed considerable time thinking of what had happened, and marveling at the variety of people who came and told her, or wrote to her, that they had read *Gone with the Wind*. There were the doctors, for example, who made it a point to get in touch with her. Did the doctors like to read about surgery? That described in Margaret's book was crude enough, and usually unsuccessful. And the psychiatrists—they were writing to her, praising Scarlett's psychological motivation. Some of these men said the heart of the characterization lay in the passage where Scarlett says to Rhett Butler after the death of Frank Kennedy, "I was so mean and now he's dead," and Rhett replies, "And if he wasn't dead you'd still be mean." Dr. John Favill, president of the Central Neuropsychiatric Association of Minneapolis, used this passage as a text in addressing a convention of his colleagues.

A letter from Dr. Hervey Cleckley, a psychiatrist of Augusta, Georgia, drew from Margaret her own view of her heroine. She wrote:

"Thank you for saying that in your opinion Scarlett O'Hara 'is a very convincing figure ... One feels, however, an inward hollowness and a serious lack of insight.' Such words, coming from a doctor like you, are very flattering to me. Perhaps most authors would not take it kindly that a psychiatrist spoke to one of their characters as a 'partial-psychopath,' but I feel distinctly pleased. Of course, I did not set out to delineate a psychopathic personality nor to do a psychoanalytical study. The novelist who consciously ventures into the realm of psychiatry does so at her peril and generally to the detriment of story and character. I set out to depict a far-from-admirable woman about whom little that was good could be said, and I attempted to keep her in character. I have found it wryly amusing when Miss O'Hara became somewhat of a national heroine and I have thought it looked bad for the moral and mental attitude of a nation that the nation could applaud and take to its heart a woman who conducted herself in such a manner. I have been bewildered and amused, too, when my book has been attacked because I pictured in detail a 'passionate and wanton woman.' I thought it would be obvious to anyone that Scarlett was a frigid woman, loving attention and adulation for their own sake but having little or no comprehension of actual deep feelings and no reactions to the love and attention of others. I suppose it takes a psychiatrist to realize this, so perhaps you can understand my appreciation of your remarks."

The study of her novel by psychiatrists struck Margaret as peculiarly astounding; but she knew it was part of a general impact that could not yet be measured as she dictated in a letter to a friend:

"Here in Atlanta, the fifth and sixth grade students are reading the book—obstetrical details and all—and with their parents' permission. I get scads of letters from school girls, ages thirteen to sixteen, who like it. And as for the old people—God bless them! There are scores of grandchildren whose voices are rasping and hoarse from reading aloud to them and Heaven knows how many indignant children have told me they had to sit up all night reading because the old folks wouldn't let them quit till after Scarlett was safe at Tara again. And in the ages between—this is what stumps me. In addition to the doctors who write and telephone, the bench and the bar like it, judges write me letters about it. And most confusing of all, file clerks, elevator operators, sales girls in department stores, telephone operators, stenographers, garage mechanics, clerks in Helpsy-Selfy stores, school teachers—oh, Heavens, I could go on and on!—like it. What is more puzzling, they buy copies. The United Daughters of the Confederacy have endorsed it, the Sons of Confederate Veterans crashed through with a grand endorsement, too. The debutantes and dowagers read it. Catholic nuns like it. Now, how to explain all this? I sit down and pull the story apart in my mind and try to figure it all out. Despite its length and many details it is basically just a simple yarn of fairly simple people. There's no fine writing, there's no philosophizing, there is a minimum of description, there are no grandiose thoughts, there are no hidden meanings, no symbolism, nothing sensational—nothing, nothing at all that made other best sellers best sellers. Then how to explain its appeal from the five year old to the ninety-five year old? I can't figure it out . . . Psychiatrists speak of the 'carefully done emotional patterns' and disregard all the history part. 'Emotional patterns?' Good Heavens! Can this be I? People talk and write of the 'high moral lesson.' *I* don't see anything very moral in it. I murmur feebly that 'It's just a story' and my words are swallowed up while the storm goes over my head about 'intangible values,' 'right and wrong' etc. Well, I still feebly say that it's just a simple story of some people who went up and some who went down, those who could take it and those who couldn't. And when people come along and say that I've done more for the South than anyone since Henry Grady I feel very proud and very humble and wish to God I could take cover like a rabbit."

In addition to the humility of that letter, Margaret had a blunt and unshakeable honesty in her view of herself. It was natural that advisers would suggest that if she did not like telegraph and special delivery messengers ringing the bell all day long, why not instruct the Post Office, Western Union, and the Postal Telegraph Company to hold up these messages, and deliver them somewhere else? Margaret answered, "I'm still country enough to get a thrill out of a telegram or special delivery letter." The main thing was that she would not alter her inner being; friends advised moving to New York, to California, or traveling abroad for a year or two. Margaret told them, "I hate traveling worse than a cat." She said, and it was true, that she had "never been west of Anniston, Alabama" and when Margaret heard a suggestion that she might fly to California for a vacation, she said, "So far as aeroplanes are concerned, I would have to be blindfolded like a mule and backed on." Margaret's lack of enthusiasm for travel may have been a reflection of her essential commitment to her native place. She wrote to a friend, "I couldn't live anywhere else in the world, except in the South. I suppose, being adaptable, I *could* live elsewhere, but I probably would not be very happy. I believe, however, that I see more clearly than most people just what living in the South means. There are more rules to be followed here than any place in the world if one is to live in any peace and happiness. Having always been a person who was perfectly willing to pay for anything I got, I am more than willing to pay for the happiness I get from my residence in Georgia."

John Marsh did not urge his wife to travel, or to give the slightest consideration to any idea of living elsewhere than Atlanta. He commented on the counsels that she might benefit from a different background by saying, "Peggy is determined to remain unchanged, and she has enough Irish in her to handle her own affairs just as she wants to handle them." Although the truth of John's statement was clear, few members of what was by now a nationwide audience accepted it as the final word. There was still much analyzing of Margaret's personality, not only by strangers who found her situation fascinating, but by old friends who were simply worrying about her happiness and health. Margaret was aware of this varied scrutiny. She wanted to tell the friends that much as she valued them, there was a part of her that nobody would ever know; she felt that this ought to be true of every mature person. She expressed her feelings in this matter to Herschel Brickell by telling him about a member of her family.

"I had a not too far distant ancestor who was a very godly man. He was a loving father and husband, a kind master and an honorable friend. If ever a man's life was an open book his was, and his nature was simple and candid. But he had one eccentricity which caused great though suppressed indignation among the females of his family. He could not endure to have any questions asked about his business, either private or public. Nor did he suffer any questions about his activities. It is related that an addled female cousin, visiting at the plantation for the first time and totally unaware of this eccentricity, observed him putting on his hat and asked politely, 'Oh, cousin, are you going out?' It is reported in the family that the look he gave her hastened her death. Once his wife asked him where he was going. This was on their honeymoon so it was pardonable. He said simply, 'Out,' and he gave her a look. Though she lived with him some fifty years thereafter, she never again asked any questions. Father told me that when he was a very little boy and the old gentleman was in his nineties, he (Father) peeked through the shutters as the old man left the house, and saw him walk down the side of the road and out of sight around a clump of trees. Father scuttled out and followed him unseen. He noted that the old gentleman walked a quarter a mile down the road before crossing the road to get to the pasture. He could have crossed the road directly in front of the house but he had no intention of letting anyone in the house have the satisfaction of knowing where he was going.

"As you can imagine, such an eccentric was not bragged about in my presence when I was young. However, when I had turned twelve and had goaded Mother about something she burst out with the fact that there was only one person in the family I had ever shown the slightest resemblance to, and it was that bewhiskered old wretch who didn't want anyone to know about his business and who couldn't bear to have a house full of women gabbling and quacking about his activities. The older I grow the more I believe in heredity, and I find myself feeling very sympathetic to the old gentleman."

Margaret could laugh at her sensitivity to being scrutinized, because she felt that even the most searching examination would not reveal everything about her. In conversation she once said, "Some of us believe we know people who are close to us but we certainly do not. No matter how long or well we know them, we do not know what that person thinks. There are always closed doors."

X

"Dear Margaret Mitchell:—"

As the autumn passed, some noteworthy magazine editors
came to Atlanta, asked permission to call, and became acquainted with the Marshes. Two who made a thoroughly
favorable impression were Kenneth Littauer, representing
Collier's, and Stuart Rose of the *Ladies Home Journal*.
Both Rose and Littauer were soon friends of Margaret
and John, and enjoyed their confidence; but neither editor
was ever able to extract any writing from Margaret. It
pleased Margaret to find that Mr. Rose was one of the
few people who had heard of the forgotten Southern novelist William Nathaniel Harben, once as popular as Mark
Twain. Stuart Rose had been in the Cavalry, and was a
noted horseman, and Kenneth Littauer had won a good
decoration in the war; these were the sort of men Margaret and John could like and respect.

They also appreciated the fairness and courtesy of the
proposals from such editors as Edwin Balmer of *Redbook*
and Graeme Lorimer at *The Saturday Evening Post*.
Wesley Stout, Graeme Lorimer's chief, suggested that
Margaret fill a page with anything she liked—fact or fic-

tion—at $1500 a week. Margaret refused all offers, though pleased to see how polite and tactful the big magazines could be. On the other hand, obscure and dubious publications by scores and hundreds continued to send Margaret peremptory letters demanding contributions and offering small payment or none at all. And these editors invariably closed their letters with something on the order of "The favor of a prompt reply is requested."

By contrast, Edwin Balmer asked Margaret to make her decision at a time suiting her convenience. He took her refusal gracefully, and told Margaret that her letter, even though a refusal, had caused more interest in his office than any document he ever handled there. The staff crowded around in excitement, he said, just to have a look at her signature. A similar agitation occurred in the *Ladies Home Journal* offices when Margaret sent Stuart Rose a doll for his young daughter. Experienced Curtis Publishing Company secretaries who would merely glance up from their work when a living celebrity passed on the way to an editor's office came from several floors, Mr. Rose reported, when news of the doll's arrival spread. What would have happened had an actual story or article by Margaret Mitchell come in the mail, he hardly dared think.

In November Sidney Howard wrote to express his gratification at the assignment to write the screenplay of *Gone with the Wind*. The playwright told Margaret he would like to have her help if it became necessary to write additional dialogue for the Negro characters. He said he thought these the best-written Negroes in all literature, and it would be impossible for anyone else to meet the original author's standard in supplying further words for them. Margaret answered this letter the day it arrived: she could not have anything to do with the moving picture script—she could not even read it before it went to the actors. This, she explained, was because of her fear of Southern indignation should anything "be wrong" with the completed picture. She said people might reproach her by saying, "You had something to do with the script, so why didn't you prevent"—whatever might have disappointed the Southern audience. This decision was consistent with

Margaret's attitude toward the entire project, and Mr. Howard accepted it with good grace.

While the playwright might have been easy to deal with—Sidney Howard was indeed, one of the gentlest of men—there was another person working for the producer who never seemed able to associate Margaret with anything having reality. This was Selznick's publicity director, Russell Birdwell. One of the great promoters of his day, Birdwell saw no reason why a publicity handout need not be a work of fiction, so long as it was also a work of art. His attitude was that if the stuff did no harm, and got in the papers with the names spelled correctly, what difference did it make whether or not it was true? This did not make him an ideal colleague for Margaret Mitchell, as she discovered at the end of November when Birdwell released to the national wire services a story that Katharine Brown was on her way to Atlanta on a mission to discover a "totally unknown daughter of Dixie" for the role of Scarlett O'Hara. The trouble lay in Birdwell's further statement: Margaret Mitchell was to help Miss Brown line up a selection of debutantes, and girls from offices and colleges, and would assist in picking "the cream of the crop" for inspection by George Cukor. Birdwell quoted Margaret as saying she "hoped it would be a Southern actress" and rounded off the story by announcing that Sidney Howard also was coming to Atlanta to consult Miss Mitchell so as to be sure the screenplay satisfied the author of the novel.

Birdwell's news release had the quality of a nightmare, like the familiar dream of frustration in which nobody will pay any attention to what one says. But within a few minutes after the story appeared, Margaret's telephone and doorbell began to ring, and that was real enough. She wired Birdwell at the Selznick studio in Culver City, California, in a commendably restrained and civil tone, to the effect that she had nothing to do with casting, and begging him to read the contract. Such a thing as a publicity director reading an author's contract had never happened in all the ages of moving pictures, but Margaret could not know that. Indeed, Birdwell probably thought he was doing her a favor when he put words in her mouth. But Margaret wired Katharine Brown in New York that unless her position could be correctly stated in Selznick publicity, she would have to leave Atlanta until the talent search excitement had died down.

Margaret's supposed remark about a Southern girl in the leading role met with approval at the Atlanta Woman's Club, and that organization issued a statement endorsing a well-known actress: "With a long background of Southern ancestry, her forebears among the distinguished Georgians in the Southern army, it is fitting that the South should see one of its favorite daughters, Miriam Hopkins, on the screen as Scarlett, the Georgia heroine of a Georgia story."

In Hollywood, Louella Parsons took note of the growing national mania for suggesting the picture's cast. She wrote that "The mail I've received on *Gone with the Wind* if put end to end, I'm sure, would extend from my home to the Selznick studio clear out in Culver City. It is well up in four figures and increasing every day." In Atlanta, Margaret reported to Lois Cole that "the telephone is screaming every minute, the doorbell has gone crazy, and it's only 11 a.m. I've been going since dawn and feel it's midnight." By December 15, Margaret had decided to retire and regroup her forces. Pausing only to send a courteous refusal to a madman who had written asking for the loan of $100,000, she quietly left town. John was with her, and their destination was the Hotel Alabama in the resort town of Winter Park, Florida. There they hoped to pass a quiet holiday season under the pseudonyms of Mr. and Mrs. John Munnerlyn. Only the Edwin Granberrys, who lived in the town, were to know the Marshes were there. Margaret recorded that this was because "I knew so many people in the neighborhood whom I would be forced to call on if they knew of my presence. Not that I minded calling but tired as I was the very idea of having to see people was appalling. With the best intentions in the world, Edwin let the cat out of the bag and we had to pack up early Christmas morning and get out of town, one jump ahead of newspapers and dinner invitations. The rest of the vacation we spent in small hotels and I had a wonderful time and gained six pounds which I lost within three days of my return home."

Back on Seventeenth Street in early January, with the millionth copy of *Gone with the Wind* on her desk, Margaret began to plan for the future. She decided she would have to make the best of living in the public eye until the moving picture of her book was completed. After that, she said hopefully to her friend, she would no longer be a celebrity, and life would be as it had been before the appearance of her novel. At the moment, the myths were continuing to spring up. A note from Stuart Rose in Philadelphia was at hand to report that the latest word from New York had her visiting Bergdorf-Goodman and ordering $10,000 worth of dresses. "I have just finished sewing up a rip in the seam of a two-year-old dinner dress to wear this weekend," Margaret replied.

Encouragement and understanding came from Alexander Woollcott, who had used *Gone with the Wind* for one of his broadcasts. "This is in answer to your letter which arrived this morning, and the first broadcast in which I took your name in vain was done last evening. It is only fair to warn you that I am likely to revert to the topic again. You may not be a good girl, but you're awfully good material. I am more than a little impressed by your sagacity about the success of your book. I never knew anyone who'd learned so quickly what some never learn and others only in time—that all the attendant huggermugger of successful authorship is neither agreeable, valuable, or necessary. I hope you will continue being tough about it and that you will spit in everybody's eye including that of yours to command Alexander Woollcott."

Meanwhile, there was settling to harness as proprietor of the foreign translation rights of *Gone with the Wind*. Dutch and Japanese pirates had already closed in; the unauthorized edition in Holland being based on the excuse that Margaret had no copyright in countries, including Holland, that subscribed to the Berne Convention. The United States was not a party to the Convention, and

American authors secured copyright by publication in Canada, which had joined in this international agreement. Macmillan of Canada had published the book on the same day as the American firm; but the Hollanders claimed this was only a legal fiction; it turned out that the definition of publishing, in the legal sense, was bafflingly vague anyhow. The subject was technical, yet of the greatest importance to Margaret, who naturally wished to be paid for the translation of her book, and who felt it a personal indignity to be robbed.

So far as the Japanese were concerned, there was a touch of legality to their theft. A villainous treaty enacted in 1905 gave their publishers the right to translate and print books by American writers without the authors' consent, and without payment. American publishers could do the same with the work of Japanese authors, for which there was about as much demand in the United States as for iceboxes at the North Pole. And in any event, here was our government giving away the property of American writers, while licensing our printers to help themselves to that of Japanese writers. Margaret did not care for this, nor was she appeased when the Japanese publishers sent her a doll with the request that she pose with it for publicity photographs. She named the doll Madame Oh So Solly and put it away on a high shelf. Madame Oh So Solly was sold at auction, in August 1942, to benefit the Red Cross.

"The problem resolves itself to whether I can last till the book stops selling," Margaret told a trusted friend. She spoke of the American sale, for she thought the publication of translations would hardly interfere with what went on in her Atlanta apartment. Settling to the task of administering the granting of translation rights, Margaret took on a New York agent who specialized in contacts with foreign publishers. Again the nomination of the agent came from officials of Macmillan, who suggested to Margaret that Marion Saunders was the right person to supply foreign representation through her European contacts. The plan was for Miss Saunders to make the sales, sending contracts to Atlanta where Margaret, John, and Stephens Mitchell would approve them.

At the Atlanta end of the business, Margaret gained an important ally, early in January 1937, when she engaged Margaret E. Baugh as secretary. Miss Baugh had been in the Atlanta office of Macmillan, and Margaret said, "She knows books. Then too, she knows enough about authors not to be too impressed with me." In the middle 1960s, Margaret Baugh could point to her case as one of the many in which *Gone with the Wind* altered the course of a life, for she was still working for the book and the family, looking after the office of the Margaret Mitchell Marsh Estate.

Making her plans for 1937, Margaret calculated that since the previous July 1, she had averaged an engagement every forty minutes from nine in the morning until after midnight. This could not go on; she would have to reduce the demands on her time. It occurred to her that she could save many hours in the week by cutting off autographing of the novel. She therefore let it be known in January that since there were now more than a million copies in existence, she would have to refuse all requests to write her name in the book. This brought the reputation of having allowed success to turn her head among persons who did not know that Margaret and Bessie Berry had to stand in line at post office windows to mail the hundreds of books that came from strangers requesting autographs.

As she often did after making an important decision, Margaret discussed this one in a letter to a friend. Her confidante was Lois Cole, to whom she wrote, "When I was a reporter, I met practically every author who came to town, including some very great ones whose books I loved and cherished. And I never once asked for an autograph and never once wanted one. Frequently when I have bought books I liked a lot and the captive author was in the book store autographing, I refused to have the book autographed. When a stranger asks me for an autograph I feel just as if he (or she) had asked me for a pair of my stepins and it makes me just as sore. I realize that other people do not intend to be insulting and are being just as nice as they know how but my feeling only grows stronger. And this feeling is one of the reasons I never go anywhere except to my office or to the library. I do not want to hurt people's feelings but, on the other hand, I do not want to get furious forty times a day. Of course, the result of this has been that people go to the most remarkable lengths to get autographs. John turns them down by scores every day, poor Father's life has been made a misery by people who sit in his office and take up his time telling him that he should force me by parental authority to sign their books. Steve and Carrie Lou and all my relatives lead hunted lives because perfect strangers descend on them, leaving copies with them and instructions that they *make* me sign them. When I make a business appointment with someone they usually turn up staggering under a dozen copies which their friends have wished upon them, in the frank hope that the caller can embarrass me into signing them. And, oh, my God the pressure that's brought to bear by charitable organizations wanting an autographed copy for raffling purposes! And they talk at a great length about the worthy cause. Usually I can get them told by asking how much they have contributed to that worthy cause in hard cash and show that I have already contributed fifty times as much and will contribute again but I will not autograph.

"Now, what do you think about this picture? *Collier's* is having an article about me and Mr. Littauer asked for a photograph that had not been published before. I had a number taken. They were all, (except the one I am enclosing) more awful than you can imagine. The expressions were unvarying. The expression was that of the Spartan Boy at the precise moment when the fox had worked his way through to the gall bladder. This one was the only one that had any possibilities, but I am uncertain as to whether it should be used. It has a theatrical look undoubtedly, and a vaguely sinister expression which is totally at variance with the sweet, simple and girlish official press photograph ... It is still inconceivable the positions people try to jockey me into on every type of thing. Every person of any large or small prominence from British generals to heads of life insurance corporations arrive in Atlanta determined to meet Bobby Jones and me ... Atlanta people have been pretty swell to me, but the out-of-town-ers seem to feel that I'm a freak, on display, something like the quintuplets and should have no objection at being roused at any hour to display myself and to autograph books ... and by callers who want to know if Scarlett ever got him back. I know that last sounds idiotic and un-believable to you but letters come in by scores, demanding to know if she got him back and people telephone and when I won't come to the phone they ask Bessie who an-swers gently in that cooing voice of hers, 'No, Mam, I can't tell you whether or not Miss Scarlett got the cap'n back or no. No, Mam, Miss Peggy, she don't know either. Yes, Mam, I've heard her say a hundred times she didn't have no more idea than the next 'bout what happened to Miss Scarlett after she went home to Tara.' And at the only tea I've been to (it taught me a lesson. I'll not go to another soon) my sash was torn off, my veil yanked from my hat, punch and refreshments knocked out of my hands as ladies from Iowa and Oklahoma and Seattle screamed the same question at me and poked me with sharp pointed fingernails to emphasize their questions. Good grief. I thought I knew human nature. But this has been a new ex-perience for me."

But the hours saved by giving up autographing, and having Bessie answer the telephone, disappeared in the crowded days. It was not that Margaret found time to do anything constructive; much of her time, and money, went to such matters as the Susan Lawrence Davis plagiarism suit, which started in February 1937. Susan Lawrence Da-vis was an eccentric who had written a book called *An Authentic History of the Ku Klux Klan, 1865–1877*. She now sued Margaret and The Macmillan Company for damages of $5,000 on each of 1,300,000 copies of *Gone with the Wind*, a total of $6,500,000,000, charging that Margaret had plagiarized her work. Miss Davis submitted a 461-page brief pointing out, among other suspicious cir-cumstances that both books were in Confederate gray bind-ing; that both used the phrase "Fiery Cross"; that Miss Davis spoke of "ghosts from the nearby battlefields" and Miss Mitchell called a character "wraithlike"; that Miss

Davis mentioned Fort Sumter, and so did Miss Mitchell; Miss Davis wrote "Charleston," Miss Mitchell, "Charlestonians"; Miss Mitchell used the words "practically destitute," infringing on Miss Davis's "utterly impoverished"; Stonewall Jackson, Wade Hampton, and Jefferson Davis were in Miss Davis' book, and also in Miss Mitchell's; Miss Davis had described a Southern home as having "mirrors above the mantel," while on page 868 of *Gone with the Wind*, Margaret Mitchell wrote of "gilt frame mirrors and long pier glasses"; and so on. The case appeared even less substantial than the famous action brought against Mr. Pickwick. Nevertheless, Margaret had to spend time and money on the ridiculous affair, and retain lawyers to prepare a serious defense to the charges. One might well ask how people like Miss Davis can find attorneys to draw up such insane accusations. They find them quite easily, as many a publisher, novelist, and dramatist can testify. This particular suit was thrown out of court on July 30, 1937, on the grounds that there was no cause for action.

Another annoyance came from a man who presumably should have known better, the veteran showman Billy Rose. Accepting a contract to produce an extravaganza for the Fort Worth Frontier Fiesta, Rose announced, "I'll make Texas the biggest state in the Union." Part of his show was based on *Gone with the Wind*, and the theatrical weekly *Variety* reported: "Harriet Hoctor is the Scarlett O'Hara of his version of Margaret Mitchell's weighty volume, and in a few minutes on her toes she wipes out a good 600 pages of the original work. The setting for Tara, schemed by Albert Johnson, is one of the most spacious edifices ever to crowd a stage. Its façade must stretch across a good 200 feet, and it towers up a full three stories. Three hundred singers, dancers and pantomimists participate in this Dixie lament which ends with Union troopers burning the O'Hara mansion to the ground."

It sounded like a splendid spectacle; but, from Margaret's point of view, Mr. Rose's production had one serious flaw, which was that he had failed to buy the stage rights to *Gone with the Wind*. She therefore referred the matter to Howard Reinheimer, a leading New York theatrical lawyer. A short time later, Margaret described the case while writing to George Brett: "Mr. Rose called John from Texas and talked for forty minutes, trying to get him or me to come out there at his expense and see the show. When John refused for both of us Mr. Rose said, 'It's pretty well known that Mrs. Marsh is averse to traveling or to newspaper publicity. Well, I'll fix her. I'll make her come to Fort Worth to testify and she will get more publicity than she wants.' To which John replied, 'Mrs. Marsh thought over that possibility before entering suit and is prepared to do what she must do.' Then Mr. Rose flew to New York to talk to my attorney. There appeared in a New York column the following item—that Rose had telephoned me and had invited me to Texas. John, according to the item, took the phone away from me and said, 'My wife is averse to publicity,' to which the clever Mr. Rose said he replied, 'Then why did she write that book?' The more I read of New York columnists the more appalled I am by the blithe way in which they print as fact things which never happened!"

Factual news was supplied, however, when Billy Rose paid Margaret $3,000 in damages, pledged a further $25,000 should he violate her rights again, and sent her a letter whose tone may be judged from the paragraph: "I realize now that I should not have used the title of your book or any of your characters, or the names of any of your characters, or alluded to your book in any way without your consent, and I apologize to you for having done so."

With that settled, Margaret announced completion of arrangements to publish authorized translations in Poland and Hungary, in addition to Germany, Sweden, Norway and Denmark.

In the spring of 1937 came two exciting accolades. First, Margaret received the annual award of the American Booksellers Association, forerunner to the present National Book Awards. And, in April, the trustees of the Pulitzer Prize conferred that honor on *Gone with the Wind* as the finest American novel of the preceding year. Margaret said, "I don't know which impressed me most—winning the Pulitzer Prize or having the city editor of the *Constitution* leave his desk." It was true: when the flash came over the wires, the city editor left desk and office to cover the story in person. Heywood Broun commented on the award: "I do not think *Gone with the Wind* is an enduring work of literature, and I not only believe but ardently hope that it will emulate its title in another twelve months." But the *New York Daily News* editorialized, "Looking back along the list of Pulitzer Prize novels down the years, we think this is the best novel that has ever won ... We've taken *Gone with the Wind* from its regular place in American fiction and parked it alongside Tolstoy's *War and Peace* . . ."

Reading that sort of praise, said Margaret, gave her "the humbles." And it made her more than ever determined to do everything she could for the people—especially the very young and the very old—who wrote to her as to a friend and mentor. Hundreds of these correspondents demanded a continuation of the story, some of them sketching out how the sequel should go, and offering to sell their ideas or to collaborate with Margaret. Two fourteen-year-old girls sent a simple and workable outline: hoping to make up the quarrel, Scarlett follows Rhett to Charleston; she finds him standing on a balcony, and the sight of her startles him so that he falls and suffers severe injuries. Scarlett nurses Rhett back to health, and they are reunited. Margaret answered the girls: "You wrote that you both would like to be authors but you felt that you were too young at present to do much. I do not think you are too young. The time to begin writing is just as soon as you are old enough to hold a pencil in your hand. If you want to become good authors, then write as much as you can. It is good practice and you will profit by it. Keep on writing about things with which you are familiar and the things you know best and understand best."

The generosity of spirit that Margaret showed in her letters to young girls reached out in equal measure to the old. By hundreds the letters in spidery handwriting sifted down like a gentle, insistent, and continuing fall of snow.

"Dear Margaret Mitchell"—and then for page after page the old people would write to her about family traditions, old diaries, heirlooms, memories. Some would tell the stories of their lives; others would ask in Southern fashion about possible relationships by way of distant kin. In these letters from the old, Margaret discerned their writers' anxieties, confusions, loneliness, and need for attention. She would reply, taking pains to make specific responses to the topics her correspondents brought up. And that would not be the end of it; the delighted old people would answer Margaret's answer, and a permanent correspondence would take form. Some of the old men and women would write to her, "I think of you as a daughter."

Another good by-product of the novel was the friendship that sometimes resulted from calls at the Seventeenth Street apartment by Northern editors and writers. Kenneth Littauer and Stuart Rose were welcome. The popular novelist Faith Baldwin, and Mabel Search, an editor of *Pictorial Review,* were visitors who persuaded Margaret to allow Miss Baldwin to write an article about her. Other friendships, like that of Herschel Brickell, started in correspondence. In this way Margaret first got in touch with such sympathetic and rewarding people as the Richmond novelist, Clifford Dowdey, the novelist and *New Republic* editor Stark Young, his friends Alfred Lunt and Lynn Fontanne, and Dr. Phelps of Yale.

Margaret later met in person most of the literary people with whom she first became acquainted by letters. The book columnist Isabel Paterson recorded how Margaret encountered Stark Young in the summer of 1938, two years after he had written to her. Miss Paterson had called at the Brickells' home and met a "Southern girl" with a fleeting but enchanting smile and a vaguely familiar face—a Mrs. Marsh. It turned out the young lady was from Atlanta, and she chatted amiably about that city until Norma Brickell said, "Don't you know, Isabel, that this is Margaret Mitchell?" Stark Young now arrived, and was delighted to meet Margaret at last. He launched into a story, then hesitated and said he had a fatal gift, perhaps some kind of malign telepathy, that made him invariably choose anecdotes that proved to be about friends or relations of those he was talking to. At the moment, he wanted to tell of a famous Southern eccentric who walked backward all the time, but added, "Perhaps Miss Mitchell knew him?" Knew, him! Miss Mitchell certainly did; she used to consult him on historical data, for he was a noted scholar; she called him Uncle Henry, and he was a close friend of her father's. "I was sure of it," said Stark Young. "He would be." Then they laughed together over the peculiarities of Uncle Henry, who insisted on walking backward even though testy residents of Atlanta tried to discourage it by peppering him with rock salt fired from shotguns.

There were some who called at Margaret's door, in the first three years of her novel's life, who brought her nothing but anxiety and distress. These were the girls without experience in the theater or movies who still felt they could play the role of Scarlett O'Hara, and who refused to believe they needed anything more than a word from Miss Mitchell to land the part. "I have lived the life of Scarlett O'Hara, Miss Mitchell," said one. Another girl told Margaret she had left her husband in order to launch an acting career by way of the Scarlett O'Hara role.

In April, George Cukor and Katharine Brown arrived, along with the assistants who held the actual auditions. Though too polite to say so, Margaret suspected the talent search was a publicity stunt. In any event, Cukor attracted considerable attention, and Margaret was astonished when she got word that he had poured gin on his salad in the main dining room at the Atlanta Biltmore. It turned out the liquid was only mineral oil, a medical fad of the time. Cukor and Katharine Brown were charming people, and made a good impression in Atlanta, some of whose citizens did not quite know what to expect in the way of ambassadors from Hollywood. The only person who endangered Cukor's poise was a visiting girl known to Kay Brown and Margaret as Honey Chile. The young lady was beautiful, and had her talent matched her determination, Honey Chile would have been greater than Bernhardt.

After Miss Brown returned to New York, Margaret

brought her up to date on this candidate for stardom: "Last night Yolande Gwin called me, practically incoherent. Honey Chile had phoned her at a quarter to six at the *Constitution*, a short while before the paper went to press. This merry romp screamed over the phone that she had discovered the train on which the badgered George Cukor was to leave and she had bought a ticket and was going to New Orleans.

" 'If I talk to him he will realize I am the only Scarlett. I must see him. I *will* see him. I will go all the way to Hollywood with him if necessary. I am now at the Terminal Station.' Yolande said she was overcome with horror and pity for the Selznickers. All of you had been so wonderful to her she could not bear to think of the weary trio* being captured by the determined belle. She rushed to the city editor and asked for fifteen minutes off so she could go to the station and warn the unsuspecting George. The city editor roared like a bull, snatched a photographer out of a trash basket, called a taxi and threw Yolande and the photographer in.

" 'Warn Mr. Cukor! You cover that story even if you have to go all the way to New Orleans!'

"In the taxi Yolande wrote a note on a bank deposit slip to give Mr. Cukor if time was short. When she arrived at the station Honey Chile was racing up and down beside the train, and she yelled to Yolande, 'Either they aren't on the train or they are in hiding, but I will find them.' She leaped on the train and the photographer banged away. Thereafter for ten minutes Yolande said Honey Chile tore through the train jerking open stateroom doors, disconcerting honeymoon couples, arousing sleeping children, and catching several gentlemen who had taken off their pants. The train was in an uproar, and the whole crew was pursuing her. Convinced that they were not on the train, she leaped off and rushed up and down the tracks, telling her troubles to all and sundry, announcing that she would make a perfect Scarlett. Yolande said that, personally, she

* Assistant Director John Darrow and Scene Designer Hobart Erwin accompanied Cukor.

was mortified as the station was packed and everyone showed an appreciative interest. One old lady sat down on her suitcase and said, with enthusiasm, 'This is every bit as good as a movie!'

"Then Yolande had an idea. The train was very long and she suggested that Honey Chile wait at the end of the Pullmans while she, Yolande, watched the stair. Honey Chile took off like a rabbit at the suggestion. In a few minutes down the stairs came the trio, all unsuspecting and weary after interviewing hundreds of applicants. Yolande jumped at them crying, 'Something dreadful has happened.' All three, bless them, questioned, 'Is Mrs. Marsh hurt?' 'No, something far worse. Miss Honey Chile is going to New Orleans with you.'

"Yolande said they evidently agreed with her that this news was far more dreadful than hearing I had been mangled by a truck. And George positively paled. He told John Darrow to hold Honey Chile off the train at any cost, and the weary John sprinted for the end of the train, with Yolande and the photographer close behind. Yolande peeped over her shoulder and she took oath that George and Hobe Erwin dived into the coal car. Miss Honey Chile leaped upon Darrow, crying, 'I don't want to see you. I have already seen you. My God, anybody can see you. I must see Mr. Cukor. This is the turning point of my life!' John soothingly took her hand and addressed her as sweetheart and told her Mr. Cukor had gone to New Orleans by motor. 'Then, I will go to New Orleans,' cried the determined Honey Chile. 'What would you advise me to do?' 'I would advise you not to chase him. Men don't like to be chased. The more you pursue him the less chance you have. Go home and forget about it, and perhaps when we come back to New York we'll see you.' He held her hand till the whistle blew and then leaped aboard.

"When Yolande got back to the paper the city editor almost threw a slug at her. 'If you had been worth your salt you'd have pushed her on that train and we'd have had a fine story.' 'But Mr. Cukor had been so nice to me.' 'Bah,' said the city editor."

Margaret's determination to have nothing to do with

casting the picture did not prevent her from privately recommending two important staff appointments. Katharine
Brown told Margaret one of Selznick's most pressing
needs was for advisers to keep him straight on historical
matters and coach the actors on Southern speech. Margaret told Selznick that "good quality stage voices" would
do very well, so long as no one used the expression "you-
all" other than in the plural. That, she said, might cause
another secession. But Selznick had been reading about
Southern accents and sensibilities, and was begging Miss
Brown to find expert help. With Kay Brown sworn to
secrecy about Margaret's part in it, the author suggested
Wilbur Kurtz as historical consultant and Susan Myrick of
the *Macon Telegraph* as coach for voices and points of
behavior.

Mr. Kurtz, though originally from Indiana, was a respected local artist, architect, and Civil War historian specializing in the campaigns around Atlanta. He proved to
be an ideal adviser, as he could show Production Designer
William Cameron Menzies how things should look by
dashing out a quick sketch. He made hundreds of pictures
for Menzies, ruled on such matters as how a well should
be constructed and a wagon sprung, and he even designed
a tombstone.

Miss Myrick was to become known as "the Emily Post
of Dixie," for she found plenty to do from the time in
March 1937 when she arrived in Culver City along with
Mr. and Mrs. Kurtz. Knowing they owed their positions to
Margaret, the Kurtzes and Miss Myrick wanted to express
appreciation, but she had to put them under stern vows
not even to mention her name. After a few weeks in Culver City they understood why, for they themselves were
forced to hide out in other people's quarters when determined persons seeking employment or introductions to
Selznick laid siege to their office doors.

Meanwhile, Sidney Howard had delivered a 400-page
screenplay to David Selznick. The producer went to work
on it with help from the well-known movie writer Jo
Swerling. They reduced the script to 240 pages. Next,
Selznick called in Oliver H. P. Garrett, once a star report-

er on the *New York World*, and now a successful Hollywood writer, to condense still further; but, when Garrett was through, Selznick found his script expanded to 250 pages. Before he got the screenplay to suit him, Selznick had retained a surprising number of writers, including John Van Druten, Ben Hecht, Winston Miller, F. Scott Fitzgerald, and Edwin Justus Mayer. It is hard to say what these gifted men may have contributed. Those who worked on the sets had the impression that a great deal of the final script was written by Selznick himself, and *he* said 90 per cent of the lines were exactly as Margaret wrote them. Indeed, in the end, the drama of the movie was Margaret's contribution; she had an instinct for confrontation, and throughout the book had not written one static scene between people with the same point of view. Selznick's extra writers did not share in the screenplay credit which went to Sidney Howard alone. But the playwright did not live to see it; he was killed, in 1939, in an accident caused by a runaway tractor at his farm near Tyringham, Massachusetts.

It was said that David O. Selznick spent $500,000 on the search for a Scarlett O'Hara—but he told Ed Sullivan of the *Daily News* the figure was more like $50,000. For this he got publicity over a period of two years. He also found two girls for small parts, and Alicia Rhett of Charleston, South Carolina, to whom he assigned the role of Ashley's sister India Wilkes. Throughout the time of searching for Scarlett, the agents and fans of female stars kept steady pressure on Selznick—and on Margaret also, still refusing to believe she would not recommend one actress over another. With Margaret, the partisans took a wheedling tone, but agents and producers with stars under contract talked definite business with Selznick, making all sorts of offers. For example, Warner Brothers suggested a deal for Bette Davis and Errol Flynn as Scarlett and Rhett. "The public wants Gable," Selznick said. Word got out that he was thinking of Norma Shearer for Scarlett. This was true: "We played around with the idea," Selznick admitted. A flood of letters insisting that this actress was wrong for the part caused Selznick to think again, and

Miss Shearer made a dignified and gracious announcement that she would not be available.

As 1937 approached its end, some of the newspaper commentators began saying Scarlett would have to be played by an unknown, because of the public's partisan feelings for the established stars. And the New York drama critic John Chapman remarked, "It looks as though the best part in *Gone with the Wind* is the publisher."

In one sense this may have been true, but it was casting the part of Scarlett O'Hara that fascinated the world. Miriam Hopkins continued to get unofficial votes from many Southerners; among others suggested by fans, or rumored to have accepted the role, were Claudette Colbert, Libby Holman, Paulette Goddard, Jean Harlow, Joan Crawford, and Tallulah Bankhead. California papers reported a test had been ordered for Mrs. John Hay Whitney, the former Elizabeth Altemus of Philadelphia society. Gracie Allen said, "I would be interested in the part, but I don't think it will go with my little blue hat."

As months passed, the matter of filling this role acquired such an aura of importance that persons not connected with show business sometimes tried to pull wires for a favorite actress. A most extraordinary example of this occurred when Margaret's telephone rang and she heard the voice of Mrs. Ogden Reid in New York City. Mrs. Reid at that time owned the *Herald Tribune* and was a person of great importance. Margaret asked, "What can I do for you, Mrs. Reid?" The lady answered that she hoped Margaret could attend a meeting of distinguished women she was organizing in New York for some reason or other. Margaret replied that she could not leave Atlanta because of business and the illness of her father, Mrs. Reid then began to speak of Katharine Hepburn, and questioned Margaret about her liking for the actress. Margaret said she thought Miss Hepburn looked pretty in hoopskirts, and she had enjoyed her performance in *Little Women*. The conversation ended. Next day, Margaret received calls from newspapers all over the country, and from the wire services, asking her about the report in New York that Mrs. Reid had said Margaret Mitchell told her she favored Katharine Hepburn for Scarlett O'Hara. The callers were reproachful: after denying them the news, why did she release it through Mrs. Reid in New York? Margaret then made a statement that the Associated Press called "polite but firm," which concluded: "I have never expressed a preference and I never will. If Mrs. Reid understood me to say I felt a strong preference for Miss Hepburn in the role, I owe her and Miss Hepburn an apology." In private, Margaret said, "The day all those calls came my father was very ill and my presence was needed at the hospital. I was unable to be with him as I had to sit at the telephone making denials. I could not help resenting Mrs. Reid's action for I had given her no cause for making such a statement. I made notes of my conversation with her and there were two witnesses to my statement."

Mr. Mitchell was not to be out of the hospital for any long period after that. But even when he was able to keep to his bed at home, his constant visitor, and his agent to doctors and what professional nurses could be obtained, was his daughter. It took time—a great deal of time, as Margaret realized; and she knew, too, that time was of utmost importance to a writer. Every day that passed without some writing done lessened the possibilities of successful writing in the future. This, perhaps, was an underlying anxiety; such intrusions as the call by Mrs. Reid were merely by-products of the great casting furor.

David Selznick could understand how Margaret felt when his butler waked him in his California home early on Christmas morning and told him he was wanted at the front door—some sort of special present was being delivered. Selznick climbed into a bathrobe and tottered downstairs, where four uniformed messengers carried into the hall an enormous Christmas-decorated box, set it down before the producer, and stood back smartly at attention. Suddenly the box opened and out jumped a girl dressed in hoopskirts, who screamed, "Merry Christmas, Mr. Selznick! I am your Scarlett O'Hara!"

Selznick knew but too well that his Scarlett would not come in a Christmas package; the fact was, casting *Gone with the Wind* hinged on Clark Gable. Not everyone understood Selznick's difficulties, and by September 1938 there was public complaint because his cameras had not yet photographed an inch of film. Selznick decided to take the public at least partly into his confidence by means of a long letter to Ed Sullivan which the columnist published. So far as delay was concerned, the producer pointed out, he had made *David Copperfield* eighty-six years after it was first published, and *The Prisoner of Zenda* forty-three years after it first came out, so he felt entitled to take his time on *Gone with the Wind*. The one character for which the public expressed a clear choice was Rhett Butler: this must be played by Clark Gable. "But you must have a rough idea as to how willing Metro-Goldwyn-Mayer would be to give up Gable for a picture to be released by another company," Selznick wrote. "The only way I could get him, was to distribute the picture through M.G.M., and this meant I had to wait to start the picture until my contract with United Artists had expired, which it does when I finish my present picture." As to Scarlett, Selznick said that his mail and a number of investigations had convinced him that "The public's choice is clearly and very strongly for a new girl as Scarlett ... Between Cukor and myself, we have seen personally every available young actress that was even remotely a possibility ... Other studios have helped me, as I promised them if they found a girl, they could use her in an occasional picture. The search is on again with renewed vigor—and the best Scarlett that shows up by the time Gable is available to start work will play the role, willy-nilly."

This was no publicity chatter. As soon as MGM agreed to loan him Gable, Selznick cast the other parts with Olivia de Havilland and Leslie Howard as the second heroine and hero, and put in support a group of seasoned character actors that included Laura Hope Crews, Thomas Mitchell, Victor Jory, Ward Bond, Ona Munson, Jane Darwell, Harry Davenport, Louis Jean Heydt, J. M. Kerrigan, Lillian Kemble Cooper, and Paul Hurst, who was to register solidly in his brief scene as the Yankee straggler. The principal Negro parts went to Hattie McDaniel, Oscar Polk, Eddie Anderson, and Kitty Lincoln, whose stage name was Butterfly McQueen. During the negotiations for these actors, the moving picture makers never stopped trying to get advice from Margaret. A crisis developed in New York when Selznick's people were testing Ona Munson for the part of Belle Watling, the brothel keeper. The question was, how should she talk? Even Eugene Mitchell on his sickbed laughed at the thought of long-distance tolls being spent on that question. Katharine Brown wondered if Margaret could think of anyone who might serve as voice coach for Miss Munson. Margaret's answer was, "I suggest that they get a professional. I mean, of course, a professional coach."

By the end of 1938, word came by way of Kay Brown that Selznick might start shooting in January 1939. The news was important to Margaret because of her belief that with the showing of the picture, public curiosity about the author would abate. As matters turned out, Selznick shot the first scene on the night of December 10, 1938— still with no one cast for Scarlett—and it was the most spectacular scene in the show. In the back lot area known as Forty Acres, Selznick's men had constructed an Atlanta Street, time 1864, following Wilbur Kurtz's specifications to the last detail. Behind and around the Atlanta street they piled the old sets from *King Kong, The Garden of Allah,* and *The Last of the Mohicans,* drenched them with gasoline, and threw on a lighted match. The sky soon glowed red over Coldwater Canyon; seeing the glare, some thought the city of Los Angeles was burning, scrambled into cars, and headed for the desert. David Selznick and his staff watched the conflagration from camera platforms while assistant directors gave orders through electric bullhorns. David's brother Myron, who was an agent, came over after dinner to have a look, bringing with him one of his lesser clients, the young British actress Vivien Leigh. At Forty Acres, Myron noticed how Vivien's eyes flashed, and the excitement and vitality of her looks in the light of the towering fires. He seized his brother's arm and cried, "David—meet your Scarlett!"

Long a respecter of Myron's judgment, David took a careful look at Vivien Leigh. And it seemed to him that the handsome dark-haired girl might be just what he was searching for. He ran a screen test on Miss Leigh the following day, and before the week was out announced that he had cast her in the role of Scarlett O'Hara.

Some of the newspapers editorialized that with this question settled, perhaps the world could get down to serious business again. Others merely reported the signing of Vivien Leigh, though on the front page rather than back in the amusement section. And every medium of news wanted a statement from Margaret. She could only say she was glad an actress had been chosen for the part, adding praise for Miss Leigh's beauty and charm. There were letters to the papers; one man wrote from South Carolina to the *New York Times*, apparently in all seriousness, that employment of the English girl was "an insult to Southern womanhood." The Florida Daughters of the Confederacy condemned the selection of a non-Southerner for a Southern part, and urged a boycott of the production. At this, Russell Birdwell issued a blizzard of press releases, and officials of Loew's Inc., selling arm of MGM, gnawed their cigars in alarm. They were counting on heavy business in the South. Fortunately for them, Mrs. Walter D. Lamar, President-General of the entire UDC, endorsed the choice of Miss Leigh as "an excellent solution of the problem in which all the country has been keenly interested." The President-General added, "I have known many delightful English people, and have often been told by them that they consider the intonations and English of cultured Southern people more like that of the mother country than is found in any other section of the United States."

With Scarlett cast and Atlanta burned, the *Gone with the Wind* company settled down to production at Culver City. Meanwhile in Atlanta, Margaret had been working like a business woman on the book's many obligations, and the decisions that had to be made. On the second anniversary of publication, the papers reported that Macmillan's American edition alone had sold 1,690,000 copies, and the bookstores of the United States were still selling nearly a thousand copies a week. Foreign language sales stood close to one hundred and fifty thousand. Negotiations were progressing with French and Rumanian publishers; and Czechoslovakia, Latvia, and China had joined the list of countries in which a translation was on sale. Chinese publishers also pirated the book in English, and caused Margaret to shake her head in wonder by sending her a copy of their three-volume edition, which contained a foreword praising the author and stating that she was a good woman, "pure, filial, and obedient."

Other things happened that passed all belief. For example, a certain Professor Castiglione came to the United States from Italy, working the lecture circuit. He sent back an article to an Italian paper, which found its way to Margaret, with the tale that he had visited "a great editor in New York" who introduced him to a "quiet inconspicuous little woman" who turned out to be Margaret Mitchell, author of *Gone with the Wind*. The professor said he found it ironical to reflect that this woman had acquired "millions of dollars"—incalculably more than the earnings of the divine Dante. Since Margaret had never seen the professor, nor heard of him before she read this clipping, she was curious as to whether he had invented the tale, or was the victim of impostors. Neither George Brett nor Harold Latham could throw light on the matter, and it remained one of the many small mysteries of Margaret's fame.

Though compared unfavorably to Dante, Margaret had the satisfaction of contributing a copy of her book for deposit in the time capsule buried fifty feet deep in Flushing Meadows at the New York World's Fair, to be opened in the year 6939. Besides *Gone with the Wind*, the capsule contained magazines and newspapers, a *World Almanac*, the Lord's Prayer in 300 languages, newsreels of Franklin D. Roosevelt, a Miami fashion show, and a selection of articles in common use, including a telephone, a can opener, a woman's hat, a wristwatch, a package of cigarettes, and a slide rule. That was in the early fall; by the end of the year, American sales of *Gone with the Wind* were within less than a hundred thousand copies of two million.

The suit against the Dutch publishers was slowly proceeding at The Hague; she called this the case against ZHUM, a shortening of the company's name, which was Zuid-Hollandsche Uitgevers Maatschappij. Margaret found that she was paying lawyers and sub-agents all over the world; but hardly had time to reflect that this must be a tribute to some universal quality that had come out of the typewriter on Crescent Avenue. She said to a friend, "The book is my own creation, but it has long since gotten out of my hands."

Out of her hands in one way, the book was now under firm control so far as business matters went. Margaret, her brother, and her husband were functioning as managers with duties clearly divided among them. John was administrator and detail man; Stephens was corporation counsel; and, after consultation, Margaret made the final decisions like the chief executive officer of any company. She paid John ten per cent of her gross income for his services, with another ten per cent going to her brother. These payments were reasonable enough, for John worked a full day at the Power Company and was sometimes so tired at home that "he could hardly hold up his head." Often the three managers had to postpone business until after dinner at night, when the telephone was quiet and they could get time to think. "Our trouble was," said Margaret, "that we were constantly meeting problems the like of which we had never seen or heard of before."

Stephens Mitchell recorded that the problems of a typical night might be as follows:

—Someone is traveling around the country, giving readings in costume from *Gone with the Wind*. Is this an infringement? If so, what shall be done?

—A striptease dancer is doing an act called *Gone with the Wind*. Same questions.

—There is a song called *Gone with the Wind*. This time the answer is easy: titles cannot be copyrighted.

—A contract has been received for translation into Hindustani. What are the copyright laws of India? Must the translation be registered there? How can the royalties be spent, and through whom? Margaret is obligated to see that a statement as to the basic Macmillan copyright appears on the title page. She also wants clauses to insure accurate and *complete* translation. Reservations of stage, motion picture, radio and television rights must be inserted. Clauses for revocation of rights in certain cases must go in. Final questions: Is there an Indian lawyer who specializes in copyrights of translations? If so, how does one reach him and how much would he charge? Is it going to be possible to adjust and control these complicated matters by cable and mail?

—There is a request for permission to do a school pageant based on *Gone with the Wind*. The answer is simple—do not endanger rights by granting permission for any sort of unpaid performance or publication. This lesson has been taught by Dutch, Japanese, Chinese, and Latin American pirates.

—There is an impostor in New York, and another in Idaho, giving interviews and autographs as Margaret Mitchell. To whom does Margaret write? Can she bring legal pressure to bear? The decision is to tell as many interested people as possible that Margaret had been in neither place, and hope for the best.

It was hard to understand the impostors. There were so many of them—and yet only a few of this number appeared to be professional swindlers, or to profit from the masquerade. But Margaret found it distressing to hear that a woman habitually rode the club car of the Congressional Limited between Washington and New York, striking up acquaintance with men, accepting drinks, and proclaiming that she was Margaret Mitchell. Another impostor caused a disturbance at the Miami Airport, ordering officials to bring out an airplane immediately for a chartered flight to the Caribbean. This woman appeared to be drunk, which heightened the embarrassment, but also caused the airline people to have certain doubts, and telephoned Atlanta.

In Los Angeles, a fraudulent Margaret Mitchell called the managers of a fashionable store after closing hours, insisted that they open for a private showing, and took away $1700 worth of goods on credit. This was a professional job, but the Margaret Mitchells who appeared at book-stores—in Milwaukee, for example—and autographed copies of *Gone with the Wind* made nothing out of it. Preening their stolen feathers, impostors appeared in the same week at Coronado, California; Nashville, Tennessee; Beaufort, South Carolina; and Winston-Salem, North Carolina, while still another was in New England, writing intimate sentiments along with an autograph in copies of the book at department stores. Kenneth Roberts advised Margaret not to mind this; he said it had happened to him, and helped sales. But, to Margaret, the frauds were pathetic as well as exasperating. She disliked the thought that her fame had attracted so much attention among weak-minded women, and she deplored it when the pseudo-Margarets behaved with arrogance and ordered people around, for beyond all things she loathed rudeness.

Margaret found she was now able to shop in the Atlanta stores without attracting so much attention that it prevented her from making her purchases. She went to Regenstern's, for example, to get a new coat. Her only difficulty was with Mr. Baum, manager of the fur department, who waited on her in person and refused to sell her a cheap coat. "I wouldn't give it to you even if I had it, Mrs. Marsh," he said. "You're out of the rabbit class." And so Margaret settled for mink.

One aspect of fame continued to show itself in the mail. There was a class of letters in which the correspondent would demand that Margaret send something to be added to a collection. One person asked for a moustache-cup, another for a miniature pitcher. Another wanted a pencil, directing that Margaret should have one side planed down and write her name on the flat surface. This impudence was exceeded by a man who instructed her to copy a verse of the Rubáiyát of Omar Khayyam; he believed that the complete poem, with each verse copied by a celebrity, would have value. Some writers merely wished to insult Margaret: "Instead of writing books, you should get a job driving a garbage wagon," said one.

There was an abundance of old-fashioned cranks; one wrote at length describing himself as a "monetary ethicist" and asked help in spreading his doctrines. Another asked Margaret to help him plan a system whereby established authors would write novels containing advertisements spoken by the characters; he felt sure there was a fortune in "Bookvertising." Margaret reaped an astonishing crop of foolish questions: a man asked, "Will you please tell me, was Melanie a strong or weak character?" Another asked, "Do you have any special aim in life?" Some other questions were, "Did you have an imaginary companion as a child?" "How often do you write a book?" "Do you enjoy your work?" "Is the income of a writer sufficient?" "If all books except one were to be burnt, not counting the Bible, which one would you choose to keep?"

Sometimes, a shotgun blast of impertinent queries would arrive in the form of a questionnaire. It might be from a student, in high school, at college, or even in a graduate course. All too often Margaret gave time and strength to answering such things, merely because the senders were young and hopeful. She also took painstaking care to answer the questions of foreigners, explaining such matters as the etymology of "Dixie," or sending maps of Atlanta and directions as to how to find the principal sights of the city.

Of course, it was hard to draw the line. One might have no trouble deciding how to answer the brisk resident of Toledo, Ohio, who shipped in thirty copies of *Gone with the Wind* along with a list of his friends, and instructions for Margaret to "Write a personal sentiment to each one." But the begging letters were a different matter. Sometimes they contained the reproach "It would mean so little to you and so much to me," and Margaret could not help feeling a certain sympathy—though most of the letters asking for money appeared to be from professional beggars or people who had lost touch with reality. Such was the case of the man who asked for a grant of $15,000 on which to finish an epic poem of universal significance. He submitted samples of his work, which proved to be absolutely incomprehensible.

Margaret grew accustomed to strange things in the mail, and observed that some insane persons had beautiful, clear, and regular handwriting. Perhaps the most extraordinary of all her fan letters came from an Englishman who had an obsessive interest in women's clothes, especially underwear; he sent ten thousand words on the subject, and urged Margaret to write a novel about lingerie. This was queer enough, but the only letters originating in abnormal minds that disturbed Margaret were the occasional threats or obscenities that she had to turn over to Post Office inspectors or to the Federal Bureau of Investigation. In a way, this steady flood of personal mail from strangers was like having strange faces looking through the window: most of them were harmless, some even had an engaging quality, but here and there would be a gross and evil one.

Commencement Day of 1939 at Smith College saw Margaret receiving an honorary Master of Arts degree. In September, the Marshes made their last move in Atlanta, to the Della Manta apartment house at 1268 Piedmont Avenue. This was in the Ansley Park neighborhood which had developed into one of the most pleasant residential quarters since the time Eugene Mitchell built his Peachtree Street house. The Della Manta was more spacious than 4 East Seventeenth Street, and the Marshes' second-floor apartment had an extra bedroom which was turned into an office where Margaret labored with Miss Baugh over contracts, correspondence, and the schedule of engagements with visitors on various errands. At last Margaret was learning not to be at everyone's disposal all the time. A few months before the move, she had written to Harold Latham, "Recently I've had a visitation of European correspondents—Danish, German, English and, finally last week, a newspaperman from Athens, Greece. I have not seen any of them. No, I take it back! I *have* seen some of them but they are not aware of it. The German ones hung around the apartment like Grant around Richmond. They wore bright green suits and Swiss yodelers' hats and each one had two small Leica cameras suspended from his neck. As they did not know me from Adam's house cat, I enjoyed standing in front of the apartment watching their frenzies. I see no sense in being interviewed when nothing of news interest has happened to me for a long time."

Margaret hoped the news interest was centered more than two thousand miles away on the Selznick lot in Culver City, where Annie Laurie Kurtz and Susan Myrick wrote from time to time with gossip of the production. And Selznick himself wrote on occasion, always hoping to get Margaret to settle some question. One problem was, "How should we tie Mammy's bandanna?" Margaret answered, "I don't know, and I'm not going out on a limb over a headrag." Her Georgia friends asked no questions in giving her the news. They told her Mr. Selznick was on the set for every scene; he soon disagreed with George Cukor as to tone and style, and Cukor resigned. His replacement was Victor Fleming, a veteran of silent pictures. Fleming had been a Signal Corps cameraman in the First World War; getting into the movies early, he became a director, turning out one of the last important silent pictures, *The Way of All Flesh*, with the German star, Emil Jannings. In talking pictures his credits included *Test Pilot* and *Captains Courageous*. Though known as an action man, Fleming had also directed Judy Garland and Ray Bolger in *The Wizard of Oz*.

An atmosphere of importance and assured success developed as the production moved along. Distinguished travelers to Southern California visited the lot: Walter Lippmann came out, and on another occasion the glittering Broadway actress Ina Claire paid a visit. "They don't need to write a script," said Miss Claire. "All they need to do is hand the actors copies of the novel. It was perfect just the way Miss Mitchell wrote it down."

The grips, or stagehands, felt the atmosphere of happiness and success. They sometimes played jokes such as putting percussive caps under boards which were to be nailed down. A workman would hammer the board, the cap would explode, and the grips would yell, "Yankees is coming!" On April Fool's Day they victimized Clark Gable. He was supposed to lift Olivia de Havilland, as the ailing Melanie, and carry her to a couch. The stage crew sewed seventy pounds of lead weights into the skirts of her costume. "What have you done to her," the actor gasped, "nailed her to the ground?" The grips knew "Dutch" Gable was a good fellow, who would not throw a tantrum at a joke of this kind. Annie Laurie Kurtz wrote that he was a delightful man; she also spoke well of Eric Stacey, an assistant director with whom she and Susan Myrick worked in coaching Leslie Howard and Miss Leigh into some resemblance to Georgia speech as they theorized it sounded in the 1860s. Mrs. Kurtz and Susan Myrick sat near the director during shooting, ready to give emergency help whenever Leslie Howard would slap his forehead and cry, "Oh, dear! Have I said bean agane?" All the workers on the picture, from stars to stagehands, came under Mrs. Kurtz's kindly eye, and all aroused her interest in some way. She was much taken, for example, by the skill of Bill Durant, a property man whom the actors called Father Time because he was responsible for aging the Civil War uniforms. One of the wardrobe girls came to Mrs. Kurtz and asked her if she would send on to Atlanta a cushion cover she had sewed together from the scraps of Scarlett's costumes because she "thought Miss Mitchell might like to have it." The gift from the studio worker gave Margaret as much pleasure as anything that came from the production. She also took delight from such items in Mrs. Kurtz's letters as the information that the spirited gray horse Thomas Mitchell rode in his portrayal of Gerald O'Hara was none other than Silver of the Lone Ranger serial.

John Marsh said Margaret wanted to live in peace with all the world, but she could "land on people" who invaded her rights or tried to take advantage of her. In fact, she did very little "landing," especially in view of the many provocations that came to her. Margaret's policy in human contacts was always to try for formal good relations at the start, and to encourage the development of dependable friendship. From the beginning of her dealings with Macmillan she had maintained formally cordial relations with George Brett, leaving it to Stephens Mitchell and John to state the differences of opinion. On her first visit to the Macmillan offices after publication, Margaret personally thanked each member of the organization for his or her contribution to the book's success. But Margaret seems to have kept the business relationship with Macmillan always uppermost in mind. Now Margaret had a new set of difficulties; Loew's Inc. was beseeching her to appear in the trailer-film advertising *Gone with the Wind*, and the Selznick organization was urging her to agree. Margaret said it appeared to her they should be advertising their picture rather than the author of the novel; of course she would no more have appeared in a movie trailer, in front of a hoked-up white column and honeysuckle setting, than she would have stood on her head at the Five Points in downtown Atlanta. Margaret wrote to Selznick, Birdwell, Katharine Brown; their answers, she said, were always on the order of "We understand perfectly now. We are sorry we did not understand before. You can count on us to respect your desire to avoid personal publicity." And then in a few days or weeks "the same old trouble"—as Margaret put it—would come up again. At last she wrote Selznick's office a letter with an indented paragraph:

I don't want personal publicity; I don't want publicity of any kind in connection with the movie except *necessary* mentions of me as author of the book; I mean this, I am not being coy, and I am tired of writing letters about it. If you occasionally say "by Margaret Mitchell" in referring to my book, and make no other mention of me in your publicity, that is what would please me most.

The publicity had a good side—it was a harbinger that the picture was nearing completion. David Selznick was editing film throughout the autumn of 1939; from time to time he would emerge from his cutting room and re-photograph a scene. While this went on, the press department issued statistics to prove the picture Selznick was about to finish the mightiest epic of the all. They announced that 4000 people had worked on it; later they increased that figure to 9000. Merely to take care of the animals in the picture—including one Jonesboro pig—took the full time of 160 people, so the press agents said. One million feet of lumber went into the sets; the property men pulverized twenty tons of red bricks to simulate the red dust of Georgia; and so on. Without question, Selznick had made the most expensive picture up to that date, spending just under $4,000,000—which, as they say in Los Angeles today, "was real money at the time." He also made the longest picture to be presented in theaters; the Technicolor film lasted four hours, including a fifteen-minute break. Historians say Erich von Stroheim's silent picture *Greed,* as photographed, would have run more than seven hours, but it was cut to less than four for theatrical release. And so *Gone with the Wind* earned a number of superlatives even before it was shown to the public. To Margaret, the cost and length of the picture meant little. But she welcomed the announcement, when it came at last, that the moving picture version of *Gone with the Wind* would have its world première in Atlanta on December 15, 1939. For more than three years she had been waiting for that day, which she hoped would be a day of deliverance.

XI

House in Order

Her performance at the opening night of *Gone with the Wind* showed Margaret had acquired skill in the art of being a celebrity. This was a way of life, in which one played an obligatory public role like a politician. On that analogy, the success of the picture was a national election that swept Margaret into an office from which she could not resign: by February of 1940, the film had played to 10,000,000 ticket buyers; by June, when its first run concluded, an audience totalling 25,000,000 had seen the show, and all at advanced prices.

Like the novel it followed so faithfully, the picture moved from a panorama of history with many characters and considerable physical action down to the confrontation of two people in an unhappy love affair. Clark Gable and Vivien Leigh gave highly satisfying performances as the lovers, and Hattie McDaniel brought Scarlett's Mammy to life in a superb feat of acting. The picture moved Margaret, for it was indeed, as Clifford Dowdey said, an illustrated edition of the novel. But some of the illustrations were out of key: Margaret said in private, for example, that the screen version of Tara was much too grand a house for the one she had described. The real Tara as it existed in Margaret's mind had been a rough sort of manor house built with slave labor by an Irish immigrant, resulting in a style that Margaret said might be called "upcountry functional." She wrote to Virginius Dabney, editor of the *Richmond News Leader,* that "In the pages of unwritten history, no fiercer fight was ever fought than the one centering around the columns of the motion picture 'Tara.' The Georgians present at the making of the film, Susan Myrick and Mr. and Mrs. Wilbur Kurtz, of Atlanta, weren't able to keep columns off of 'Tara' entirely, but they managed to compromise by having the pillars square, as were those of our upcountry houses in that day, if they had columns at all."

Still, the Selznick Tara was the essence of authenticity compared to the screen Twelve Oaks, seat of the Wilkes family. Margaret said she "rolled on the floor screaming with laughter" when she first saw studio photographs of the Twelve Oaks set, and could think of nothing to compare it with except the State Capitol at Montgomery, Alabama. She went on, to Mr. Dabney, "I believe we Southerners could write the truth about the ante-bellum South, its few slaveholders, its yeoman farmers, the rambling, comfortable houses just fifty years away from log cabins, until Gabriel blows his trump—and everyone would go on believing the Hollywood version. The sad part is that many Southerners believe this myth even more ardently than the Northerners. A number of years ago some of us organized a club, The Association of Southerners Whose Grandpappies Did Not Live in Houses With White Columns ... Its membership would be enormous if all the eligibles came in. Since my novel was published, I have been embarrassed on many occasions by finding myself included among writers who pictured the South as a land of white-columned mansions whose wealthy owners had thousands of slaves and drank thousands of juleps. I have been surprised, for North Georgia certainly was no such country—if it ever existed anywhere—and I took great pains to describe North Georgia as it was. But people believe what they like to believe and the mythical Old South has too strong a hold on their imaginations to be altered by the mere reading of a 1037-page book."

The romantic license taken by the producer did not handicap the film at the distribution of awards by the Motion Picture Academy, generally known as "Oscars." On March 1 of 1940 the front pages announced that *Gone with the Wind* and its makers and actors had won ten awards: first, the entire production was Best Picture of 1939; then came Oscars for Vivien Leigh, best actress of the year; Hattie McDaniel, best supporting actress; Victor Fleming, for direction; Sidney Howard, for the screenplay; awards to the technicians for art direction, film editing and color photography; a special plaque to William Cameron Menzies for "outstanding achievement in the use of color for the introduction of the dramatic mood"; and the Irving Thalberg Memorial Award for distinguished work as a producer to David O. Selznick. The picture also won many critics' awards, exhibitors' polls, and so on; and the National Association for the Advancement of Colored People presented Hattie McDaniel with a statuette in recognition of her achievement.

By the time the newspapers announced the Academy Awards, Margaret had accepted the sad realization that the appearance of the picture, rather than easing her work load, had increased it. While closing the contracts for the Bulgarian translation, she observed that the mail was heavier than ever, and that the rumor crop was especially luxuriant. She read that Selznick had been willing to pay $250,000 for film rights, but that she had leaped at an opening bid of $50,000, to the discomfiture of Stephens Mitchell, who had planned to hold out for $100,000. Over and over Margaret explained in conversation and in letters that she was satisfied with $50,000 (at that time the highest price ever paid for a first novel), the offer an agent obtained for her some time before the final agreements were signed; that what had concerned her most were the terms of the contract, and that she had insisted on having many of them rewritten before she signed. Yet rumor persisted that David Selznick had taken advantage of Margaret "before the book was a success." The facts wee that it had enjoyed a tremendous advance sale and was a Book-of-the-Month selection, at the time Margaret agreed to let Selznick buy it. One can understand why Margaret would want this known. She objected to being pictured as an odd little thing who did not realize the value of her work.

The summer of 1940 came on, and Margaret heard or read other rumors: she had lived in Glasgow as a girl; she had been a file clerk in an Atlanta insurance office, writing *Gone with the Wind* on company time; before the novel came out, she had canvassed Atlanta bookstores and begged them to order three copies each; she had dyed her hair black as a disguise; Louis B. Mayer of MGM had sent her a blank check, to be filled in with any amount she wanted, for a sequel to her story; she was putting in every moment writing another novel; she did not live in Atlanta at all, but was hiding on a mink farm in Alaska; she had an advanced case of claustrophobia; she had made all the Margaret Mitchell autographs in existence with a rubber stamp; she had appeared here, there and everywhere under the influence of liquor; and, in some ways the most irritating of all, the actual Tara was the old Fitzgerald place near Jonesboro, now occupied by one of Margaret's uncles. Edwin Granberry had said, "To find that there was not and never had been a Tara is like the sadness for the vanished scenes of a dream." Not everyone was willing to accept this sadness, and it appeared that the uncle was willing to assuage it by showing off the Jonesboro house as Tara and telling visitors he was Scarlett O'Hara's son. And Alex Stephens was not the only resident of Jonesboro who showed a Tara to strangers. A filling-station attendant once directed Margaret herself to Tara, and when she told him there was no such place, and she could speak with authority because she had written *Gone with the Wind*, he simply refused to believe she was the author. Jonesboro was proud to be the scene of a world-famous book; before long, its movie house was named The Tara Theater. In spite of Margaret's efforts to keep the record straight, eventually the old road in front of the Fitzgerald house—

formerly Bumblehook Road or Hebron Church Road—was renamed Tara Road.

Rumors and the denials of false Taras were only a small portion of a day's work. There was an extraordinary number of suggestions for commercial tie-ins with the book. Mercifully, after July 1937, Loew's Inc. became responsible for commercial schemes involving the movie, and from that date on, Margaret was able to refer the proposals to New York. As one might suppose, doll-makers were prominent among those in whose heads there danced visions of prosperity upon reading *Gone with the Wind*. One woman made sample dolls representing twenty-five characters in the book. A man in New Orleans offered a royalty of one per cent per doll sold. Others thought the characters would make excellent pin cushions; from the garment district of New York came a bid for children's masquerade outfits based on the clothes supposedly worn by Scarlett, Mammy and Rhett—this company having a license from Walt Disney to make Snow White and the Seven Dwarfs costumes; The Loom Tex Corporation of New York wanted to name a knitted rayon pantie "The Scarlett O'Hara"; makers of scarves, handkerchiefs, dress goods, costume jewelry, charms, cosmetics, boxes and figurines were constantly asking Mrs. Marsh to license their products. Several parlor-game promoters got the notion that *Gone with the Wind* would make a basis for one of their Parchesi-like diversions. This struck Margaret as an impractical idea. Nor did she take any interest in plans to endorse a fountain pen, and a mechanical pencil. It was not that Margaret looked down on advertising—it was her husband's business; she merely felt there was nothing about her book that justified commercial adaptation, and nothing in her own life and personality that would add glamor to an endorsement.

Unsolicited endorsements of Margaret's book, however, continued to come from the highest quarters. Visiting the United States, H. G. Wells remarked, "One hardly dares say it, but I believe *Gone with the Wind* is better *shaped* than many of the revered classics." That must have impressed Margaret, for Mr. Wells had outlined all human history in one book.

In spite of her daily chores she managed by November 1940 to get time off for a trip to Richmond, and to John Marsh's home town of Maysville, Kentucky. Writing to Lois Cole she told of visiting the battlefields around Richmond with Clifford Dowdey as guide. On another day "Douglas Southall Freeman had us out to lunch and there we met Mr. and Mrs. James Branch Cabell, and it was all I could do to keep from falling into a swoon. Miss Ellen Glasgow, who is in bed after a heart attack, let me come over to see her, and I never had such fun.* Not knowing Miss Glasgow had been ill, I phoned her house and spoke with a Miss Bennett. When I asked for an engagement I was told that Miss Glasgow would be glad to see me, but of course I knew she had been ill in bed for some time. I did not know and I was embarrassed that I had intruded. I said that I would stay only fifteen minutes. Thereafter, everyone in Richmond told me how ill she had been following several heart attacks. Miss Bennett told me the doctors let her up a few minutes every day and that she works a little then. But she is so full of energy and so anxious to finish the book she is writing that she does not relax and lies there with her motor going full tilt until she can get up and work another fifteen minutes ... When I went to see her, I discovered to my horror that I had stayed over an hour. But I was having a wonderful time and she was talking away as if she were enjoying the visit and I just forgot to go home.

* These people were notable throughout the country as well as in Richmond and the South. Ellen Glasgow was famous for her impeccably finished regional novels, and had been one of the first well-known writers to praise *Gone with the Wind*. Dr. Freeman, scholarly editor of the Richmond *Times-Dispatch*, had astonished Margaret by offering her membership in the Society of American Historians; at the time of her visit, he was engaged in the prodigious labors that resulted in monumental biographies of Washington and Lee. James Branch Cabell had been an author of national renown since the appearance of *Jurgen* in the 1920s.

"She looked so well and was so pretty and full of pep that you would never have known she was ill except for the fact that she was in bed and the pillows were quite flat. If I had not been told that she was ill, I would have thought her a very pretty and witty Southern lady who was taking her afternoon rest. I cannot tell you how much the visit meant to me."

After these visits with eminent literary people in Richmond, the Marshes went on to Maysville, and Margaret reported that although John had not been there for twenty years, "Not only Maysville but all of Mason County turned out, it seemed, and we had a marvelous if exhausting time, for company began arriving at breakfast and did not stop till midnight. We went to Lexington on a little one-car train which was heated by a coal stove. We stopped at every wide place in the road and at some of the stops both old friends of John's and perfect strangers came aboard. The telegraph operators up and down the line had been gossiping with the Maysville operator and they spread the news. After hanging over the back platform for three and a half hours, I did not know whether I felt more like a fugitive from justice or Mrs. Roosevelt. At one stop, just as the train was pulling out, a girl dashed frantically out of a house and jumped on the platform, crying breathlessly, 'Is Clark Gable really darling?' I assumed as rapturous an expression as I could under the circumstances and said, 'He's simply divine. Get off the train before you break your neck.' She said, hoping for the worst, 'Is it true he's in love with his wife?' I assumed an expression of complete dejection and said, 'My dear, I never saw a more devoted couple.' 'Oh, my God,' said the young lady, and fell off backwards. It didn't hurt her, and she waved good-bye from a pile of frost-covered rocks."

By that fall of 1940, Americans had begun to feel that this country might not be able to stay out of the European war which had started when Hitler attacked Poland the previous September. By now the British army had left the Continent, and Italy had attacked Greece. As they watched the tragic events in Europe, many American college boys did not have the uncomplicated reaction of those

237

in Margaret's generation, some of whom had gone to Canada to enlist in the First World War for fear the fighting would be over before this country was involved. A youth of the modern generation, a friend of Margaret's, wrote her that in his opinion he and his college mates "had been cruelly cut away from the faith of our fathers by solid facts ... We have found it hard to look ahead to any good world for ourselves. We have cried out for security, have yearned for it more than any other blessing. And we have been constantly warned that, of all things, security was the one we were least likely to find." The young man went on to say that he thought this a bad state of affairs.

Margaret's reply is a careful statement of her philosophy of life. It is also interesting because after writing it, she did not mail it. But immediately after reading the young man's complaint, she wrote, "I arise to ask, in a loud, hoarse voice, 'Who the hell ever promised you and your generation security? And, most important of all, why should any youth want security? Let the old and the tired, who have fought the good fight and run the race, think of security, not the young.'

"What bothers me about some of the young is that, to the best of my knowledge, they are the first younger generation I ever heard about who not only yearn for security but confidently expected it as their lawful right and were bitter and disgruntled when it was not handed to them on a silver platter. There is something very frightening about the young people of a nation crying out to be secure. Youth has been, in the past, thrusting and willing and able to take chances. If the youth of today wants to be safe and secure and leave to the older people the tough job of fighting the fights and taking the hazards, then we are all in a bad way.

"My family is very long-lived and I can remember that when I was a little girl I had the privilege of listening to a relative who was in the Forty-nine gold rush, and he remembered very clearly talking to his older relatives who had gone through the Revolutionary War, the War of 1812 and the Seminole Indian troubles. I know a great deal about my own family, and my friends here in the South are just as well informed about the doings of their long dead people and the attitude of those people. I do not recall a single instance where any of these old timers ever expected security or even thought they might attain it. In fact, I am sure they would have given you a bewildered look if you had discussed the matter with them, and they would have been as angry as if you had accused them of the rankest cowardice. Certainly the youngsters who went out with Washington weren't promised anything but the privilege of freezing or dying in the British prison ships. And their children who came after them, when the currency of these United States 'wasn't worth a continental' expected nothing except the opportunity to work like hell and not get anywhere. Those who came along in the 1812 time, with our ports blockaded and workmen dying of starvation, did not look for security or expect it. When Andy Jackson wrecked the banks and there were no Federal Reserve System or insured bank deposits, I don't believe these young people sat around being bitter about an insecure world. I know my kinfolks didn't. Certainly the people who went into South Georgia and North Florida and Alabama to build their homes when the Seminoles were taking scalps, would not have gone there had they expected security. All they wanted was a halfway chance to scalp Seminoles. As for what young people faced in the South after Appomattox, not even half of the horrors have been told. There was no money, no opportunity, and hardly as much hope as the Belgians under Hitler now have. I personally knew that generation very well. They were a tough and hard-bitten lot; they knew there was no safety anywhere in the world; I doubt if it ever occurred to them that they merited security; they knew that the race was not to the swift nor the battle to the strong; they knew they could break their backs working and give their lives to rebuild their section and yet in the end lose everything, even their lives. But the ones I knew certainly enjoyed scrapping, and they rebuilt our section with no more security than their own guts to build it on. We now come to the next generation, which was my mother's—well, I think she would have laughed if you had talked about security for youth, for she married in the panic of the mid-nineties, in times more bitter than the present depression, and she brought up her children through the successive panics of 1907 and 1914. I myself saw the 1914 one and the hard times of 1920. Perhaps the North didn't have that 1920 panic, but I remember it very vividly.

"Now that I come to my own age and generation, I am on very firm ground. Even if someone had been silly enough to talk to us about security or to tell us that we merited it, we would not have been silly enough to believe them. Furthermore, we would have been furious because doubts would have been cast upon our courage and our capabilities. I recall that the worst insult which could be flung at my generation was, 'Oh, so you want it safe.' We didn't want it safe. Most of us fought against safety. Even the girls who came from sheltered homes wanted to get out and take their chances, and most of them did. The ones who didn't were looked upon as weaklings. You spoke of seeing your father's world come tumbling down. Well, we certainly saw the world crash, and, except for the Restoration Period in England, I cannot think of a similar world, for we saw the Victorian Age crash about our feet. And, far from feeling disgruntled or bitter that life was not going to be what we might have expected, we were pleased to death, for here was something new, a land without landmarks, a country to be pioneered—spiritually, at least.

"So that brings us down to your generation. You aren't the only boy who has spoken to me as you have written, but you are far above most of them because you are thinking your way through this matter. Ever since the New Deal came into being the young ones have been told that they are God's chosen creatures, that the world not only owes them a living but a good living and an awfully good time. Granted that your generation has been told this, why on earth have you believed it? Surely, your generation can't be so foolish as to swallow all this whole and then feel that you have the right to be bitter and frustrated when things don't work out as promised. Surely, common sense and the experience of your elders and the perspective of history and the knowledge of human nature should have made you realize that these things were untrue and unenforceable.

"People like my husband and me will not often say or write the things I have written. It's just too much trouble and we generally feel that the young persons we are talking to will not comprehend what we are saying or, having comprehended, will say indignantly that we are Tories standing in the way of the more abundant life. But these are the things we think ... We are alarmed at seeing a generation of young people, who should be full of courage and daring, having the mental attitudes of the old and the tired and the bitter who want nothing more than a warm chimney corner and a sense of security.

"Probably by now you have forgotten what you wrote in your letter and will wonder at the length of my reply to one small item you wrote, but I had it in mind and I like you, so I had to write it. Come to see John and me when you are in Atlanta next. We will make a large pot of coffee and talk till dawn if you like."

She had many things on her mind, and during this same autumn of 1941, found herself writing thousands of words to the New York offices of MGM in an effort to protect her ownership of the stage rights in *Gone with the Wind*. The difficulty arose when MGM, through Loew's Inc., announced a "second première" of the moving picture in Atlanta for December 1940, for the benefit of British War Relief. Margaret got a laugh from the phrase "second première" but otherwise the business was all migraine. In writing to Lois Cole, Margaret summed it up: "I will not undertake to give you all the horrors of this situation, but for two weeks we have had a terrible time with the Metro-Goldwyn-Mayer people. They had never even told me the date of the 'première' or consulted me in any manner, and then, without warning, they announced that Vivien Leigh and Hattie McDaniel would appear on the stage and do the corset lacing scene. It so happens that I own the dramatic rights and they should know it. Of course I could have sued the hell out of them, and I would have done it except for the unfortunate and innocent ladies of the Atlanta British Relief Unit. I gave, without charge, this portion of my dramatic rights for the benefit of the British, and asked only that Metro-Goldwyn-Mayer and Selznick guarantee me copyright and copyright protection ... Finally, the whole thing blew up. The reason for this was that Hattie McDaniel could not get away from the picture she was in. A wire sent to Hattie three weeks before would have revealed this but it had not occurred to any of these screwballs to send such a wire ... These movie people are crazy."

At the height of the "second première" turmoil The Macmillan Company announced they had sold 2,868,200 copies of the book, a total not including foreign editions. Arriving at this sale after two and a half years convinced Margaret she was indeed a public figure, which was further confirmed by the invitation to christen a new cruiser which was to be called *Atlanta* after two earlier fighting ships. There were several postponements of the launching date, but it was set at last for September 6, 1941, and Margaret left Atlanta on the previous day bound for Kearny, New Jersey. Before leaving she told reporters how she planned to handle the champagne bottle. "I am going to hold it low," she said, "and sort of bunt it against the side, and if it explodes it will splash on Jesse Draper [an Atlanta naval officer] who will be standing nearby resplendent in a white uniform." In New York before the launching, Margaret faced the metropolitan press corps in a large conference. The *Constitution* wrote that she was "dauntless, composed, and scintillating" for sixty minutes before this critical audience. Later that day she christened the ship with style. Afterward the reporters asked what she thought of as she swung the bottle of wine. "I was thinking, what if I miss it?" Margaret answered. "And then I thought what if I hit it and it doesn't move, and the admiral has to push!—Or suppose I hit it and rip a hole in it and I'm arrested for sabotage. Seriously, it simply was tremendous to feel the ship begin to live." As always, the reporters asked what plans she might have for further writing. Margaret would give varying answers to such questions. This time she said, "I'd rather pick cotton than write. But all I need is opportunity."

Back in Atlanta, Margaret found among the many letters waiting for her a note from a young man who said he was in trouble with his girl for comparing her to Scarlett O'Hara. Margaret's painstaking answer was typical of her behavior toward anyone she thought she could help. "You have set me a difficult problem, when you asked me to help soothe the injured feelings of your Southern girl friend whom you compared with Scarlett O'Hara. The reason the problem is so difficult is that I can understand her feelings perfectly and sympathize with her. Not long ago when I was in New York a newspaper reporter, with the best intentions in the world, asked me if I had modelled Scarlett after myself. I must admit to a sense of indignation and insult and I said before I thought, 'But Scarlett was a trollop, and I am not one.'

"I am glad you liked Scarlett and thought she was 'a determined and exciting girl.' I thank you for writing and telling me this. But, to me, she was a far from admirable character, so I can understand your girl friend's reactions.

"But now, let's see what we can do about straightening out your problem. Here are some of the things other people have written and said about Miss O'Hara. They have said that, selfish as she was, she had the invincible courage that is part of the Southern heritage. They have written that she took care of her own, both black and white, even if she had to go hungry herself. And this, too, is a very fine Southern trait, which I think we must inherit from the old Scottish clan spirit, for most of us in this section have Scottish blood. Others have written that she had charm plus, where men were concerned. Still others liked her for the reason you mentioned, that she had the determination to see things through to the finish, a trait rare in any era.

"I do not know if the foregoing will be helpful to you but I hope it will. If worst comes to worst, why not say that your girl friend reminded you of Scarlett because she looked like Vivien Leigh? Goodness knows, Vivien Leigh is one of the most devastatingly attractive women I ever had the pleasure of meeting. Good luck!"

Other matters were not so easy to handle; one in particular gave Margaret much concern. This was the suggestion by David Selznick that Margaret allow him to produce a musical version of *Gone with the Wind* for the Broadway stage. Margaret had no doubt that Selznick could do this well; but the negotiations coiled round and round, growing more complicated by the day and week. Among other things, the producer suggested a nationwide talent hunt for new faces and voices. At last, just before Christmas 1941, Margaret asked John to write Katharine Brown and bring the Broadway-musical project to an end. John asked Miss Brown to give Selznick Margaret's thanks for his interest, but to "tell him that Peggy just doesn't feel like making the trade on the basis he has proposed. What you said about a talent search wasn't the only reason for the rejection of the offer but it was one reason, and I am going to make one more effort to explain our position. Apparently we did not succeed in doing that before, judging by your statement that you understood Peggy's objection was only to a talent search in Atlanta.

"No amount of money would ever induce Peggy to go through another experience like the one she was subjected to by the talent search for the movie. It was a fine buildup for the movie, it got publicity for the movie which you might not have gotten otherwise, but it was hell on earth for Peggy. I doubt that Mr. Selznick has ever gotten the faintest conception of what it did to Peggy ... Your idea that Peggy might escape a similar experience simply by not having a talent search *in Atlanta* disregards the fact that the United States mails and the telegraph and telephone lines are still operating. Even if there were no publicity about the search in Atlanta at all, Peggy would still have to deal with a swarm of pitifully unqualified humans demanding her assistance in obtaining roles in the show.

"It is the fact that a talent search stirs up the pitifully unqualified—and is intended to do so—that makes it offensive and distasteful and a burden to her ... It also uses up innumerable hours of time, and time is the only working capital of an author, by still further postponing the time she can begin writing again, as she ardently wishes to do."

John's saying that Margaret wanted to get writing again was significant. Amid her humorous exaggerations about the hard labor of writing, and her references to herself as "a lucky amateur," she would also say "writing is my trade"—to Governor Ellis Arnall when he asked her to serve on the state board of education—or "I have been writing since I was five and a half years old, and until I got so busy cleaning up after *Gone with the Wind*, I always had something going."

But now two catastrophes intervened to keep Margaret from her writing table in the time she could take from administering the worldwide business of her novel. One was the universal tragedy, the war. The other trouble was personal—Eugene Mitchell had returned to the hospital, with a variety of serious ailments, and needed Margaret's attention every day. Mr. Mitchell came of a generation that could call on a seemingly bottomless pool of colored labor; and he did not understand that there was no longer an unlimited supply of Negro hospital workers, in particular the orderlies whose services he needed twenty-four hours a day. There were better-paying jobs in the war industries, to say nothing of the army. Yet Mr. Mitchell could be so demanding that his orderlies would quit, and Margaret would tear her hair. "Even at death's door," she said, "Father is just as easy to handle as a wildcat in his prime. He does not like hospitals, to put it mildly, and resents the ministrations of nurses. Two months ago he reached the point where he would not even take an aspirin unless I administered it. And I suspect this was done only to harass the nurses and put the doctors in their places."

Caring for Mr. Mitchell and finding orderlies and nurses in wartime Atlanta took hours of Margaret's day. In the rest of the time, she served as a member of the Red Cross, a worker in the Civilian Defense, as a war bond salesman, and as a hostess, seamstress, and letter writer for American and Allied service men. Sometimes she would invite a soldier or sailor for a meal at the apartment or the Piedmont Driving Club.

One young soldier who came to supper brought his guitar, which he called Betsey, and played and sang for the Marshes. Later they got word the boy was on orders to go overseas, and somehow higher authority ordered him to leave Betsey at home. Margaret pulled wires, the guitar followed the young man by special shipment, and in a couple of months a postcard arrived to tell them that Betsey was going through Italy with the soldier and his outfit. On another occasion, Margaret heard that P.X. officials at a certain place in the Pacific had refused to stock snuff and chewing tobacco, though Southern marine enlisted men had requested they do so. Knowing the rural South, Margaret knew these materials were as necessary as food to the men; she took direct action, shipping a generous supply directly to the marine battalion.

The correspondence with men overseas grew to large proportions. Some of the soldiers who wrote to Margaret, and received her prompt, cheerful answers, were old Atlanta and Georgia friends. Others had introduced themselves by mail because of their admiration for *Gone with the Wind*. Sometimes when a man went on patrol or on flight over enemy territory, and did not come back, the others would find a letter from Margaret in his store of personal effects. Her willingness to write became sufficiently well known to cause the GI artist Bill Mauldin to draw the well-known cartoon which showed his familiar exhausted and dirty combat soldier licking a pencil and writing to "Dear Miss Mitchell." Margaret wrote to Mauldin that the appearance of this cartoon had "raised her stock to extravagant heights."

It has been asked why Margaret did not employ secretaries to answer letters in her name. The reason is simple: as a lady—especially as a Southern lady—Margaret had an ingrained reaction to any personal letter, which was that it demanded a personal reply. Obviously, the time and effort that went into millions of words in answer to thousands of letters was subtracted from the time and strength that might have gone into writing more novels. Coupled with the demands of her invalid father, it may have been the prime reason why she wrote no more. It was certainly one of the main reasons why Margaret had not proceeded with the plans she was known to have when suddenly all plans were ended.

Margaret's ability to charm men became evident when an Army show and demonstration unit camped in Piedmont Park near the Marsh apartment. The Red Cross set up a canteen for this outfit, and groups of ladies went there to help soldiers keep their gear in order by mending uniforms, sewing on new chevrons, reattaching buttons and reknitting gloves. They also would chat with the men while they worked. When Margaret was in the work party, there would always be a crowd of young soldiers around her chair, sitting on the floor, or against the wall, laughing and rallying with her, or listening quietly while she told a story. One day Margaret returned to the canteen after a trip to New York where she had seen her friends Alfred Lunt and Lynn Fontanne in a new play, *The Pirate*. She wrote to the Lunts, "I was appropriated and taken into a quiet corner by a half-dozen who had New York connections with broadcasting companies, the theater and the music world. They said they had heard I had just returned from New York and they were so homesick they wanted to hear anything I had to tell. When I told that I had seen *The Pirate* they took the sewing out of my hands and gave it to another worker in the vineyard and kept me talking for an hour. So I told them everything I could think of—the gorgeous flounces of Miss Fontanne's petticoats when she took off her dress and the way she held her head in the hypnotism scene and the delightful yet heart-tugging quality of Mr. Lunt who can poise so delicately between romance and rueful laughter. I was so glad I had a photographic memory, for these homesick New Yorkers turned my mind inside out about you both and the play. They said they'd never see it but it felt like home to hear about you . . ."

During the war Margaret overcame her fear of public speaking, though she continued to dislike it. She would appear as speaker for the Red Cross or at bond sales; and she would attend fund-raising parties where the noise, according to her report, equalled that at the fall of Atlanta.

In her Red Cross uniform, with the cap tilted at a becoming angle, Margaret sold war bonds to a great number of adults, and savings stamps to a multitude of children. Her account of the business was graphic: "If anyone had told me a year ago that I'd be gallumphing about the countryside making speeches and selling bonds, I would have fallen on my rear screaming with laughter and kicking my heels up. But, oddly enough, war brings out the best and the worst in one (take your choice, dearie), and that's what I've been doing. The other day Rich's department store busted loose with a full-page ad announcing that I'd be selling bonds in their booth and would *not* give autographs. By now I'm convinced that no one ever reads anything aright. Shoals of people decided I was going to autograph, and so we had quite a crowd—$212,000 in four hours. Many mothers brought their two-year-olds to buy their first 10¢ stamp, and held the babies up to the counter to lick the stamps I was holding. Abjured to 'Now lick, sugar,' they enthusiastically and obediently licked me on my cheeks. Several infants reached delightedly for the stamps and swallowed them. I was kept busy running my hands into infant throats and retrieving stamps. One little boy licked, and pasted the stamp on my hand. God knows how many children I kissed. I had started out in high-heeled slippers, but seeing that it was not a sit-down job, telephoned Margaret Baugh to bring my oldest and largest shoes. This she did, arriving with all the celerity of the marine corps, but by that time the crowd was so thick I couldn't change. Fifty or sixty comfortable matrons were loafing about determined to see whether I was going to pull off my shoes then and there."

A war bond speaking engagement before the inmates of the Atlanta federal penitentiary brought a new interest. In order to encourage the editors and contributors of the prison magazine, Margaret established an annual cash prize for the best essay or story by a prisoner. Though sympathetic to these men, many of whom had gotten into trouble because of theft, she could still make it hot for anyone who helped himself to her literary property. Such an offender was Al Capp, the cartoonist whose grotesque

"Li'l Abner" was popular with many newspaper readers. When Capp infringed on *Gone with the Wind* he got a shock from the same high-voltage legal battery that had galvanized Billy Rose. To straighten things out, Mr. Capp found he had to publish an apology, and transfer to Margaret Mitchell the copyrights in the cartoons in which he had used her characters without her consent.

At about the same time in 1942, something pleasant happened in connection with the exploitation of *Gone with the Wind;* Selznick and J. H. Whitney, liquidating Selznick International Pictures with profit to all concerned, decided to send Margaret a token of esteem in the form of a check for $50,000. Acknowledging the check, Margaret wrote to Messrs. Whitney and Selznick that she had come home tired, and found their envelope "on the bottom of the pile." At the sight of their appreciative letter and their check, Margaret said, "weariness left me." She added that the gesture raised her spirits immeasurably, but at the same time almost made her cry; and that she planned to devote a large part of the money to defense bonds and assistance for the Red Cross and the United Service Organizations.

The war made it impossible for Margaret and her associates to keep track of a great deal of the foreign business. Publishers were liquidated where the Germans or Russians came in; but this did not mean the book lacked readers or influence. Jean-Paul Sartre reported that at first the occupying Germans allowed the French to circulate and read the book, thinking it would make them hate the Yankees whom the Nazis equated with the contemporary United States. Then the invaders realized Margaret's story glorified a conquered but resisting, never-really-surrendering people, and they forbade further publication and confiscated all copies they could find. Members of the first American force to reach Lyons, in southern France, told Margaret that tattered copies of her book, read almost to pieces, were selling on the black market for 3500 to 4000 francs. The Russian state publishing house did not bring out *Gone with the Wind;* and the Soviets forbade reading of the book in all territories they conquered in World War II.

For a long time Margaret had endured pain in her back which doctors told her came from the spinal injuries she had sustained in her riding accidents as a girl, and in the automobile collision of 1935. In March 1943 Margaret went to the hospital of the medical school at Johns Hopkins University in Baltimore for an operation on her spine. Four weeks later she was back in Atlanta, not at all certain that the surgery would result in permanent relief. Margaret had tried it as a last resort; she confided to a friend, "I have been in pain so many years that I am willing to do anything to get well." Two months later she reported that "leaning over was bad," and that she understood from the doctors that "it might take two years for my back to get right." As soon as she was on her feet, however, she returned to the war bond speeches, the Red Cross and Civilian Defense work, and the correspondence with soldiers and sailors.

By September, Eugene Mitchell was so weak that Margaret had to lean over his hospital bed and put her ear close to his lips to understand what he was saying. But he clung to life with characteristic determination. The nursing problem grew acute. "As fast as we find a nurse," Margaret said, "she marries a soldier. We are running a matrimonial agency." At this time Margaret was sad because of the recent death of a good friend, Professor William Lyon Phelps. She wrote that "It is hard to believe that there will be no more undecipherable messages coming from Augusta announcing his arrival in Atlanta. We were always happy to have these cards covered with his large scrawl, but we once met three trains for we were unable to figure out from his writing when he would arrive."

The long watch over Eugene Mitchell ended when he died, early in the morning of June 17, 1944. Looking back over his life, the newspapers added up his contributions to Atlanta as a lawyer, a patron of the library and the historical society, and as a man of integrity in the city's councils. Margaret took pride in her father's memory and sorrowed at his death; but she also wrote to Dr. Freeman, "I realize now that most of my time and energy during the last six years have been centered around my father, and it is now possible that some day I might be able to get back to my writing desk." But, as the end of the war approached, the daily business of the foreign editions of her book grew more complicated than ever. It was obvious that the enemy would withdraw from areas he had destroyed and occupied, and Allied military governments would then take charge for an indefinite time. Like so many business aspects of *Gone with the Wind,* this state of affairs would have no guiding precedents. The questions would be, have any publishers survived, and if so, what laws govern them? Margaret now hoped that when the war was over, she could conduct her international publishing business through agents and lawyers in the individual countries, watched over on her behalf by the reliable accounting firm that had been keeping her books since 1936, and had offices all over the world.

The multitude of war activities was exhausting and in December, 1945, brought on an attack of bursitis in both shoulders and arthritis that disabled her right hand and put her arm in a sling for a time. The overseas business began to mount again, as she wrote a friend. "During the last four months we've had heavy work upon us, for my European publishers, storm battered, have been checking in. Still no news from Poland, where I know my first set of publishers were Jewish. Nothing from Latvia, but the Russians have them. No news from Finland at all. They were a fine set of people, and I recall that, when the Russians were almost at the gates of Helsinki and the old gentleman of the firm was running the business while his boys were at the front, they still came through and paid me my royalties.

"The foreign stuff keeps us busy because there have been some incredible sales of *Gone with the Wind* in occupied countries—most of the sales under the ban of the Nazis and sold on the black market. Neither John nor I have done very well in the last six months. He is always so fatigued it frightens me, but there is nothing much to do about it except 'supportive' treatment. Perhaps by spring this new drug, streptomycin, will be out of the experimental class and we can try it. As for me, my inability to use my right arm throws too much extra work on John and Margaret. We never seem to get caught up on our work."

For some years the Marshes had known peace and beauty at the Georgia sea islands, which they visited from time to time for refreshment of body and spirit. In the early hours of December 24, 1945, John and Margaret got off the train at Jesup, Georgia, intending to change for Brunswick and Sea Island. It was raining, there was nobody to meet them; their Pullman had stopped, and the porter had put down their bags, some distance from the station. Margaret hurried to cover and urged John to leave the bags, but he carried them out of the rain. When the station wagon from the Cloister Hotel picked them up, John was very tired and his face had a crumpled look. He tried to rest at the hotel, but later in the day a bad heart attack struck him. Writing two months later from Atlanta to Lois Cole, Margaret recorded:

"Yes, John has been very ill. He nearly died Christmas at Sea Island. He had a coronary occlusion that was complicated by my inability to get a doctor for what seemed an eternity. He was in the Brunswick hospital almost three weeks, and this was made very difficult by the scarcity of nurses and the fact that Sea Island orderlies hide in different places than these upcountry ones, whose hiding holes I know of old. John is still at Piedmont Hospital here in Atlanta, and there is faint hope that he may be home in a week by ambulance. How long he will stay upstairs I do not know. It seems to me he has made a remarkable recovery but the whole truth of his recovery will not be apparent until he starts to take up normal or semi-normal life again. You know that I am the least optimistic of people. So when I say that I am happy at his good progress and have hope for a decent life for him if he is very careful—then you know that he is doing very well. He ran a temperature from last June until he collapsed at Sea Island. It was diagnosed as undulant fever. There was nothing to be done for it, so he just went on working. He was in pretty bad shape when his heart gave out. During the attack his lungs had filled with fluid and, fearing pneumonia, he was given penicillin. He has had no whiff of fever since then, which proves that he did not have undulant fever, for penicillin availeth naught with that disease."

Slowly, John got better. At first, his only concern was to get through the day. Then he became strong enough to sit up and study the birds outside the windows of the Della Manta. Margaret put out peanut butter, according to her belief the favorite food of mockingbirds; she said, "Mockingbirds are beating on the windows all day long yelling to John for peanut butter." Some friends brought Margaret a lost kitten, which she christened Maud and introduced to John as a sickroom campanion. He would lie propped on pillows, reading his daily chapter of Angela Thirkell, while the little cat scampered up and down the counterpane or sat and looked at him. Miss Baugh observed that the household which had always centered around Margaret now functioned solely for John's benefit and comfort: Margaret wanted it that way. Stephens Mitchell thought that "John knew he could never work again, and that his interests must be confined to what he could do at home." It was not until near the end of 1946 that he was able to cross the street and dine at the Driving Club. Until John could get to the Club, Margaret would sometimes order a dinner or cocktails brought to the apartment. If the employees had a favorite member, it was probably Margaret, for she was known to write even a club servant a note of appreciation. At the end of an especially hard and exasperating day, Margaret sometimes would pick up the telephone and order a tray of champagne cocktails brought across the street, laughing at herself for the indulgence.

There was an occasion for drinking champagne toasts when news came, near the end of the war, that the highest court in Holland had decreed a satisfactory settlement of Margaret's claim against the Dutch publishing house. Relations thereafter were cordial. Publication in French started again; in Italy the presses again began turning out the story of Rossella—their translation of Scarlett. Publishers in Czechoslovakia and Poland resumed business briefly until the Russian authorities stopped them; and a new Hungarian edition did well until the Russians banned it in 1948. As Stephens Mitchell remarked, "All the nations that had suffered defeat and privation wanted to read *Gone with the Wind*." Word would come from Estonia, Latvia, and Bulgaria—there was no trouble selling the book, for everyone wanted it; then the Iron Curtain would come down. In the free countries, sales continued at a good rate.

There were few American companies transacting foreign business on as wide a scale as Margaret's licensing enterprise. One thinks of great corporations with battalions of clerks, translators, and foreign experts, all working in some cases to bring about less penetration of overseas markets than Margaret achieved with the help of three people, only one of whom worked for her full time. And Margaret's product had impact—reading *Gone with the Wind* caused an emotional reaction in Europeans just as it did in citizens of the United States. As soon as the mails began functioning European readers, fresh from the war experience, would write to the author. Typical of hundreds was the letter from a Hungarian woman who compared herself to Scarlett and added, "Like her, I have no job and no money. And the way things are going in my country I am not likely to get one or the other ... I have enough to live with my child for a few months more ... Perhaps you will be able to help me. There is no earthly reason why you should of course. Except that you wrote 'Scarlett' ..."

Margaret did what she could in every case where there was any way to help the writers of these touching letters. Since early in 1945, she had been sending food packages to England and Europe, a practice she continued until her death. "Spread over the years," Margaret Baugh recalled, "the volume of packages grew without our realizing it." The parcels went to individuals for whom Margaret had addresses—translators, publishers, agents, and even to readers. She sent packages to Angela Thirkell in gratitude for the pleasure and refreshment her books had brought to John.

Margaret shopped for the items she put into her parcels, brought them home in her car, and carried them up the steps to the apartment. In the night when she could not sleep for worrying about John she would get up and fill a few packages to quiet her nerves. Miss Baugh helped fit the articles into boxes and filled out customs declarations—some countries required four forms. Then Margaret would load her car with addressed parcels and take them to the post office. Into each parcel went a few toys and favors for children. Margaret said, "I remember my disappointment as a child when a parcel would be opened, and there would be nothing in it for me."

In September 1947 John resigned from the Georgia Power Company. Margaret wrote to Helen Dowdey, "If you should in future weeks come across any small garbled item in a gossip column that John is desperately ill, you'll know the truth is that the doctor said John must not ever go back to his job at the Power Company, or any similar job where deadlines had to be met and where John would have to keep working regardless of how tired he was. We had been expecting this news and it did not bother us. I would never have had an easy moment if he had gone back part time. Just now John is able to go across the street to the Driving Club every afternoon, have a drink, stay about forty minutes and see a friend or two. If you think John is retiring to a life of leisure, you are mistaken, for I am just panting to get him well enough to take back on his shoulders my foreign affairs. The doctor said it would be very good for him to do this work if he could. Really, the work seems to get heavier and heavier as time goes on instead of getting lighter, and any hope of ever having an opportunity to do more writing is something I never even think about."

About this time, the Marshes cancelled their listing in the telephone directory. Stephens Mitchell recorded, "People called me and asked, indignantly, why Margaret had done this, or they tried to get her number from me. All of this was wearing on Margaret. She was tired, she was nervous, she was irritable. I had never known her to be like that in all her life. The worry told on her, and she began to look older and a strained look came into her face."

Gray had appeared in Margaret's hair at the time of John's siege in the Brunswick hospital. Arthritis, a hurting back that refused to get well, and the continuing irritation of reading fantasies about her life and work in the gossip columns—throughout 1947, for example, an ineradicable crop of items that she had completed another novel—contributed to the exhaustion and strain that Stephens Mitchell noticed in her. But John began to improve, now that he had dropped the burden of his job downtown. He was able to work not only on foreign business, as Margaret had hoped, but took a hand in their American affairs as well. He was himself again when, on November 23, 1947, he wrote to George Brett on the old topic, Margaret's royalties from Macmillan, and made what was to stand as a final statement on another matter. There had been a miscalculation in one of the royalty payments on the American edition. Mr. Brett corrected it, and in so doing referred to something that he might better, perhaps, have treated on the principle of letting sleeping dogs lie. At any rate, John responded:

"Your promptness in acknowledging the error and making the adjustment was characteristic of you and we are glad to have that misunderstanding behind us. I wish I could close this letter with our thanks, but I am forced to go further because of your remarks about the $50,000 payment to Peggy for the motion picture rights. At their mildest, they were slurring.

"Peggy was offered $50,000 for her motion picture rights in 1936 and she accepted this price. If, at some later date, some other author received a higher price for motion picture rights in some other book, that is no reason why Peggy should be dissatisfied about the price she received. In 1936, we thought that $50,000 was a lot of money and we still think it is a lot of money. Peggy has never been dissatisfied and she has never complained, either publicly or privately. But everybody else seems to complain for her. Everybody else seems to think she ought to be dissatisfied and unhappy about the $50,000. It all carries the suggestion that she would wish to welsh out of a trade which she has made, and we don't like it. Now you have joined your voice in that chorus.

"Our dissatisfaction with the motion picture contract did not arise from the amount of money and nobody has the right to attribute to Peggy the qualities of a welsher or a whiner. Our dissatisfaction did arise from very different factors and you are in a better position than anybody else to know what they are."

Both Margaret and her husband had too much common sense to let recurring contractual annoyances blind them to the fact that eleven years after publication, *Gone with the Wind* was still a superb success. The moving picture that had caused so much trouble had run for five years in London—straight through the war. The book had done equally well both at home and throughout the world; by the end of 1946, the Marshes had tallied the sale of 1,250,000 copies of foreign translations. These were in the authorized editions. Nobody could guess the number of copies sold in unauthorized printings; the Japanese and Chinese pirates claimed sales in millions. In New York, Macmillan announced in 1946 that the public had now bought, through April, 3,713,272 copies of the American editions.

The greatness of this achievement had established a special place of esteem for Margaret in the South, and throughout the country. If she had wished, she now could have cut herself off from all annoyance, and taken a position above the battle in any conceivable public dispute. Margaret did dislike controversy; but she did not use her fame as an excuse for not taking a stand when she thought a question of right and wrong had arisen. She showed this moral courage during the spring of 1947, when she became interested in the case of a man accused of murdering his wife—Paul Refoule.

Refoule was a French artist who married an Atlanta girl, served in World War II, and returned to Atlanta to teach and paint. The Refoules bought an abandoned thread mill in suburban Atlanta, which they converted into a picturesque residence with Peachtree Creek the lower boundary of its lot. On May 14, 1947, Mrs. Refoule was found dead, hanging by a rope from the limb of a tree near the creek. Paul Refoule came home from an art class to confront this tragedy and find reporters and police searching the premises. Next day a morbid crowd overran the funeral, and the newspapers began plastering front pages with headlines about police seeking a motive and "grilling" Paul Refoule. On June 13 the police were still bringing Refoule in for lengthy examinations, while the sensational stories and headlines continued in the press. Stephens Mitchell recorded, "The town went into an orgy of hatred against the unfortunate young man and against French people in general. No one would have known that we and the French had recently been allies. In the midst of all this, Margaret went out of her way to stand up for Paul Refoule in public and in private."

Paul Refoule came to Stephens Mitchell, who advised him to go into Federal courts for relief from the police, and referred him to a lawyer experienced in Federal practice. Stephens also asked the editors of the *Constitution* and *Journal* to go easy until charges were brought in court—something the police had not yet done. The editors told Mr. Mitchell his advice was unwelcome. At this point, Margaret appealed to James M. Cox, who now owned both the surviving Atlanta newspapers, and was living in Miami. She asked the publisher if he knew what was going on, and suggested that the papers were not the place to try Paul Refoule—if, indeed, he was to be tried at all. To his credit, the Governor listened and took action. And Stephens was able to record that "A splendid reporter, George Goodwin, was put on the case, and the story was told as it really was." That story was simply that affidavits of a number of impeccable citizens established Refoule's innocence beyond question, and the police had no case. A Federal court found they had violated Refoule's rights in trying to build one. Paul died soon afterward; during his time of anguish, he had numbered the dead wife's family and Margaret and Stephens Mitchell among his few friends.

Her defense of Paul Refoule was characteristic, but an account of Margaret's controversies would miss the mark if it gave an impression that she was usually in a fighting mood. In fact, Margaret was seldom in contention, except over business matters, and her day-by-day approach to life and the people in it was one of sunny geniality, gayety, good humor, and good will. "She made you laugh," her friend Samuel Tupper, Jr. once remarked. Indeed, where Margaret was, there was nearly always laughter, and she was as ready to be entertained as to furnish entertainment. Anyone who enjoyed the Marx brothers as Margaret did would have a nice taste in slapstick, and she once amused Mr. Tupper with a cardboard camera from which a green cloth snake jumped out—she knew Sam Tupper would think it funny. Her sense of fun had its part in her popularity with men of all ages, but Margaret also took pains in maintaining friendships with women, and was grateful for their company.

Once she said, "The longer I live the more convinced I become that the ability to get along with people in a simple and pleasant way is better than great riches." But she would do more for friends than merely keep in touch with them in an agreeable manner. As her brother put it, "Margaret always turned up when there was illness or grief, and did the practical things." She sometimes felt the call for help by something on the order of extra-sensory perception. A friend remembered an example of this. Waking in a hospital before dawn after a major operation, in pain and anxiety and too weak to reach the nurse's call-button, the sufferer became aware of someone standing in the doorway. It was Margaret, who advanced into the room asking, "What's the matter?" It developed that Margaret had waked suddenly with the conviction that her friend was in trouble, and had thrown on her clothes and hurried to the hospital. At another time, Margaret wrote to a friend in New York, "I have waked on three successive nights with a feeling of anxiety about you. Are you all right? Are you working too hard?" During this period, the friend had suffered a collapse from overwork.

Margaret understood the importance of friendship so

well that she would take the initiative if a good relationship seemed to be coming to an end without good reason. Sometimes a friend's falling out of touch could mean he had come to a barren period of life, and needed help he might be ashamed to ask for. On behalf of herself and John, Margaret wrote to a man in trouble, "Our main business with you is that we consider you one of our best friends and we don't want to drift apart ... Your life is dislocated; hold out a few more months. Bury your troubles in work. I never thought to be intruding on your privacy and telling you how to run your life, but I want to point out your assets of courage, fighting spirit, endurance and common sense." Though she kept it a secret, Margaret would sometimes supply friends with money in the form of a gift or a loan; she dreaded these necessities, knowing that money was the world's most dangerous commodity between friends or members of a family. All the same, there were times when nothing but money would help.

Never compromising her inner dignity, Margaret did not worry too much about appearances; once when caught by a flash flood walking to a nearby party, she simply took off her shoes and put them in John's pockets, held up the skirts of her dinner gown, and, with great enjoyment, waded through the overflowing gutter. Margaret admitted she was only four feet eleven inches tall; her remark that she did not on that account *feel* small is well known, though she got no pleasure from newspaper references to her as the little woman who wrote the big book. But her small size never embarrassed her. Sometimes when going to a party she would take along a copy of Bartlett's *Familiar Quotations,* which had exactly the thickness she needed for a footstool, and she would sit with her feet resting comfortably on Bartlett, listening more than she talked, but talking with flavor and point. As she did so, her friends would admire her black-fringed Irish-blue eyes and her fair skin with its sprinkling of light freckles across the nose. William Howland observed that this face was mobile, and "disclosed emotions as though they were cast on it by a projector." Another friend said, "When you saw

Peggy, you knew that here was a person." But the lasting quality in Margaret, the one that mentioning her name would always summon up, according to Medora Perkerson, was "unquenchable gayety."

Stephens Mitchell wrote, "I cannot give you her bad points, for to me she had none. She had her sorrows, and they were many. She bore them well. She had her illnesses and accidents. They were many, and she bore them well. Most people liked her, but she had her enemies, and they and she remembered each other like elephants." It was true that Margaret could hold a grudge. For example, she was able to recall a certain piece of discourtesy thirteen years after it took place. About another person who had offended her, Margaret said, "It's wrong, I know. But I don't forget things and I'll take my time about seeing her."

Even with the oldest friends, who loved her most dearly, the closed doors of which she had spoken could sometimes be felt. It was not that Margaret had anything to hide. It was simply that according to her principles, personal life was private life. But that conviction does not prevent students of her career from being both complete and specific in summing up her public accomplishment. This was: that she created living characters, and with those creations, through the printed story and the moving picture, she reached more people than any other writer of a single book in the history of the world; while doing this she preserved her integrity; and she caused Atlanta, a man's town and a business town, to accept a woman and a writer as its leading citizen. It will be a long time before anyone else achieves that combination of victories in one career.

Late in 1948, Margaret called Stephens Mitchell into conference on several nights. She wished to put her house in order. First she had made a new will replacing the one she had asked Stephens to draw up for her in the flush of success ten years before. She wrote this later will in the simple language of a business letter, leaving all domestic and foreign rights in *Gone with the Wind* to John Marsh, and modest bequests to nieces and nephews, friends, and various institutions; the rest of her estate, at that time about $300,000 in cash and securities, was to go one quarter to Stephens Mitchell, three quarters to John Marsh.

Margaret and Stephens went over business files and made decisions about investments. Then they discussed what was to be done if Margaret died before Stephens, and if John was incapacitated and unable to carry out her wishes. She wanted her manuscripts and notes destroyed; and there were to be no sequels to *Gone with the Wind*, no comic strips, no abridgments. Late into these few nights, after they put aside their business papers, brother and sister talked of other things. Margaret asked Stephens how he was doing in his legal practice, aside from her work. He said his practice was increasing—he had not been able to give it as much time as he would have liked during the crowded years they now thought were coming to a close. He had, however, found time to write a 776-page book, *Real Property under the Code of Georgia and the Georgia Decisions*, the authority in its field. Margaret asked why he had insisted on putting his fees for her work into the firm, of which his father and uncle were members, and so cutting down his own income. Stephens said he thought that only fair. She said she had hoped to make him rich, but now could see that if he got rich it would be on his own account. Stephens answered that he was doing fairly well in Atlanta real estate, a good way from starvation. But he went on, "I have never taken any pride in the work I did for you, nor in the money I made from it. I have taken pride in my specialty—real estate law—and that's the thing on which I want to base my reputation." Margaret said she understood, and it made her both happy and sad—happy that he could do it, and sad that she had not helped his career, but stopped it in mid-flight. Their conversation turned to religion, and Stephens recorded that Margaret said, "We never talked about it, you and I, since I gave up my religion. A good part of my giving it up was due to the fact that I didn't think I'd ever get anywhere or that you'd get anywhere. It looked like a hopeless job, it looked as though you were just going to stay in this town and fight a hopeless fight all your life.

Well, I'm glad to see that even outside of what I may leave you, you haven't fought a hopeless sort of fight. And you'd get along all right if you never saw me or had any money from me any more. Perhaps what you did was the right thing after all." Stephens said this sounded as though her religious sentiments might be returning. Margaret replied, "That's something I don't want to talk about. I'm just going to say one thing about it. When you make a bargain with the devil, you had better stick to your bargain. I may have made one, but whenever I give my word on something, or whenever I take a course of action, I am not going to try to crawl out of that course of action because I may have made a mistake in starting it. It is not the fair thing to do." They said goodnight, and Stephens Mitchell went back to 1401 Peachtree Street.

As the early months of 1949 went by, Margaret began to tell her close friends that it seemed as though at last the pressure of business was becoming lighter; there now might be time to think—even to write. Margaret asked an editor of *Harper's* to correct a statement that she had said she would never write again. Admitting a certain inconsistency, for she had often said she would write no more books, Margaret pointed out that it was inability to find time that had kept her from writing as much as any decision never to attempt further work. On occasion Margaret had also made remarks about having been scribbling all her life, with the implication that she had acquired an unbreakable habit. At any rate, her correspondence was writing, and it totaled a prodigious, incalculable number of words. In the summer of 1949, as that correspondence at last began to diminish, Margaret did think of other writing. She had spoken to John and others about a novel, or perhaps two novels, that would continue the history of Atlanta to the time of World War I. But she was certain the characters of *Gone with the Wind* would not make a second appearance, for that would be a sequel, which she was determined not to have. Margaret also considered writing a play; she thought there might be something in the drama of a woman writing a successful book—a book so successful that it gets out of control.

In June, Margaret and John had a quiet visit in New York and saw a few friends. Back on Piedmont Avenue in early August, they began to sort over their social commitments, and lay plans for what they would do when the dry, cool, and bracing Atlanta autumn came again. There would be work, and it might well be new work; whatever it was, it could be planned. Margaret had come to one of those pauses in life, when a mature person can draw a breath, look ahead, and see some kind of order in the next few years.

August 11 had been a hot day and Margaret had stayed out of the sun. In the evening, the reliable breeze came across town, and Margaret and John decided to go to the movies. There was a British picture called *A Canterbury Tale* at the Arts Theater. This theater, specializing today as it did then in imported films, stands at the northeast corner of Thirteenth and Peachtree Streets, near The Dump where John and Margaret had lived in their Crescent Avenue days. They drove three quarters of a mile to the neighborhood of the theater. Margaret parked the car on the west side of Peachtree Street, and with John at her elbow started over to the movie on the other side. It was 8:20 p.m. As they got a little more than halfway across, an automobile came north on Peachtree, traveling too fast and momentarily hidden by the curve in the street. When it burst into view, bearing down on them, Margaret drew back and the driver jammed on his brakes. The car skidded and seemed to pursue Margaret, knocking her down near the curb she had just left. Police arrived at once and arrested the driver, an off-duty taxi operator.

Dr. Edwin Paine Lochridge, the intern riding Grady Ambulance No. 1, was the son of Margaret's friend Lethea Turman, who had been a schoolmate and fellow member of the Debutante Club. When the young doctor bent above her, he saw that she was badly hurt and unconscious. Margaret never regained consciousness, though she was still living five days later, on the 16th. During those intervening days, lying in the shock and coma of terrible injuries to her head, Margaret made Grady Hospital a center of worldwide concern. Large crowds waited outside for news; calls of inquiry over-whelmed the hospital switchboard and special lines had to be installed. Friends volunteered to answer calls, working around the clock in four-hour watches: "Can you tell me about Miss Mitchell?" "Her condition is serious but she is still alive." President Truman in Washington, the governor of Georgia, the mayor, asked to be kept informed. On the morning of the 16th, as a last resort, the doctors de-cided to attempt an operation on the brain.

Stephens Mitchell came downtown that morning, briefly consulted a colleague about a legal matter, walked from his office down Edgewood Avenue to Coca-Cola Place, and spoke to Frank Daniel of the *Journal*. Someone asked for Margaret's full name, and Stephens said, "Margaret Munnerlyn Mitchell Marsh." Frank Daniel said, "Steve, I'm terribly sorry, but she's gone." He had his office on an open line, and said into the telephone, "Margaret Mitchell is dead. Time of death, eleven fifty-nine a.m. Repeating time of death, eleven fifty-nine a.m."

In the *Journal* office, the red light on the newsroom clock flashed for exactly noon as rewrite man Bill Key re-peated Daniel's message to the city editor. Throughout the big room, there followed a minute of silence. As Key remembered it later, "Margaret Mitchell's death was a news event of worldwide importance, but the *Journal's* people did not react to it as Hollywood might convention-ally have pictured it—with confusion, excitement, shouting, running about. There was, for at least a minute, only this dull and empty meaningful silence." A few weeks before, Margaret had sauntered into this room and passed the time of day with Key, Daniel, and other old friends.

John Marsh's doctor telephoned Bessie Jordan and told her to make sure John was in bed for his afternoon rest with no radios on. He then went with Stephens Mitchell to the apartment. "Doctor Waters told John she was dead," Stephens recorded. "I remember little of the exact words. There was a request from the doctor for an autopsy, which John granted." John suggested that the funeral be conducted by a family friend, Dean Raimundo de Ovies of the Protestant Episcopal Cathedral. Stephens then called on the Dean in his study. "I told him what we wanted. He asked what the service should be, and I said, 'The Service for the Dead from the Book of Common Prayer.' He said, 'What gentlefolk would like.'" And Margaret's brother nodded, afraid he would break down if he tried to speak. Stephens Mitchell's record goes on: "Next day the funeral service was held. The Dean read the service in his best manner, clearly and sweetly. The long train of automobiles went to Oakland Cemetery. It is the old city cemetery, set up in 1854. Across the valley loom the great buildings of the new city and the sun bounces back from the ranks of their windows to the country town graveyard near their midst. They buried her there beside her father and her mother and her little brother who died in babyhood. There was a grave space left for John. The flowers were banked high. I forgot to tell the caretakers to give the flowers to the crowd. I did it the next day. There was a crowd there for two or three days. She had said something to her people and they had answered.

"And when I looked across at the city riding high in the sunlight on the long ridge, crowded with towers, I broke and cried. I do not remember anything else for the next week.

"So we say goodbye. I said at an earlier place that we were closer than most sisters and brothers. We were, until the end. May her soul, through the mercy of God, rest in peace."

Epilogue

When a person whose name is known to millions dies, it seems reasonable to use the length and number of newspaper obituaries for a rough measurement of that person's stature. On this scale, Margaret ranked as one of the prominent figures of our time. But more to the point was the emotion that came through in the newspaper writing. The *Manchester Guardian* mourned "this woman of courtesy, generosity and good sense." The *Charleston News and Courier* wrote of Margaret that she was "a dear, sweet woman who had the charity that vaunteth not itself. Her life and her book were the realization of genius, goodness, and modesty." The *New York Times* said, "The South and the Nation have lost one of their most beloved and admired personages. Certainly she will always be one of our most remarkable literary figures." The *Montgomery Advertiser* showed the unforgettable quality of Margaret's novel by writing, "She provided an enchantment with her story of a woman scoundrel and her man in a war that, for range and durability, had no counterpart in the history of American literature. She was thus a great author and only a literary fop would argue the point." And the *Saturday Review of Literature* said of her book "It has a love story so imperatively moving that Rhett Butler and Scarlett O'Hara have become the lineal descendants of all the great fictional lovers of the past, and the fall of Atlanta in our Civil War has become one with the siege of Troy." So it went, in every daily and weekly newspaper in the United States, and most of those in the rest of the world.

Public opinion was bitter against Hugh D. Gravitt, the man who had run Margaret down. The police reported that in the ten years since he had come to Atlanta, Gravitt had compiled a list of twenty-eight citations to traffic court, and had been convicted on eight of them. He admitted having taken some beer during the afternoon before the accident, but blamed his fast driving on the urgency of his errand, which was to get medicine for his stepson. Released on bail, Gravitt came to trial in October on several charges adding up to criminally reckless driving. His attorney could not make much of a defense beyond pointing out that Margaret would still be living had she stepped forward instead of back in the moment when she saw the car sliding toward her. The defense also maintained that Gravitt's record of traffic violations was normal in the occupation of taxicab driver. Gravitt was convicted, and sentenced to eighteen months in jail. The court allowed him six days to arrange his affairs before starting to serve the sentence, and next day he managed to become involved in another accident, though not a fatal one.

Sorrow and anger over Margaret's death made newspaper editorials and columns throughout the country try to arouse a demand for more stringent safety regulations, and more care in the granting of driver's licenses. On the first anniversary of the tragedy, the National Boy and Girl Scouts promoted a "Margaret Mitchell Minute," a moment of silence to think of the careless hand at the steering wheel; and, for many years, the National Safety Council cited Margaret's death in its annual campaign. In Atlanta, a traffic safety board became the Margaret Mitchell Safety Council until it turned into the Georgia Safety

Council. A glance at national street and highway death toll figures, however, will show that from a public safety point of view, Margaret's death was a tragedy as useless as it was senseless.

Nevertheless, in a way which had nothing to do with her death, Margaret was to have influence in a field of public regulation. In 1952, Congress passed the revenue law known as Code Section 107-C, intended to give some relief to taxpayers who collected in one year the returns for several years' work, thus landing in confiscatory brackets. This legislation reflected recognition by Congress of "injustices that had prevailed to authors such as Margaret Mitchell," and was generally known as the Margaret Mitchell Law. The tremendous taxes she paid for the years 1936 and 1937 had dramatized the plight of all creative people who asked only that their incomes be averaged over the years of work in which they earned them. In 1962, it seemed that the problem Margaret personified was receiving further attention with the passage of the Authors and Self-Employed Individuals Retirement Tax Act. This legislation allowed self-employed persons a tax deduction for retirement plans they financed from earned income. But, in 1964, the Internal Revenue Service ruled that authors' royalties were not "earned income". This would have given Margaret a hearty but rueful laugh, thinking of the ditch-digger's labor of writing *Gone with the Wind*.

Margaret and her book had influence on two other important laws. One was the fair trade or price protection act, known as the Tydings-Miller bill, signed into law by President Roosevelt in August 1937 after long debate and much postponement. Supporters of the bill made *Gone with the Wind* a dramatic demonstration of what they wished to correct; in the summer of 1936 the novel's rocketing popularity had set off a fantastic price war in New York City. Book and department stores ran out of stock practically as soon as a shipment came in. But in spite of the sure sales, several department stores began advertising the book at cut prices as a loss leader. One store would offer *Gone with the Wind* at $2.89, another would respond at $2.49, and the first store would then cut to $2.19 for the book supposed to sell at $3.00. When the price went below what the stores paid the publishers, the war continued, with merchants sending runners to the store with the lowest figure rather than buying fresh stock from Macmillan—even at the extra discount allowed for large quantities. The war spread to the Middle and far West, where drug stores and other outlets drove the price as low as 89 cents. When the Tydings-Miller bill became law, it covered drugs, cosmetics, food, jewelry, tobacco, and many other products, as well as books. But the best-known single product in the country was Macmillan's edition of *Gone with the Wind.*

The other law Margaret helped to establish was that which made the United States government a member of the Universal Copyright Convention. From shortly after the time her book was published, Margaret had been working with legislators and State Department people to demonstrate American authors' need for this protection. In 1954, after the deaths of both Margaret and John, Stephens Mitchell submitted a statement, summarizing the foreign copyright problems of *Gone with the Wind,* as evidence in favor of this country's entering the copyright agreement—which finally came about in 1955.

John Marsh moved from the apartment, buying a house nearby at 26 Walker Terrace, where he would not have to climb stairs as he did at the Della Manta. To his distress, shortly before the move Maud the cat disappeared, probably a victim of Piedmont Avenue traffic. John equipped an office in the house, where he worked each day on the affairs of *Gone with the Wind* and the Margaret Mitchell Estate. There were offers to write sequels to refuse; offers to make stage plays and musicals to consider; and there was, above all, the worldwide business of the many translated editions to administer.

On July 26, 1951, John Marsh deposited a large sealed envelope in the vaults of the Citizens and Southern National Bank, together with a codicil to his will explaining why he had done so. This document said the envelope contained some undestroyed pages of the original manuscript of *Gone with the Wind*. These were "certain chapters, typewritten by my wife, and with many changes and corrections in her handwriting. Also two or three drafts of chapters, showing their development and changes as she wrote and rewrote." In addition were proof sheets with corrections in both John's and Margaret's handwriting; chronologies prepared by Margaret while writing the book, giving events in the novel and historical happenings in parallel, together with the ages of characters as the story progressed—"pregnancies and other time-important situations." Also included were samples of Margaret's notes, and her lists of items to be checked at the library, and "notes made by her father and brother, who were asked by her to read the manuscript and let her know of any errors they found." Lastly, John put in some of the manila envelopes in which Margaret had stored chapters of her book during the years she was working on it; the envelopes were labeled in Margaret's handwriting, and had her scribbled ideas for changes and corrections on them. "With this material," John said, "I am confident it can be proved not only that my wife, Margaret Mitchell Marsh, wrote *Gone with the Wind*, but that she alone could have written it." The package of notes and manuscript pages was to be opened, he instructed, only if need to prove Margaret's authorship should arise.

In 1952, Stephens Mitchell sold the family house and lot at 1401 Peachtree Street. He had promised his sister that no one was to occupy the place as a home. The neighborhood had been zoned for business, and in accordance with the purchase agreement, the buyer razed the house to put up an office building. Souvenir hunters swarmed over the lot, picking up fragments, buying blinds and mantels, lighting fixtures, even the hexagonal stones of the front walk. Of the rest, nothing remains; and the Georgia Historical Commission has marked the site with a bronze plaque. The scene of Margaret's accident is a few blocks to the south.

John Marsh lived quietly; and he died quietly, on May 5, 1952. His will left all rights in *Gone with the Wind* to Stephens Mitchell. The Walker Terrace house was sold,

Stephens moved the office of the Margaret Mitchell Marsh Estate to a downtown building, and the business of *Gone with the Wind* went on, with Miss Baugh working full time as office manager. Mr. Mitchell came in daily from the nearby office of his law firm, sometimes to reply, as his sister would have done, to such young people as the German girl who inquired about the prospects of pioneering to Atlanta, hoping to enjoy success like that of "the brave Scarlett O'Hara." Stephens Mitchell suggested that times had changed since the days described in the book.

The novel's tremendous readership continued to increase. By 1956, its total sale passed 8,000,000; by the end of 1962, more than 10,000,000 copies had been sold. That year, editions in English alone sold 570,000 copies. By late 1965, *Gone with the Wind* had been translated into 25 languages in 29 countries, and was being published in twelve countries besides England and the United States, with the sale of all authorized editions reaching 12,000,-000 copies. And the enormous sale of pirated editions cannot be calculated. What this means in human terms is that every day, all over the world, hundreds of men, women, and children are delightedly reading for the first time that "Scarlett O'Hara was not beautiful, but men seldom realized it when caught by her charm . . ." It is one of the universal good experiences, like reading the opening lines of *Treasure Island,* or beginning *The Adventures of Huckleberry Finn.*

Since Margaret's death, Atlanta has grown into a sparkling metropolis, filled with glitter and shine. But Margaret Mitchell is still the leading citizen, and her name continues to appear in the newspapers, while friends often speak of her as though she had just stepped out of the room. Her brother noted that she had said something to her people. Indeed, Margaret said many things to Atlanta, to the country, to the world. For all her modesty, she did bring a message to mankind. And she allowed the unconquerable Scarlett to put the essence of it in words: "Tomorrow is another day."

Index

AVON ⬢ THE BEST IN
BESTSELLING ENTERTAINMENT!

THE BIG BESTSELLERS
ARE AVON BOOKS

Humboldt's Gift Saul Bellow	29447	$1.95
est Adelaide Bry	29652	$1.95

The Relaxation Response
   Herbert Benson, M.D.
   with Miriam Z. Klipper
	29439	$1.95

Freedom at Midnight Collins and Lapierre	29587	$2.25
The Nude Diana Hunter Rowe	29090	$1.75
Dawn of Desire Joyce Verrette	27375	$1.95
Rommany Florence Hurd	28340	$1.75
Freedom's Thunder Michael Foster	29058	$1.95
Castles in the Air Patricia Gallagher	27649	$1.95
Something More Catherine Marshall	27631	$1.75
The New Body James Fritzhand	27383	$1.95
Getting Yours Letty Cottin Pogrebin	27789	$1.75
Fletch Gregory Mcdonald	27136	$1.75
Shardik Richard Adams	27359	$1.95
The Promise of Joy Allen Drury	27128	$1.95
Anya Susan Fromberg Schaeffer	25262	$1.95
The Bermuda Triangle Charles Berlitz	25254	$1.95
Dark Fires Rosemary Rogers	23523	$1.95
Watership Down Richard Adams	19810	$2.25

Available at better bookstores everywhere, or order direct from the publisher.

THE
SUPERB
GOTHIC
EPIC

A TOWERING MANSION
AND ITS TANGLED LEGACY
OF EVIL AND DESIRE

THE STORMY ROMANTIC SAGA BY

FLORENCE HURD
ROMMANY

It began with Eustacia, first mistress of Rommany, whose love
for Duncan Blackmore was not to be denied. But the inn-
merable rooms and sins of Rommany drew her into the grip
a sinister plot that spread its evil stain across seven decades. .

Until, in the life of Constance, her granddaughter, three generations of mystery converge in a fateful decision to love th
hypnotic Leonard, a man cruelly linked to the shadowy pas

Suddenly, the gloom of Rommany is punctuated by ominou
thumpings in the night, and Constance must pierce the ve
that enshrouds her hopeless passion—so the ultimate secret
Rommany can be unmasked at last!

 28340/$1.75

THE SWEEPING ROMANTIC EPIC
OF A PROUD WOMAN
IN A GOLDEN AMERICAN ERA!

PATRICIA GALLAGHER

Beginning at the close of the Civil War, and sweeping forward to the end of the last century, CASTLES IN THE AIR tells of the relentless rise of beautiful, spirited Devon Marshall from a war-ravaged Virginia landscape to the glittering stratospheres of New York society and the upper reaches of power in Washington.

In this American epic of surging power, there unfolds a brilliant, luminous tapestry of human ambition, success, lust, and our nation's vibrant past. And in the tempestuous romance of Devon and the dynamic millionaire Keith Curtis, Patricia Gallagher creates an unforgettable love story of rare power and rich human scope.

AVON   27649 $1.95

CIA 5-76